US MILITARY STRATEGY
AND THE
COLD WAR ENDGAME

US MILITARY STRATEGY
AND THE
COLD WAR ENDGAME

STEPHEN J. CIMBALA

FRANK CASS

First published in 1995 in Great Britain by
FRANK CASS & CO. LTD.
Newbury House, 890–900 Eastern Avenue, Newbury Park,
Ilford, Essex IG2 7HH, England

and in the United States of America by
FRANK CASS
c/o International Specialized Book Services, Inc.
5804 N.E. Hassalo Street, Portland, Oregon 97213–3644

British Library Cataloguing in Publication Data
Cimbala, Stephen J.
  US Military Strategy and the Cold War
  Endgame
  I. Title
  355.033573

  ISBN 0-7146-4556-7 (cloth)
  ISBN 0-7146-4117-0 (paper)

Library of Congress Cataloging in Publication Data
Cimbala, Stephen J.
  US military strategy and the Cold War endgame / Stephen J. Cimbala.
    p.   cm.
  Includes bibliographical references and index.
  ISBN 0-7146-4556-7 : — ISBN 0-7146-4117-0 (pbk.)
  1. United States—Defenses.   2. Europe—Politics and
  government—1989–   I. Title.
  UA23.C5437   1995
  355'.033573—dc20   94-17487
                                                           CIP

Typeset by Regent Typesetting, London
Printed in Great Britain by
Bookcraft (Bath) Ltd, Midsomer Norton

Contents

List of Tables

Introduction

It is now a truism to restate Santayana's aphorism that those who do not remember the past are condemned to repeat it. For historians and political scientists, among other interested students of public policy, the more subtle question is how the past is to be interpreted. Which past is relevant to the present? For a Europe looking forward into a potentially new security community in which the expectation of major war among great powers might be almost non-existent, the Cold War past offers only some of history's full brew. Nevertheless, because the Cold War is so recent, it has been subjected to the normal risk of historical and political misconstruction attendant upon any recent event.

This study argues that the future of European security will not completely escape the clutches of Cold War experience and recent past decisions taken by the great powers, especially the Americans and the Russians. The Soviet Union gave way in 1991 to the Commonwealth of Independent States and to Russia as a great power, symbolized in Russia's inheritance of the Soviet United Nations Security Council seat. A power- and policy-vacuum now exists in east and central Europe as a result of Soviet disintegration and military retrenchment also passed along to Russia. Russia finds itself hard-pressed to maintain economic and political viability, including the challenge of internal stability and border security. The fulcrum of conflict in Europe shifts eastward as a result of Cold War termination, from the inner German border to the lands of east, central and southern Europe. Although the shifting axes of potential conflict differ considerably from those of the Cold War years, the post-Cold War period carries forward from the past difficult and unresolved security issues.

Among these issues carried forward is the post-Cold War responsibility of the Americans for European security, and within that broader question, the narrower question of how any future American security guarantee for Europe can be implemented. From 1945 until 1990, it seemed self-evident that the US, through its membership in, and domination of, the North Atlantic Treaty Organization (NATO), would provide for the territorial integrity and political independence of Western Europe. After 1967 and the official adoption of

1

flexible response strategy by NATO, the alliance sought to deter an outbreak of war in Europe by making certain that it had options, including if necessary nuclear options, for repelling any aggression or for inflicting unacceptable punishment on the aggressor. Although providing the forces and plans to carry out these missions was demanding of political leaders and military planners, the obvious Soviet challenge of political advancement through military intimidation forced a cohesion within NATO which kept the US connected to European security.

As discussed in Chapter 1, the Cold War armed forces of the United States were sized and shaped to meet this commitment to deterrence and defense in Europe. As a result, these forces were historically unprecedented by American standards.[1] Preparedness for global war against the Soviet Union, a war which in all likelihood would begin in Europe, mandated numbers of standing divisions, fleets and air wings which would allow the United States to fight one major war in Europe and one or more wars outside of Europe, say in Korea and/or the Middle East/Southwest Asia theaters of operations. During the Kennedy years this ambition extended to two and a half wars which the US would be able to fight simultaneously: major wars against the Soviet Union and against China, plus a half war in the Middle East or South Asia. Kennedy's successors scaled down these ambitions in the aftermath of US Vietnam disengagement. A notional one and a half war strategy prevailed during most of the 1970s and 1980s, on the assumption that forces adequate to hold off Soviet attackers in Europe would also be adequate to win rapid and decisive victories outside of Europe.

The assumption of transferable power among theaters of strategic military action may have been reasonable for conventional wars. But low-intensity conflicts, including insurgencies and revolutionary movements which were sometimes supported by Moscow, posed a challenge to the US and its NATO allies of uncertain dimensions. Therefore, it called forth an uncertain response. Some US diplomats, political leaders and military planners felt that the focus of defense and security preparedness should remain uppermost in Europe. Other US leaders felt that low-intensity conflicts now took center-stage once the basic Cold War alignments on either side had settled in. It could not be denied that low-intensity conflicts were more numerous than interstate wars, but it was far from obvious what the US or other developed armed forces could do about them.

US Vietnam experience was subject to a variety of interpretations in this regard. Some contended that the US had actually inflicted military defeat on the Viet Cong insurgent forces, but lost the war owing to political opposition and decision mismanagement at home.[2] Others, including those in the first group, also indicted the US Army for its disregard of classical military strategy and campaign proficiency in favor of theories of graduated deterrence and political action. As Colonel Harry G. Summers, Jr., US Army (Ret.), wrote in his widely acclaimed book:

> In justifying strategy in civilian strategist terms, the Army surrendered its unique authority based on battlefield experience ... there was an increased emphasis on technical, managerial, and bureaucratic concerns. Instead of being experts in the application of military force to achieve the political ends of the United States, we became neophyte political scientists and systems analysts and were outclassed by the civilian professionals who dominated national security policy.[3]

Much of this professional military disinterest in classical strategy was the result of military men understandably looking to their civilian superiors for clues about the kinds of analyses that the civilians would find most congenial. The nuclear age had made major war too risky and the problem of preserving stability in Europe or globally became defined as one of making deterrence work. The omnivorous potential of US and Soviet nuclear weapons did not, despite the lay image of overkill, make governments on either side complacent about deterrence stability. Instead, during the Cold War years each side sought to increase its own deterrent potential and to hold constant, or to decrease that of its opponent. The architecture of deterrence and arms control became understandable, and in some ways unavoidable, substitutes for military art.

The probable future of nuclear deterrence after the Cold War is that it will be less relevant than it was from 1945 to 1990, but not irrelevant. Both the first and fourth chapters help to explain why. US grand strategic objectives for the early part of the next century include deterrence of attack on the American homeland, the retarding of nuclear proliferation inside and outside of Europe, and the protection of vital sea lanes of communication to Europe, North and South Asia, and the Persian Gulf. But the availability of ample numbers of US nuclear weapons, making America self-sufficient for deterrence, and the gradual decoupling of American and European political fates after the Cold War, changes the equation of European security. Europeans must become more self-reliant for the creation of a security community which is less dependent both on American 'extended' nuclear deterrence and on a willingness among the great powers of Europe to fight large-scale conventional wars.

Chapter 2 argues that nostalgia for the return of America's nuclear umbrella over Europe is largely misplaced. Confidence in nuclear deterrence placed excessive faith in the ability of political leaders to make brinkmanship

3

work. Evidence from Cold War crises suggests that leaders muddled through several crises despite, not because of, the risk of nuclear war. Cold War American and Soviet leaders showed little interest in nuclear brinkmanship when truly vital interests were at stake, as they were in Berlin in 1961 or in Cuba in 1962.[4] This did not mean that nuclear weapons were irrelevant to Cold War stability, as some writers have suggested.[5] Instead, nuclear weapons contributed to the avoidance of deliberate war between the US and the Soviet Union or their European allies. Nuclear weapons did not preclude escalation from conventional to nuclear war or an outbreak of inadvertent nuclear war during a breakdown of crisis management.[6]

Because they oversold deterrence, governments failed to recognize that nuclear deterrence worked for reasons other than the rationality of leaders who would obviously refuse to enter into the nuclear shadow of death. Instead, deterrence worked because the probability of escalation, either from conventional to nuclear war or from smaller to larger nuclear wars, was neither certain nor impossible. Either certain or impossible nuclear escalation would have doomed nuclear deterrence to defeat, especially extended deterrence guarantees on behalf of America's European allies. Certain escalation would have precluded a resort to war on the part of any sane leaders in Europe. Impossible escalation would have made Europe safe for conventional war. The region in between certain and impossible escalation was ideally suited for the success of nuclear deterrence: it rested, as Chapter 2 explains, on the psychology of uncertainty and on the threat that left something to chance.

However, it was not realized what a slender reed this was. One fatal misconstruction of the Cold War era would be to assume that because nuclear deterrence was not fundamentally tested in Europe between 1945 and 1990, it will be as robust outside of Europe after the end of the Cold War. Superpower strategic nuclear forces of the Cold War years imposed a bipolarity and a tightness in bloc politics which will not reappear in our political lifetimes. The manipulation of nuclear risk in order to make deterrence work presupposes that leaders will be more impressed with the uncertainties of an aggressor's calculus than they will be with the uncertainties of a defender's risks. Any nuclear exchange between Cold War US and Soviet forces placed a greater burden of uncertainty on the attacker: the defender holding a survivable second-strike force could guarantee unacceptable retaliation under almost all conditions. Therefore, risky bargaining tactics did not favor the attacker.

In a post-Cold War situation of attacker and defender uncertainties in which the defender lacks good warning systems or survivable forces, the uncertainties attending first strike may seem less daunting to the defender than the uncertainties of awaiting the first blow. Such a perception on the part

4

of leaders faced with timely nuclear decision-taking could be self-defeating of stable deterrence. And as Chapter 3 argues, even conventional military forces can be so poised for surprise attack and large-scale offensives that the forces themselves contribute to instability. Recognizing this, European security analysts and governments have begun to take more seriously the notion of defensive or 'non-offensive' defenses as components of any stable European security community including the former members of NATO, the Warsaw Pact, and neutral and non-aligned states.

There are many varieties of non-offensive defense strategies, and not all are applicable to the requirements of large states on the Eurasian continent. In the discussions leading up to the conclusion of the CFE (Conventional Forces in Europe) reductions agreed to in 1990 by the members of NATO and the former Warsaw Treaty Organization, the relationship between non-offensive defense strategies and force structure was made quite explicit. Earlier and unilateral force reductions announced by the then Soviet President Mikhail Gorbachev in 1988 emphasized, as did the CFE reductions, the reduction of force structure components which could be used for surprise attacks and large-scale offensives: tanks, armored personnel carriers, mobile artillery and so forth. Along with these force reductions, states in Europe have also agreed to engage in operational arms control, in the form of confidence and security-building measures (CSBMs) growing out of the CSCE (Conference on Security and Cooperation in Europe) process.[7]

Structural and operational arms control in Europe became a great deal easier once the Soviet Union had turned to 'reasonable sufficiency' or 'defensive sufficiency' as a criterion for the adequacy of its armed forces. Accepted with reluctance by the senior armed forces leadership of the former Soviet Union, defensive sufficiency was Gorbachev's way of establishing the primacy of political détente with the US over military redundancy in case of East–West conflict, as favored by the old guard among military leaders. Gorbachev took the argument for détente beyond the old standard of mutual deterrence, toward a concept of mutual security in which both sides would reduce nuclear and conventional forces to levels sufficient for defense only. Apart from the domestic political controversy that this caused within the former Soviet Union, Gorbachev's transition from mutual deterrence to mutual security also disconnected military preparedness for Cold War political values. Elites in the Soviet Union and in the United States were not all quick to catch on to this agenda until it had overtaken them.

Liberalization in Eastern Europe turned into revolt in 1989 and 1990: either date can reasonably be used to denote the official end of Cold War. Would defensive sufficiency unencumbered by the potential for large-scale

5

offensives be a viable approach for the powers of Europe in the remainder of this century or in the early years of the next? Much depended on the kinds of security structures or architecture Europeans chose to build to replace the old NATO–Warsaw Pact cathedral. Both simple and rococo designs have been proposed. Some build incrementally on past accomplishments and others involve radical departures from recent past experience. Chapter 4 discusses some of the options available to Europe for preserving security after the Cold War and their implications for US security policy.

Europe has a variety of institutions which can engage in structural and operational arms control, provided that the major European powers agree that further progress is both necessary and desirable. The Western European Union has had a rebirth and was called forth in 1992 to assist in implementing a UN blockade against the rump of Yugoslavia (Serbia and Montenegro). Some proposals call for the WEU to become the military arm of the European Community, itself given federalist aspirations by the Maastricht agreement of 1991 on political and monetary union. Other proposals envision a transformation of NATO from a bloc defense alliance to a regional peace-keeping organization. One especially interesting plan called for a modern version of the Concert of Europe, formed in 1815 to preserve stability in Europe after the conclusion of the Napoleonic wars. In this proposal, the leading NATO powers and Russia would form an executive committee primarily responsible for peace-keeping, in consultation with other states. The medium and smaller states would be involved more directly in non-military and non-coercive security activities, including the monitoring of confidence- and security-building measures and in crisis management.[8]

NATO adheres to the view that there is no necessary incompatibility between its continued existence as a bridge between European and North American security, on the one hand, and its transformation into one among several pillars of a post-Cold War European security architecture on the other. This facade of best-of-both-worlds may be preserved for the duration of the 1990s: eventually, NATO will have to give way as the primary security guarantor in Europe on account of the vanishing threat for which NATO was first constituted. NATO needs to evolve into some form of pan-European security organization that includes former NATO, Warsaw Pact and non-aligned states plus those newly independent states of the former Soviet Union.[9] Although the inclusiveness of CSCE makes it attractive to some for this role as NATO's security successor in Europe, CSCE's prior experience is more pertinent to consultation than to decisive action in the field of peace enforcement.

Combined with an activist West European Union in the field of collective

6

security and arms control, CSCE could serve as a second pillar of consultation and verification with regard to new confidence- and security-building measures, including the monitoring of military exercises and the preventive intervention in potentially destabilizing crises. Not too much should be expected of either organization in the way of military assertiveness against the will of a major European power. Whether the WEU and CSCE together can provide the institutional mechanisms necessary for a post-Cold War security community in Europe also depends on a favorable political and economic climate in Europe.

This favorable political and economic climate in future Europe, permissive of NATO-substitution by some version of Euro-multilateralism, assumes a Russia without revanchist ambitions toward Poland or other states in East Central Europe, and a Germany which is willing to be contained within a new European security system pointed not against Moscow but against some generalized fear of instability. Germany's future political and military ambitions are unknown, but some fear a more nationalist and unilateralist German foreign policy in the aftermath of unification. Relations between future Germany and Russia, so obviously central to European peace and security, will be influenced not only by their political inclinations, but also by their economic performances. Germany's ability to absorb former East Germany without a rebirth of self-destructive pseudonationalism, and Russia's ability to shift from a command to a market economy without unacceptable political turmoil, will set much of the agenda for security and foreign policy issues in the new Europe.

Stability in Europe does not only depend upon events within Europe. The countries of Europe may stabilize their relations between the Atlantic and the Urals only to find threats emerging from outside European territory proper. States located from the Mediterranean littoral to the mountain passes of South Asia may bring to the table grievances among themselves or against European powers which cannot be resolved short of armed conflict. One additional danger is that many of these non-European states capable of making trouble on the Eurasian periphery will be armed with more capable weapons, including long-range delivery systems and various weapons of mass destruction. Chapter 5 discusses one aspect of the growing military power of Third World states, in terms of its implications for regional and global stability: nuclear proliferation and civil–military relations.

The literature on the spread of nuclear and other weapons of mass destruction and the academic studies of civil–military relations have remained in separate compartments. In addition, the non-proliferation literature has emphasized almost exclusively the measures which can be taken by nuclear

7

suppliers and world organizations to prevent non-nuclear powers from acquiring nuclear weapons. The study of civil–military relations suggests that state actors may be driven by powerful domestic imperatives to acquire weapons of mass destruction. In addition, governments outside of Europe which may acquire or develop nuclear or chemical weapons and long-range delivery systems by the year 2000 may not be accountable to duly constituted civil authority.

The joint occurrence of praetorianism and proliferation presents an especially dangerous combination for regional stability. Nuclear weapons in the hands of an immature and unaccountable command and control system could be the proximate causes of war instead of deterrence. Praetorian regimes with vulnerable arsenals could be prone to brinkmanship and first-strike strategies. States acquiring small and vulnerable nuclear arsenals would also, in all probability, lack the redundant checks and balances built into mature nuclear command and control systems against accidental or inadvertent nuclear use. Apart from the problem of accidental war, the command system itself could be corrupted by general staffs totally committed to one political faction in a situation of civil strife.

The former Soviet Union offers a case of potential nuclear proliferation, and much depends on what is learned from it by scholars and policy-makers. The coup attempt of 19–21 August 1991 was an unexpected reminder of the vulnerability of governments even in developed and formerly authoritarian systems. The replacement for the Soviet Union, the Commonwealth of Independent States, is still cobbling together its political apparatus and military command and control system. In the spring of 1992, the Russian Federation President Boris Yeltsin announced the nationalization of the formerly Soviet armed forces in Russia, partly in response to similar measures already taken in the Ukraine. A draft Russian military doctrine was issued in May 1992, which included, among the enumerated security interests of Russia, the fate of peoples of Russian nationality in non-Russian former Soviet republics and the status of non-Russians in the same republics who identify with Russian culture and heritage.[10]

Fortunately the coup and its aftermath, although resulting in the official demise of the Soviet Union and its replacement by a collage of free-standing former Soviet republics, did not lead to disaggregation of the command and control system for nuclear weapons. Years of experience with negative control (prevention of unauthorized nuclear use or inadvertent launch) had allowed the Soviet armed forces to develop procedural and electronic or mechanical safeguards which carried over through the coup and post-coup periods. Bush administration officials worried, none the less, that the transition from Soviet

8

Union to Commonwealth might be marked by rivalry in the officer corps and devolution of nuclear command authority over tactical nuclear weapons scattered among the various former Soviet republics.

Strategic or long-range nuclear weapons were concentrated in four of the former Soviet republics at the time of the official collapse of communism in Russia in December 1991: in Russia, Ukraine, Belarus and Kazakhstan. Fomerly Soviet strategic nuclear weapons were thought by US experts to be under more reliable centralized control than tactical weapons were. The problem remained whether the political and military center would hold. Agreements reached by Russian President Boris Yeltsin with other republic presidents called for tactical nuclear weapons outside of Russia to be removed to Russian territory by the summer of 1992; by January 1992, all but Ukraine and Belarus had completed this task.

Strategic nuclear weapons remained under the centralized command and control of the 'Commonwealth' armed forces: by spring 1992 this meant, to all intents and purposes, the armed forces of Russia. Russian President Boris Yeltsin reorganized the Russian defense ministry in the spring of 1992. In April, Yeltsin appointed Colonel General Pavel S. Grachev, former commander of Soviet airborne divisions, and Andrei Kokoshin, former deputy director of the USA and Canada Institute, as first deputy defense ministers. In the same month, Yeltsin appointed the State Commission for the Establishment of a Defense Ministry, Army and Navy of the Russian Federation. The commission was chaired by the noted historian Dmitri Volkogonov. The next month, Yeltsin designated General of the Army Grachev as Minister of Defense.[11] Following his appointment as Defense Minister, Grachev announced that 'We must in essence create a Russian army from nothing', and he stated (at a meeting attended by NATO officials) that the sphere of interest for the Russian Federation included all former Soviet republics on the land borders of Russia.[12]

Thus for purposes of deploying major elements of ground, tactical air and nuclear forces, the commanders and command systems formerly subordinated to Soviet authorities have now been Russified. The recreation of the Russian armed forces and their explicit concern with potential security dilemmas around Russia's vast borders, in addition to internal strife not fully dealt with, opens old military planning dilemmas not seen in Russia since the late nineteenth century.[13] Russia then confronted a situation of difficult trade-offs between economic modernization and continued indulgence of a bloated military bureaucracy. Finance ministers, such as the assertive Sergei Witte, clashed with war ministers who sought to protect their bureaucratic turf against infringement from external sources, including external forces who

9

might intrude on the military subject of war plans. Russia's nineteenth-century war planning became an even more vexatious subject at the turn of the century, when the Russo-Japanese war exposed the military and political weaknesses of the Tsar's regime.

Between the Russo-Japanese war and the outbreak of the First World War Russia faced military-strategic dilemmas not unlike those into which it may be headed in the multipolar world of the year 2000 and thereafter. Extensive frontiers offer both opportunity for imperial expansion and vulnerable arteries for the flow of aggressors into Russian territory. As foreshadowed in Chapter 3, future Russian general staffs will have to choose, as did those in the late nineteenth and early twentieth centuries, between a mobilization and a deterrent paradigm. A mobilization paradigm would rely on a small professional force operating at a high degree of peacetime readiness for combat and capable of prompt response to attack. The force would be supported by deep pockets of reserves drawn from Russia and perhaps from associated Commonwealth states. A deterrence paradigm, dominant during the Cold War years, required large numbers of immediately deployable and offensively poised ground and tactical air forces to storm fortress Europe before the US could arrive with its rescue mission and before NATO could take its decision in favor of nuclear escalation.[14]

Some have written off the significance of nuclear deterrence as a result of the growing amity between Russia and the West. For the immediate future, however, it appears that deterrence remains a significant issue for the Russian general staff and political leadership. This is so for several reasons. First, Russia is a global power only by virtue of its large nuclear arsenal, and especially by virtue of its strategic nuclear weapons. Its general purpose armed forces are in a state of political uncertainty and military personnel turbulence. Second, nuclear deterrence is more predictable than conventional deterrence. Whereas the historical record of nuclear deterrence is so far unblemished, albeit with a few scary near misses such as Cuba, 1962, the record of conventional deterrence in this century admits of two world wars and a large number of other highly destructive military conflicts.[15] Third, the US and Russia must be concerned about the crisis and deterrent stability of their respective strategic retaliatory forces unless and until those forces are no longer aimed at targets in one another's territorial homeland.

Chapter 6 offers detailed quantitative assessment of various possible arms reduction agreements between Russia and the US. Our purpose is to ascertain whether stable deterrence is as likely at lower levels of armament as it was at higher levels. It will be recalled from Chapter 2 that the degree of deterrence stability during the Cold War years has sometimes been exaggerated. None

10

the less, both the US and the Soviet Union since at least the late 1960s deployed forces of such redundancy and diversity that a credible first strike was inconceivable for either side. Reducing strategic nuclear weapons to minimum deterrent levels, well below START and perhaps down to as few as 1,000 weapons, does not automatically make for a safer world or more secure relationship of mutual deterrence.

Detailed simulations of nuclear exchanges between hypothetical US and Russian arsenals were performed for the following force levels on both sides: START-accountable; 'true' START or 6,000 actual strategic re-entry vehicles; 3,000 RV; 2,000 RV; and two 1,000 RV cases. The analysis considers the significance of different levels of alert for the two sides' forces and the implications of different operating tempos, such as those which distinguish American from Russian submarine forces, for readiness and survivability. Simulations permitted examination of counterforce targeting options until hypothetical forces were used up, allowing the user to compare the 'remainder' US and Russian forces left over. Although minimum deterrent forces might not actually be used against counterforce targets, the methodology forces the important question whether surviving forces after counterforce exchanges can still inflict unacceptable damage on the attacker.

The analysis reveals that under reasonable assumptions about survivability and other aspects of weapons performance, the US and Russia can preserve assured retaliatory capabilities even at levels as low as 1,000 warheads. However, the consequences of reductions are not necessarily symmetrical below the level of 3,000 or so. Below that level, the lower alert levels and higher vulnerabilities of Russian submarine and bomber forces compared with US forces (based on experience of the Cold War years, which, if anything, *overestimates* probable future Russian capabilities) leaves the Russian deterrent much more dubious than the American one. Each side under any condition retains enough survivable nuclear force to inflict numerous 'disasters beyond history' on the other side's economy and society, apart from the strategic reserves arbitrarily set aside from US and Russian nuclear forces.

There is both good news and bad news in these findings. The good news is that force reductions even greater than those agreed to in START, and even below the levels of 3,500 to 3,000 mentioned in the Bush–Yeltsin initiatives of 1991 and 1992, can be carried out without necessarily placing in jeopardy stable deterrence. On the other hand, deterrence stability is not automatically better at lower than at higher levels, and it may be worse unless Russia can modernize its bomber and submarine forces or acquiesce in dropping out entirely from the strategic nuclear deterrence competition. The Russian general staff may be very reluctant to do so unless its conventional military

11

power is much more secure against all probable enemies than it now appears to Russian military leaders.[16]

The concluding chapter summarizes our findings and cautions against two kinds of simplicity in efforts to project the future of US and European security from the Cold War past.[17] The first kind of oversimplification dismisses the Cold War experience as totally irrelevant. In this view, a demilitarized security agenda dominated by supranational economic interdependence and liberal political pluralism will rule out any resort to major war in Europe.[18] Along with this is the related assumption that nationalism, at least nationalism of the virulent kind that spawned two world wars in this century, has been dampened by the experience of both wars and by the stamping out of recividist tendencies toward belligerence in European domestic societies.

The opposite version of security simplicity is the assumption that what will follow the end of Cold War is anarchy. While the importance of economic interdependency and liberal institutionalism can be exaggerated, both must be acknowledged as significant components of a new European security community. The experience of the European Community and its potential for acquiring a usable military-security arm, by means of a revived Western European Union, argues against a return to security autarchy in Europe. So, too, does the peaceful reunification of Germany and the inclusion of united Germany in NATO. Franco-German military cooperation and the continued presence of some US troops in continental Europe, albeit reduced to about 50,000 or so, are additional pillars of support against any renewal of the kinds of tendencies so evident in the 'gathering storm' of the 1930s.

In between the polar futures of debellicized Europe and security anarchy is a third, which is security pluralism combined with concert diplomacy. Security pluralism allows to Europe the option of maintaining nationalism and statism in high politics while economic integration proceeds apace, pursuant to those aspects of the Maastricht agreement which call for greater coordination of monetary and other economic policies. Political union is further off, but some expression of federalism is apparent in the growing significance of the European parliament and in the revival of the WEU as a security instrument for the EC. Through CSCE, WEU and NATO, Europe has available institutions for the 'multilateralization' of any conflict and its dampening through concert diplomacy. Concert diplomacy exploits the interest of the larger powers of Europe and the United States, including Britain, France, Germany, Italy and Russia, for the purpose of dampening conflicts elsewhere.

Before the idea of concert diplomacy in support of security pluralism is dismissed out of hand, it serves to recall that the original Concert of Europe operated with exactly this kind of setting. The conclusion of the Napoleonic wars did not result in one hard and fast prescription for postwar security, and the Congress of Vienna admitted many compromises for ordering the post-war world. The concert was not far off the ground when it subdivided into two security blocs: the 'eastern' and more authoritarian group of Prussia, Austria and Russia, and the 'western' group of Britain and a restorationist France.[19] Ideological differences divided the northern courts from the more democratic British and French players in the concert system: Britain, for example, was against forceful intervention to suppress democratic revolutions. Neverthe-less, the concert system held together by means of a broader consensus against any major adjustment of interstate territory and in favor of balance of power politics as a means of preserving the status quo.

As Craig and George have noted, this consensus prevailed over ideo-logical and other differences among the powers from 1815 to about 1854.[20] It also merits recalling when this system first began to break down in a major way. The Crimean War ended with a majority of European powers in favor of revising rather than preserving the system of toleration for ideological diver-sity in order to preserve a stable balance of power.[21] A war fought over few if any of the powers' intrinsic interests far from the center of Europe became the gateway through which a working system of concert diplomacy fell into irrelevance.

The preceding point is significant in view of events in former Yugoslavia in 1992 and the possibility that this and other regional or civil wars could draw into its vortex the great powers of Europe now that they have been liberated from nuclear thrall and Cold War bipolarity. A middle way of security pluralism supported by concert diplomacy that we have forecast here is permissive of meaningful success in the avoidance of war, or of significant failure to bring about security community. The destiny of Europe remains in the hands not of systems of diplomacy or strategy but of persons who will be required to adapt those devices to a new international environment.

NOTES

1. Samuel P. Huntington, *The Soldier and the State* (Cambridge, MA: Belknap Press/Harvard University Press, 1957); Huntington, *The Common Defense* (New York: Columbia University Press, 1961); and Morris Janowitz, *The Professional Soldier: A Social and Political Portrait* (New York: Free Press, 1961).
2. Harry G. Summers, Jr., *On Strategy: A Critical Analysis of the Vietnam War* (New York: Dell Publishers, 1984).
3. Ibid., p. 73.
4. For details, see Stephen J. Cimbala, 'Behaviour Modification and the Cuban Missile Crisis: From Brinkmanship to Disaster Avoidance', *Arms Control*, No. 2 (Sept. 1992), pp. 252–84.

5. John Mueller, 'The Essential Irrelevance of Nuclear Weapons: Stability in the Postwar World', *International Security*, No. 2 (Fall, 1988), pp. 55–79.
6. Richard Ned Lebow, *Nuclear Crisis Management: A Dangerous Illusion* (Ithaca, NY: Cornell University Press, 1987).
7. For a discussion, see Richard H. Ullman, *Securing Europe* (Princeton: Princeton University Press, 1991), Ch. 4, esp. p. 71.
8. Charles A. Kupchan and Clifford A. Kupchan, 'A New Concert for Europe', Ch. 8C in Graham Allison and Gregory F. Treverton (eds), *Rethinking America's Security: Beyond Cold War to New World Order* (New York: W.W. Norton, 1992), pp. 249–66.
9. A European security organization very much along these lines as an outgrowth of NATO is discussed in Ullman, *Securing Europe*, Ch. 4.
10. *Osnovy voennoy doktriny Rossii* (Proekt) (Fundamentals of Russian Military Doctrine) (Draft), *Voennaya mysl'*, May 1992, Special Edition, esp. pp. 3–9.
11. Richard F. Staar, *The New Russian Armed Forces: Preparing for War or Peace?* (Stanford, CA: Hoover Institution, 1992), pp. 16–18.
12. Ibid., p. 19.
13. For historical perspective, see William C. Fuller, Jr., *Civil–Military Conflict in Imperial Russia, 1881–1914* (Princeton: Princeton University Press, 1985).
14. One might argue, following this distinction, that Russia failed to manage successfully the crisis of July 1914 on account of its inability to choose successfully or decisively between a mobilization and a deterrent paradigm. Its Foreign Ministry sought to use partial mobilization for deterrence of Germany and Austria, but the Russian general staff distrusted any plan for partial mobilization and effectively stonewalled orders for partial mobilization until the Tsar could be talked into general mobilization. See L.C.F. Turner, 'The Russian Mobilisation in 1914', Ch. 11 in Paul M. Kennedy (ed.), *The War Plans of the Great Powers, 1880–1914* (London: Allen & Unwin, 1979), pp. 252–68, and D.C.B. Lieven, *Russia and the Origins of the First World War* (New York: St. Martin's Press, 1983), esp. pp. 139–54. Turner and Lieven offer interesting and somewhat contrasting views on certain aspects of Russian First World War mobilization.
15. John J. Mearsheimer, *Conventional Deterrence* (Ithaca, NY: Cornell University Press, 1983), pp. 19–20, enumerates some significant modern failures of conventional deterrence.
16. See, for example, the discussion of potential dangers in the draft Russian doctrine of May 1992 cited in note 10, *supra*.
17. For an informative and balanced assessment of the post-Cold War world, especially with regard to the relationship between technology and politics, see Donald M. Snow, *The Shape of the Future: The Post-Cold War World* (Armonk, NY: M.E. Sharpe, 1991).
18. For commentary and critique of this perspective, see Mearsheimer, 'Disorder Restored', Ch. 8A in Allison and Treverton (eds), *Rethinking America's Security*, pp. 213–37.
19. Gordon A. Craig and Alexander L. George, *Force and Statecraft: Diplomatic Problems of Our Time* (New York: Oxford University Press, 1983), pp. 34–5.
20. Ibid., p. 34.
21. A.J.P. Taylor, *The Struggle for Mastery in Europe, 1848–1918* (Oxford: Clarendon Press, 1954), p. 61. See also Craig and George, *Force and Statecraft*, p. 36.

1

The Cold War Armed Forces of the United States: Atypical Past and Uncertain Future

The issue of military legal and political subordination to duly constituted civil political authority has long been a decided issue in American politics.[1] Nevertheless, the Cold War presented to US policy-makers and military planners some unexpected and unprecedented challenges.[2] The Cold War US military was qualitatively as well as quantitatively different from its predecessor.[3] The following discussion identifies some of the most important attributes of the Cold War US armed forces and their political setting in terms of their implications for civil–military relations.[4] These are: bipolarity and US–Soviet hostility; nuclear weapons and mutual deterrence; defense reorganization and developments in command-control technology; the experience of Vietnam and other cases of low-intensity conflict; and, finally, the development of an all-volunteer armed force. Some comments will also anticipate the future international environment and its implications for civil–military relations.

BIPOLARITY AND US–SOVIET CONFLICT

The international system of the Cold War was an unexpected outcome of an unexpected war. The US had hoped prior to the outbreak of the Second World War to withdraw to its stance of splendid isolationism which had supposedly characterized its foreign policy before the First World War. However, this effort at inter-war military self-effacement was already compromised by several factors. First, the US imperialist experience in the aftermath of the Spanish–American war gave to Americans a heady sense of world engagement, however selective that engagement might be. Second,

15

European security concerns would not go away from American national interests. To the contrary, during the 1930s the two became inextricably linked. The major significance of Franklin Roosevelt's election to the Presidency was not apparent at first blush; lauded by his partisans as an economic savior, his actual innovation was to guide brilliantly an isolationist Congress and polity toward European engagement.

A third force driving the US away from its inter-war isolationist reverie was the development of well-armed imperial dictatorships in Germany and Japan with world-class political ambitions. Given the size and competency of its military establishment during the 1930s, the US could not extend deterrence on behalf of the status quo in Europe and Asia against rising hegemons in Berlin and Tokyo. The League of Nations proved to be feckless. The power vacuum that resulted when Britain and France only belatedly grasped the ring of anti-fascist resistance had to be filled from outside of Europe. Russia was a possible source of rescue, but Hitler's initial diplomatic moves had neutralized Stalin as an opponent until Germany was ready to deal with Russia. As France crumbled and Britain scrambled to evacuate Dunkirk, American political leaders were forced to confront their responsibility for global political order. The Japanese attack in December 1941 influenced the timing of US national awakening, but the content of that awakening had already been settled.

Forced to re-arm on a scale unprecedented before or since, Americans divided in their assumptions about the probable shape of the postwar world and of US civil–military relations within that world. Some maintained that wars were caused by renegade states and perverse ideologies. Once these states and ideologies had been defeated and discredited, a return to normalcy in US overseas commitments and in the size of the US military establishment could be expected. Others who saw the causes for the Second World War as more complicated doubted that the US could extricate itself from postwar responsibility for world peace. President Roosevelt and his advisors, clearly in sympathy with the internationalist viewpoint of postwar global engagement, expected that the US and other great powers, including the Soviet Union, could cooperate through the United Nations to deter irruptions of world peace.

This expectation was to be disappointed, and bitterly so. There are various explanations for why events turned out so much against the optimism of US wartime leaders. Most important for the discussion here was the immediate postwar distribution of global military power. The bipolar international system which followed the collapse of Axis military power left the US and the Soviet Union in a position of uniquely global reach. US and Soviet Cold War leaders began to perceive that world politics was a constant sum game in which the winnings of one side would have to take place as a consequence of the other's losses.[5] As suspicion hardened into hostility during crises over Greece and Turkey, Iran, Czechoslovakia and Berlin, President Truman was persuaded that only diplomatic firmness and military preparedness would deter further Soviet adventurism. The Truman doctrine and the Marshall plan declared US universal and regional interests in keeping friendly regimes outside of the Soviet political orbit. But Truman was not prepared to pay the defense costs for these expanded commitments until the outbreak of war in Korea in 1950.

The US postwar military establishment was not returned to a status similar to that awaiting the US armed forces after the First World War. Although more than ten million men were demobilized as rapidly as possible, the Truman administration did not foresee the peacetime period ahead as one of pacific deterrence through international organization and US disengagement, as had been the expectation of President Woodrow Wilson following the First World War. Instead, the US committed itself to oversee the postwar reconstruction of Japan and Germany, the former as a political democracy and the latter according to the four-power division of the pie agreed to during wartime conferences. In the event, Germany was permanently divided and rearmed, but not before the US confronted the need for the rearmament of Europe along with the economic construction of it.

The rearmament of free Europe had to be undertaken with some sensitivity to US and European sensitivities: US body politic neuroses about overseas commitments in peacetime, and European sensitivities about being dominated by American guns and capitalism. The solution for incorporating Western Europe within an American strategic protectorate was NATO, a voluntary alliance of unprecedented scope and inclusiveness in peacetime Europe. NATO grew up along with the maturing of the US nuclear arsenal and the hardening of Cold War lines between the Soviet sphere of interest and the Western one. Eventually the Soviet side copied NATO's approach and organized the Warsaw Pact as a belated answer to NATO's European rearmament, although decisions were not taken by democratic consent within the Pact as in NATO.

The extension of US peacetime defense commitments to Western Europe, followed by the stationing of permanent American garrisons there, was a politico-military strategy for Cold War competition. But it was also a strategy for freezing the status quo in the center of Europe, thereby reducing the risk of inadvertent war between the US and the Soviets. NATO was to contain the independent proclivities of the British, French and Germans to fight with one another as a by-product of its importance for deterring Soviet attack. Although not fully appreciated even now, NATO's political role was as

17

important as its military one. Most US foreign policy influentials did not anticipate an actual shooting war in Europe during the latter 1940s or early 1950s. As George F. Kennan had anticipated, what was more probable was the slow squeeze of Kremlin pressure against American and allied interests both directly, as in the Berlin crisis of 1948, and through surrogates, as in Korea in 1950.

Before the outbreak of the Korean war, the Truman administration had a hard sell for military buildup, including a rapid expansion of the US nuclear arsenal. NSC-68, a high level policy study calling for major US rearmament in view of an imminent Soviet military threat to Europe and Asia, had been completed shortly before the eruption of North Korea's forces across the 38th parallel in June 1950.[6] US defense spending shot across the previous ceilings imposed by the Truman administration and the Chinese entry into the war only convinced many Americans that a Sino-Soviet bloc now threatened US global interests. However, Korea was an improbable war for which American strategic planners had scarcely prepared. Expecting a global war against the Soviet Union begun in Europe, planners had given little consideration to the possibility of US involvement in limited wars supported by the Soviet leadership but fought by other governments and forces.

Korea posed strategic and policy-making dilemmas in Washington. The Truman administration's decision to fight a limited war was controversial on several grounds. Field commander Douglas MacArthur chafed at political restrictions on military operations. Truman neglected to ask for a formal declaration of war against North Korea or against China after Chinese troops later entered the fighting on the Korean peninsula. The war was fought under the auspices of a United Nations collective security operation. Since the precedent had been set for commitment of US forces to limited war without a Congressional declaration of war, the precedent would be repeated to disastrous effect in Vietnam.

NUCLEAR WEAPONS AND MUTUAL DETERRENCE

The paradox of nuclear weapons was that they made the United States homeland vulnerable to destruction for the first time in more than a century. In addition, this destruction could be accomplished without first destroying US military power or occupying the country. At the same time, nuclear weapons gave to the United States the retaliatory power to strike back at any aggressor, inflicting unacceptable damage. Therefore, a perceived sense of imminent vulnerability to possibly devastating surprise attack went hand in hand with a conviction on the part of leaders that mutual deterrence would guarantee strategic stasis. This vulnerability–invulnerability paradox left some persons confident in US security based on the threat of nuclear retaliation. Other persons were equally confident that nuclear weapons would cancel themselves out, and that meaningful military competition between the US and the Soviet Union would occur below the nuclear threshold.[7]

The US nuclear stockpile was relatively small when Truman left office, and control of nuclear weapons in peacetime remained with the Atomic Energy Commission. This situation became unacceptable to the armed forces once the Eisenhower admininistration had embarked on its preferred strategy of massive retaliation, emphasizing the employment of nuclear weapons instead of conventional forces even in contingencies other than total war. The acquisition of nuclear weapons by US military commanders was a strategic necessity even as it posed problems of civil–military relations and problems for the relationship between the President and Congress.

The Korean war had seen the US commit combat forces overseas without a Congressional declaration of war. The judgment of the Truman administration had been that a formal declaration of war was neither necessary nor desirable. Nuclear weapons posed another kind of challenge to established civil–military relations. The National Security Act of 1947 had established a national military establishment headed by a Secretary of Defense and responsible for the administration and combat performance of all US arms of service, including the newly independent Air Force. Amendments to NSA in 1949 created the Office of the Secretary of Defense and removed service secretaries from cabinet rank. Defense reorganization is considered at greater length below, but the preceding points about the initial unification of DOD and the assumptions on which that unification was built are pertinent for the present discussion.

For reasons well understood by the framers of the US Constitution and accepted by most nineteenth and twentieth century Presidents, the US could not have a Presidential military force. The armed forces belonged to the people, and to this end were subdivided into active duty forces, reserve forces (trained service reserves and individual ready reserve pools) and unorganized militia (potential draftees). The US Congress had rejected Universal Military Training prior to the Korean war despite President Truman's strong support for UMT. The US Constitution lodged the power to declare war in the Congress because the authors of that document distrusted executive power acting without legislative oversight. But the framers also required a Congressional declaration of war for another reason: it would empower the President to conduct a war on behalf of the entire aroused nation in arms. Public opinion was thought to be the bedrock on which effective commitment of US forces had to be based, and Congressional assent to war was deemed improbable unless broad public support was available.[8]

Nuclear weapons called into question this carefully circumscribed relationship created by the Constitution between the Executive and Legislative branches of the US government. They did so in two ways. First, they made necessary the avoidance of total war. Since it was easier for the public to perceive that total war was more threatening than limited war, Presidents found it harder to make the case for those kinds of wars which the nuclear constraint would permit. Second, nuclear weapons promised unprecedented destructiveness in a short time. Especially once the Soviet Union had acquired a strategic nuclear retaliatory force capable of destroying many targets in the continental United States, the US had to devise warning and assessment systems and to create a nuclear decision-making process which by implication circumvented the Constitutional luxury of a declaration of war. In case of Soviet nuclear attack against targets in the continental United States with ballistic missiles launched from land or sea, the US effective warning would be measured in minutes rather than hours.

The Constitutional bypass created to deal with this situation of unprecedented danger was that the President was recognized as commander-in-chief and that this status permitted him to retaliate against surprise attack without immediate Congressional authorization. The Congress had other ways of reviewing and controlling the development of US nuclear weapons programs and military budgets too. Therefore, the legislative branch was not frozen out of the process of force acquisition and general military–strategic planning. But the arcana of nuclear weapons target planning and the packaging of strategic and other nuclear options remained largely within the compass of the executive branch during the Cold War years.

By itself this might have been regarded as an unavoidable necessity, but the nuclear habit of Presidential initiative unencumbered by legislative oversight spilled over into Cold War Presidential approaches to other security and defense issues. It was no surprise that maintaining a state of permanent military preparedness raised the status of the Pentagon relative to other cabinet departments, which themselves grew in stature on the coat-tails of Cold War Presidential power. In addition, the play of power within the national security community in response to activist Presidents, to the visibility of Cold War crises, and to the possibility of prompt nuclear surprise attack was important in its own right. As discussed in the next section, the implications of instant readiness for deterrence and for total war were far-reaching for

20

defense reorganization. This section emphasizes the implications of the strategic paradigm shift from mobilization to deterrence for military strategy.

Nuclear weapons affected the means of defense preparedness and the expectation of surprise attack. But they did not provide usable forces in battle. Therefore, Cold War Presidents and their advisors confronted the problem of what to do if deterrence failed. This problem was partly diverted by the expectation of 'extended' deterrence: nuclear weapons would deter any Soviet conventional attack against NATO Europe or other vital American interests. However, there were several problems with extended deterrence of this sort. First, not all Europeans wanted it; the French, for example, quite vociferously rejected any reliance on American nuclear protection. Second, the absolute character of nuclear weapons did not lend themselves to military separatism: self-defense by threat of nuclear retaliation was intimately bound up with notions of sovereignty. Third, Presidents wanted usable options in times of crisis, so that they could up the ante by using coercive measures short of war, as President Kennedy showed by his choice of blockade during the Cuban missile crisis of 1962.

Because nuclear weapons implied separate sovereignties, they complicated NATO alliance cohesion unless NATO Europeans were prepared to play only the role of US military satellites. West European economic recovery subsequent to the Marshall Plan and the creation of the European Communities led to assertive self-confidence within NATO deliberative bodies for policy consultation and for military planning. By the 1960s US military strategy had to be marketed aggressively if it were to be adopted consensually by America's NATO European allies. In 1967 NATO settled on a declaratory doctrine, flexible response, which carried it to the end of the Cold War. It was a political success wrapped in a military enigma. Europeans were allowed to believe that flexible response was something other than graduated escalation, whereas American expositors contended that graduated escalation was exactly what flexible response was all about. Although NATO represented singular success in the area of peacetime military planning and coordination, under the stress of actual crisis or war the political diversity of its member states could have prevented consensual response to any Soviet challenge. Fortunately for NATO, such a challenge was not provided by Moscow.

DEFENSE REORGANIZATION

The preceding section noted that nuclear weapons and deterrence theory forced US military planners to shift from a mobilization to a deterrence paradigm in force and policy planning. The requirement to be ready for instantaneous response and global military operations meant that both plans and budgets would have to be coordinated across service lines. This caused civilians in the Office of the Secretary of Defense to interfere in decisions about military procurement and war planning to an extent without precedent in peacetime American history.

The battles over Planning, Programming and Budgeting Systems (PPBS) during the McNamara years in the Pentagon do not require retelling. The political controversy during those years was not really about budgeting techniques, but about preferred strategy, doctrine and prerogatives in determining force size. During the latter years of the Eisenhower administration, it was recognized that separate service planning for nuclear retaliation was not acceptable. The Single Integrated Operational Plan (SIOP) was established by McNamara's predecessor as a method for the coordination of Navy and Air Force strategic target planning. It followed that the same model might be extended to general purpose forces: defining objectives and asking what mixes of forces, regardless of service ownership, would most effectively and efficiently fulfill those objectives.

McNamara and his associates knew that the battle between OSD and the services over conventional forces programs would be more difficult than that over nuclear.[9] Nuclear weapons lent themselves to tight Presidential control: release would be obtained only in the gravest circumstances. The readiness and structure of conventional forces were other matters, and military leaders felt with some justification that they were the experts in residence on war fighting with armies, navies and air forces apart from nuclear deterrence. Civilians in the McNamara Pentagon doubted openly that there was any such thing as military science or military art and disparaged combat experience as a necessary constituent of fruitful policy analysis. Although the military services outlasted some of McNamara's more ambitious exertions into their domains, his lasting impact on defense decision-making was to exploit the National Security Act of 1947 and the subsequent amendments of 1949, 1953 and 1958 to make the Office of the Secretary of Defense the most powerful of cabinet departments.

None the less, the post-McNamara Secretaries of Defense would have their hands full. One source of trouble was the previously mentioned tradition of decentralized military decision-making within each service. Another was the growth of Presidential power and the derivative raising in stature of the President's advisor for national security affairs. The first person to hold this title formally was McGeorge Bundy in the Kennedy administration, and the significance of the NSC advisor and his staff grew proportionately as the

Cold War demands for US preparedness thrust Presidents into the cockpit of military decision-making. Not all of Bundy's successors necessarily enhanced the power and prerogatives of the NSC advisor, but one who surely did was Henry Kissinger. As NSC advisor to President Nixon, Kissinger became the President's *éminence grise* for all matters of security and foreign policy, eventually eclipsing Secretary of State William Rogers and finally pre-empting his job.[10]

Kissinger's NSC *apparat* represented a threat not only to the Department of State, but also to the Pentagon. In defense of the Pentagon it must be said that Kissinger was a formidable and relentless bureaucratic opponent whose grasp of policy and power-mindedness in Washington were uncommon. Kissinger also profited during Nixon's second term from that President's preoccupation with domestic policy, especially with Watergate. But Kissinger's special talents for self-aggrandizement foraged into two areas of great military sensitivity: crisis management and arms control. In addition, the failed US military strategy in Vietnam was by the time Nixon took office all too apparent, and the US program of phased withdrawal for American forces from South Vietnam, termed Vietnamization, required the orchestration of military and diplomatic instruments to exploit coercive diplomacy in reverse.

Laird's and Schlesinger's Pentagon fought off the NSC about as well as any bureaucrats could have, but the legacy left by Kissinger was an empowered NSC with the prerogative to exert control over the coordination of all matters touching upon foreign and defense policy. Once power had flowed in the direction of NSC, Presidents no longer had the choice of reinstituting a weak NSC organization and depending upon cabinet departments to take up the slack. Reagan attempted just this solution at the outset of his first term, and it failed. The NSC emerged during the Reagan administration as the locus for highly sensitive covert operations, in part because the CIA wanted to avoid Congressional investigations related to covert action, and in part because the expectations of experienced bureaucrats were that NSC was the place to get things done.

The tendency to empower NSC reappeared during the Bush administration. Brent Scowcroft, formerly NSC advisor in the Ford administration, accepted the same position under George Bush. The NSC retained its status as a second policy-planning and crisis-management department for national security affairs. Scowcroft served as Bush's most articulate expositor of US security policies, confident that defense management would be carried out according to the President's wishes by long-time Bush political colleague Dick Cheney. However, one important change from the Reagan to the Bush administrations had been Congressional passage of defense reform in the

23

form of the Goldwater–Nichols legislation. This added to the power of the Chairman of the JCS, who became the principal advisor to the President and the Secretary of Defense on matters of military strategy and force structure. The Joint Staff was also reorganized and made more responsible and responsive to the Chairman. In addition, Goldwater–Nichols mandated that future officers aspiring to general or flag rank must have career defining experiences wearing 'purple' in specified joint assignments. Finally, the Goldwater–Nichols legislation mandated that the various commanders-in-chief of the US military unified and specified commands (LANTCOM, PACOM, CENTCOM, and so forth) be given more weight in the process of developing combat and crisis management plans.[11]

Throughout the Cold War history of defense reorganization, one could with some justification divide policy-makers, military professionals and scholarly observers into two schools of thought: those who were structural optimists and believed that defense reorganization was actually related to improved policy outcomes; and bureaucratic pessimists, who rejected the possibility of any direct connection between structural reorganization and better defense policy.[12] In defense of the optimists, one could point to McNamara's introduction of PPBS and its avoidance of waste and duplication in some high technology, expensive service programs. In defense of the optimists, one could also cite the Goldwater–Nichols legislation and its apparently favorable implications for the conduct of US defense planning and war-fighting strategy during the Gulf crisis and War from August, 1990 through February, 1991. Pessimists could argue, to the contrary, that the reach of McNamara's reforms frequently exceeded their grasp, as in the eventual demise of the TFX. Pessimists could also note that 'servicism' remained, even after the Goldwater–Nichols reforms, an unavoidable barrier to jointness in planning and procurement: command and control systems usable by more than one service provide excellent illustrations of the pervasiveness of single service opportunism.[13]

PERSONNEL POLICY AND MILITARY DOCTRINE

The US military experience of the Cold War years was marked by unprecedented beginnings and endings with regard to personnel policy and military doctrine. The beginnings and endings in personnel policy and doctrine were related. The early Cold War years saw conscription carried over into the peacetime armed forces in the form of selective service. This went hand in

24

hand with the concept of permanent preparedness for global war. The Army was of course more dependent than the Navy (including Marines) or Air Force on conscription. Large forces permanently stationed in Europe, Korea and elsewhere served as trip wires to deter Soviet attack on American allies. US strategy for global war during the Truman administration, given the relative scarcity of nuclear munitions and delivery vehicles compared to forces available to Truman's successors, did not envision an air–atomic offensive against the Soviet Union as capable of fulfilling US wartime objectives by itself. It was assumed in the war plans of the late 1940s that air–atomic attacks by both sides would be followed by protracted conflict between Soviet and opposed armed forces in Europe and worldwide.

The availability during the Eisenhower administration of larger numbers of nuclear weapons supported the shift to a declaratory strategy for general war of massive retaliation. While administration officials were eventually forced to retreat from this formulation in cases of less than total war, for global war against the Soviet Union Eisenhower defense planning relied mainly upon promptly delivered and massive air atomic offensives. Special study committees such as the Gaither committee pointed to the need for a larger menu of military responses, and Army officials chafed at the allocation of defense resources within arbitrary ceilings and under planning assumptions favoring Air Force and Navy procurement. NATO's declared objective of 96 active duty and reserve divisions went far beyond any commitment that its members were actually willing or able to provide. Thus, reliance on nuclear weapons for extended deterrence became all the more necessary as a result of allied as well as US domestic budgetary priorities.

The Army emerged from the 1950s as the fourth wheel of a defense establishment whose preferred military doctrines favored the more technical and less manpower-intensive arms of service. Under the Kennedy administration things would soon change. Kennedy preferred the strategy which became known as flexible response, calling for improved US conventional forces for crisis response, forward presence and, if necessary, actual war fighting in order to raise the nuclear threshold in Europe. This last rationale was pushed hard within NATO by McNamara, to the detriment of alliance solidarity on doctrine until the French departure from NATO's military command structure in 1966 and the promulgation of flexible response in 1967. Flexible response arguably allowed a greater role for the ground forces in US military doctrine and force planning, but by the time flexible response became official NATO doctrine, the lines between Cold War 'east' and 'west' had solidified and neither side seemed interested even in limited probes against the other. The outcome of the imbroglio over the Berlin crisis of 1961 and the Cuban missile crisis of 1962 had been to establish a mini-détente between the superpowers on matters of high politics and security, especially on the likelihood that either side would instigate even a crisis in Europe, let alone a war.

If strategic stasis reigned in Europe, Khrushchev's insistence that wars of national liberation could be loosed against Third World regimes supportive of US policy, called forth from the Kennedy administration a burst of doctrinal innovations. Special operations and low-intensity conflict studies, as the term was later denoted, led to an emphasis on sub-conventional warfare, psychological operations and nation building as constituent elements of US military strategy.[14] But only a fringe of the armed forces officer corps, such as the Green Berets, committed themselves to careers along these lines. The more traditional arms of service lacked serious interest in special operations and regarded their counterinsurgency brethren with undisguised distaste. As the US commitment to Vietnam escalated well beyond the engagement of special operations forces and intelligence operatives, conventional military mind-sets displaced the political side of the politico-military equation on which special operations had been predicated. US conventional forces in Vietnam, on the evidence, fought well against North Vietnamese conventional forces and Viet Cong units when the latter were willing to stand and fight pitched battles.

However, it became apparent by 1968 even to the Department of Defense that the US could not win the counterinsurgency or propaganda wars at an acceptable cost: Johnson's resignation and Nixon's phased disengagement followed. Many arguments can be started in bars whether US conventional or unconventional military strategy failed in Vietnam. The present discussion bypasses that temptation and emphasizes the implications of counterinsurgency displacement by conventional strategy for military personnel policy. Having decided that escalation from limited commitment to a major US military campaign in South Vietnam was necessary, President Johnson none the less sought to balance the requirement for military escalation against his other priorities in domestic politics, especially his cherished Great Society programs recently passed by Congress. Johnson's 'guns and butter' policy filled the armed forces ranks of enlisted personnel by expanded conscription of young persons while forgoing the option to mobilize the organized reserve forces. The result of this approach was to create nationwide dissent against the war, first across US college campuses, and then to wider audiences.

The draft more than anything else had brought the US military escalation in Vietnam to a stopping point. When US Commander-in-Chief William Westmoreland asked for several hundred thousand additional troops in 1968, then Secretary of Defense Clark Clifford suggested to Johnson that he pull the plug. Johnson did so, announcing his intention not to seek another term of office and thereby conceding the failure of US policy and strategy in Vietnam. However, Johnson left the nation with a major force and policy commitment to a war which would continue without complete US disengagement until 1973, and with war between the Vietnamese until 1975. With military disengagement from Vietnam went another look at US conscription policy, and the Gates Commission recommendation to end conscription was adopted and put into effect in 1983. In effect the US had come full circle to its pre-twentieth century peacetime standard of raising armed forces by voluntary enlistment (except for the American Civil War, when both sides were drafted).

The onset of the AVF coincided with post-Vietnam doctrinal revisionism. The Nixon administration changed the 1960s strategy of being able to fight two and a half wars simultaneously to one and a half wars, and Nixon emphasized that US support for besieged allies would stop short of involving American ground forces. Voluntary enlistment dictated a strategy of selective rather than ubiquitous military engagement. Selective engagement was also facilitated by the full-blown emergence of US–Soviet détente during the 1970s and Sino-American rapprochement. It was perceived by US foreign and defense policy élites that diplomatic containment of Moscow's ambitions was more cost-effective than overpromising of US military involvement in regional conflicts. US and Soviet leaders worked to stabilize the Middle East and to create new expectations about their mutual interests in avoiding nuclear war and inadvertent military escalation.

The Carter administration ended its term of office on a sour note in US–Soviet relations: the invasion of Afghanistan caused Carter to ask that the US Senate suspend consideration of the SALT II treaty he had negotiated. In addition, Carter called for the creation of a Rapid Deployment Force for prompt intervention in the Middle East/Persian Gulf: this force would grow into the Central Command which US Army General Norman Schwartzkopf would take into battle against Iraq in 1991. But Carter's démarches against the Soviet Union did not revert to ubiquitous commitment. Carter maintained the path of selective engagement of US military power previously established under Nixon and Ford. Thus, Carter was disinclined to call for a return to conscription, and Reagan was even less interested in doing so.

Nor was the Reagan administration very interested in commitment to large-scale counterinsurgency wars. It preferred to direct US commitments toward counter-terrorism, covert action, and investment in conventional high technology supportive of 'air–land battle' between the Warsaw Pact and NATO. The all-volunteer force, so badly underfunded that it could scarcely meet its recruitment goals during the 1970s, fared better in the 1980s after enlisted

27

TABLE 1.1

DISTRIBUTION OF ARMY AND ARMED SERVICES RECRUITS BY EDUCATION
AND ARMED FORCES QUALIFICATION TEST CATEGORY 1980 AND 1987

Year (Army only)	Education	Cat. I, II	Cat. IIIA	Cat. IIIB	Cat. IV	Total
1980	H.S. grad.	10.2	5.4	10.9	28.1	54.5
	Non-grad.	3.6	4.0	12.2	25.7	45.5
1987	H.S. grad.	35.2	22.6	29.4	4.0	91.2
	Non-grad.	3.4	5.3	0.1	0.0	8.8

Year (All-Services)	Education	Cat. I, II	Cat. IIIA	Cat. IIIB	Cat. IV	Total
1980	H.S. grad.	19.0	9.8	17.2	22.1	68.1
	Non-grad.	4.8	4.3	9.8	13.1	31.9
1987	H.S. grad.	38.4	23.2	28.0	4.0	93.6
	Non-grad.,	2.7	3.7	0.1	0.0	6.4

Source: Adapted from Congress of the US, Congressional Budget Office, *Social Representation of the US Military* (Washington, DC: Congressional Budget Office, 1989), p. 63.

and officer compensation were raised significantly by Congress. A comparison of Army and all-service recruits in 1980 and 1987 shows that high-school graduates by 1987 were a significantly larger proportion of all-service recruits, and especially, of Army recruits. (See Table 1.1.) From 1980 to 1987, the proportion of high-school graduate non-prior accessions to the Army rose from 54.5 per cent to 91.2 per cent: the all-service proportion rose from 68.1 per cent to 93.6 per cent. In addition, these larger numbers and proportions of high-school graduates fared much better in 1987 than in 1980 on the Armed Forces Qualification Test.

Congress also supported the administration's emphasis on firepower-intensive as opposed to manpower-intensive military strategies, although the DOD and services emphasized the need to make firepower smarter through precision-guided munitions, improved capability for electronic warfare, and eventual applications of sensors and weapons based on other physical principles.

Reagan's high-tech strategic focus extended even into the heavens, where he assumed his proposed Strategic Defense Initiative would eventually yield deployments of space-based battle stations and other accoutrements of post-nuclear deterrence. This vision also seemed to require technology-intensive, not manpower-intensive, forward planning, and the vision of massive man-power wars was pushed even further from planning consciousness. A war which began in Europe might, according to Reagan planning guidance, extend into a world war, but US and allied NATO strategy did not envision a repeat of any conflict as extended in time as the Second World War. NATO's campaign on the central front in Europe would be based on conventional deep strikes, aided by modernized sensors, battlefield computers and precision weapons, and it would be designed to disconnect the tail of the Soviet offensive from its teeth in short order. The template for this NATO game plan could be perceived clearly even by lay readers who picked up a copy of Tom Clancy's *Red Storm Rising:* it remains interesting even though experts now suspect that the Red Army was far less capable of carrying out any offensive action in Europe in the 1980s, or earlier, than government and media alarmists supposed.

The modernized US air–land battle template also remains interesting for its subsequent application to the Persian Gulf, against Iraq in 1991. Here US military planners who contemplated how to prevail in a war between NATO and the Warsaw Pact, and who were confounded by the commingling of conventional and nuclear forces in Europe, found a more amenable theater of operations for the application of US military power. A five months' period of grace for military buildup in Saudi Arabia did no harm to US readiness for war in January, 1991 and US air–land battle doctrine played successfully before a packed house.

The results of the Gulf War of 1991 seemed to vindicate not only US conventional military strategy and technology, but also the decision in favor of the all-volunteer force taken decades earlier. Columnist Charles Krauthammer, celebrating the 'unipolar moment' in which the US had allegedly found itself by virtue of the collapse of the Soviet Union, noted that:

> in 1950 the U.S. engaged in a war with North Korea: it lasted three years, cost 54,000 American lives, and ended in a draw. Forty-one years later, the U.S. engaged in a war with Iraq: it lasted six weeks, cost 196 American lives, and ended in a rout. If the Roman Empire had declined at this rate, you would be reading this in Latin.[15]

However, experts recognized the ironical character of the vindication of US strategy, since the air–land battle doctrine had been intended for a force structure which was obviously not going to be preserved intact into the post-Cold War era. The US might not even be able to repeat Desert Storm by 1997 with forces drawn down considerably from 1990 levels even following the Bush plan of 1991, which Congress might choose to modify. In addition, the Congress and some politico-military strategists in the executive branch were also planning to employ US military capability for non-traditional-non-combat missions, including operations designed to preserve sanctuaries

29

from attack for besieged ethnic or national populations (such as operation Provide Comfort for the Kurds in Iraq). The Bush strategy for more traditional uses of US military power emphasized the performance of forward presence and crisis response missions intended for regional contingency operations outside of Europe, not for global warfare or for large inter-state wars in Europe.

PREVENTIVE DIPLOMACY AND MULTILATERAL MILITARY INTERVENTION

The US had created a conventional force structure of unprecedented size in order to fight the Cold War. That force structure was backed by nuclear deterrence which conveyed the threat of unacceptable retaliatory punishment for any Soviet attack on North America or Europe. US experts now declare that the Cold War has ended and that the US has won it. It would be more accurate to say that the US successfully overstated the Soviet threat from the beginning to the end of the Cold War and that this overstated threat never materialized. Whether this was due to successful deterrence or crisis management, or to good fortune, we will never be certain. The point is that, whether success was designed or fortuitous, the sizes and kinds of forces appropriate for Cold War will be less suitable for the next century. As force sizes and character change, so, too, will the politico-military context within which forces are used for deterrence or compellence.[16]

Recent experience suggests that nuclear deterrence will be less significant in future US policy planning. The improved capabilities of long-range, precision-guided conventional munitions allow policy-makers to escape nuclear dependency even for some missions requiring strategic depth. Although the technology spin-offs of SDI are not altogether clear at the time of writing, the US and allied experience with SCUD attacks and Patriot interceptions in the Gulf War suggest growing military interest in theater missile defenses for US allies. Limited non-nuclear defenses for the US homeland have also been authorized by Congress in the form of support for the Bush GPALS (Global Protection Against Limited Strikes) program. There is little apparent Congressional interest in overturning nuclear deterrence based on offensive retaliation, even at greatly reduced force levels.[17]

US military interventions of the future will favor the use of tailored forces for rapidly concluded contingency operations, as in the Bush administration Panamanian intervention (Just Cause). Selective unilateral intervention will in all likelihood be combined with increased post-Cold War willingness to support multilateral military interventions or preventive diplomacy, through the United Nations or by means of regional international organizations. One can distinguish in this regard *peacekeeping* and *peace enforcement* operations. In the case of peacekeeping, the UN or other multinational body authorizes the positioning of neutral forces between combatants, in order to separate their armies and to provide time for negotiations that must precede any conflict resolution. Peace enforcement means that the forces of a multilateral organization impose a solution on reluctant combatants. The United Nations Emergency Force (UNEF) deployed in Egypt from 1956 to 1967 illustrates the UN use of a peacekeeping force; the UN operation in the Congo, involving the forcible reintegration of secessionist Katanga province, is a case study in peace enforcement.

The participation of US forces in peacekeeping and peace-enforcement operations is not without difficulties. During the Cold War it was necessary for American and Soviet forces to be excluded from United Nations peacekeeping or peace-enforcement operations for obvious reasons: a regional crisis would be turned inadvertently into a superpower conflict. This difficulty no longer obtains. The end of the Cold War opens the door to Security Council peacekeeping or peace-enforcement operations backed by both the United States and Russia, among other permanent members. However, the involvement of US forces in multilateral operations will not be without controversy on the home front. The commitment of US combat forces under the command of any other governments, even under the umbrella of an international organization, creates potential problems of operational integrity and political accountability. These problems did not really arise in Korea or in the Gulf War of 1991 because, although authorized by the UN, they were essentially US-designed and -directed military campaigns.

The civil war in Yugoslavia leading to the breakup of that country in 1992 provided a case study of the difficulty in obtaining commitments by the great powers to multilateral military intervention. Reports of widespread genocide and the potential for this conflict to escalate beyond the Balkans called for some kind of concerted European or UN action, either to separate the combatants or to impose a cease-fire and return to the status quo ante. However, none of the European security organizations seemed able to take the lead. NATO had been designed for an entirely different mission. The Western European Union was enjoying a welcome rebirth, but it had not yet matured as a center of gravity for preventive diplomacy or for multilateral military intervention. The Conference on Security and Cooperation in Europe (CSCE) was the most inclusive body capable of taking a stand, but its

31

very inclusiveness precluded harmonious action of a military sort. Sadly, the recognition dawned in 1992 that only a military organization with the capabilities of NATO or the former Warsaw Pact, without the aura of Cold War illegitimacy that either of those organizations would carry, could intervene effectively to put a stop to the slaughter in Croatia and Bosnia.

But even if effective intervention could be obtained, the question remained on whose side intervention should be undertaken. Collective security is the political umbrella under which multilateral military intervention takes place. Collective security presupposes that one can identify an aggressor and a defender, a good guy and a bad guy.[18] In a multinational civil war of the Yugoslav type, the problem of identifying aggressors and defenders would be one that defied consensus or political objectivity. Prominent US politicians and media pundits called for military interventions of various kinds in 1992, and some made compelling cases that the chaos in former Yugoslavia could not be ignored. However strong the imperative, the 'how' remained difficult if not impossible to answer. The *necessity* for multilateral intervention was easier to demonstrate than the *feasibility* of any military operation involving multinational ground forces under UN or other auspices.

The questions about operational feasibility of post-Cold War contingency operations, for US or for multinational military forces, are the same. What is the political objective? What are the military objectives which follow from this political objective? Are these military objectives attainable with the forces which the US or the UN are willing to commit? Similar questions, in case of US unilateral or US commitment of troops to multistate operations, must be answered with regard to American domestic politics and its unavoidable connection with foreign policy. The Cold War experience, with a much more evident global military threat facing each administration from Truman through Reagan, was marked by great contention between Congress and the Executive branch over the prerogatives held by each in security policy. In addition, the acceptability of unilateral or multilateral interventions to the US public would be relevant to the Congress and, for this reason and others, to the administration.

It is instructive to recall how thin was the margin by which the US Congress in January 1991 voted to authorize President Bush to use force in order to expel Iraq from Kuwait. Bush wisely avoided the trap into which President Johnson had fallen in Vietnam: marching into battle without getting Congress explicitly committed to the nation's war aims. However, in insisting on getting the explicit endorsement of Congress for Desert Storm, Bush risked a negative vote and a greater domestic obstacle course against the effective use of force. The vote in Congress was close despite the following aspects of the situation, all presumably permissive of intervention: Saddam Hussein acted the role of a textbook villain; the threat to oil supplies provided an obvious and tangible interest; the US acted with the support not only of its former Cold War allies but also of a majority of Middle East and Southwest Asia Muslim societies; and the Soviet Union endorsed the use of force if necessary in the UN Security Council.

One might argue, therefore, that the UN support for Desert Storm represents a 'best case' of international consensus behind US war aims.[19] None the less, public opinion polls during the US Gulf military buildup and before the outbreak of war suggested that the American people were anxious about the feasibility of going to war and divided about the desirability of doing so. Congress reflected this ambivalence in public perceptions of the desirability and feasibility of using force: Congressional and public opinion, fortified by some expert testimony on Capitol Hill, contained strong support for continued economic sanctions as an alternative to war. In the aftermath of the rapid and decisive coalition victory over Iraq, of course, public ambivalence turned into overwhelming approval. But a less successful military campaign would, on the evidence of Korea and Vietnam, have produced a more divided and contentious public policy debate.

In any event, the kinds of forces required for future multilateral or unilateral US military intervention will be, compared with their Cold War predecessors, more mobile, technically advanced, and élitist. As the armed forces are drawn down in size and as decades of voluntary service make the armed forces less familiar to average Americans, the degree of dissociation between the armed forces and the larger society may increase. Objective civilian control of the US armed forces may become more necessary as the assumption of a military embedded in societal values is less sustainable. Careerist and vocational motives for recruitment and retention can be expected to assume even greater importance for the military services in the 1990s and thereafter than they did from 1973 through the 1980s. The AVF of the twenty-first century will therefore constitute a paradox for Presidents. It will be easier to set in motion small interventionary or protective reaction strikes, such as those against terrorism. But it will be as difficult as it was during the preceding four decades, if not more so, for any sustained commitment of large numbers of US forces to unilateral or multilateral military interventions. US long-range conventional maritime and air power will become the makeweights of the US strategic deterrent, with smaller, residual nuclear forces kept in the background. Europe will either pacify itself or not, but in either case eventual US disengagement of all but token US combat forces from Western Europe seems unavoidable. US forces remaining in Europe could be incorporated

33

into multistate military frameworks such as WEU or a WEU-deputized remnant of NATO.

FUTURE PROSPECTS

One can take as a point of departure an essay written by Robert E. Osgood in 1983, published in the Naval War College Review and entitled 'American Grand Strategy: Patterns, Problems and Prescriptions.'[20] In this essay Osgood discusses the history of Cold War US security policy from the perspective of the gap between American interests and American power. According to Osgood, this gap is inevitable in any state's foreign policy, but the gap may be larger for countries with global stakes and commitments. This 'interests–power gap' is related to the tendency of US foreign policy to oscillate between periods of activism and passivity, or in Osgood's terms 'augmentation' and 'retrenchment'. Military build downs go along with retrenchment, of course, and up with augmentation.[21] Osgood disagrees with those who say that the US suffers for lack of any grand strategic concept:

> The American problem is not the lack of grand strategy but an undifferentiated and excessively abstract view of US vital interests and of the Soviet threat to them, crisis-born fluctuations in perceptions of the threat, spasmodic responses to crises, and the disparity between proclaimed security interests and actual capabilities.[22]

Approximately one decade after Osgood wrote this essay, Robert J. Art attempted to define American grand strategy for the post-Cold War era.[23] Art's essay is usefully bracketed with Osgood's, for it looks backward to the US security struggles of the period 1945–90 in the aftermath of Soviet collapse, German reunification and outbreaks of democratization in East Central Europe. Art's use of the term grand strategy is rather specific and differs from some other and more traditional uses. Grand strategy, according to Art, is used: (1) to specify the goals that a state ought to pursue, both security and non-security objectives; and (2) to outline how military power can serve those goals.[24] This leads Art to ask four main questions about preferred US grand strategy after the Cold War. First, what are US interests? Second, what threats to those interests can be foreseen? Third, which military strategies are best suited to counter those threats? Fourth, what kinds of forces are necessary in order to carry out those preferred strategies? Using these dimensions of interest, threat, strategies and forces, Art develops the following schematic as shown in Table 1.2.

34

TABLE 1.2

INTERESTS, THREATS AND REQUIREMENTS FOR US OVERSEAS FORCE
DEPLOYMENTS

US Interest	Primary Threat to US Interest	Major Purpose for Overseas Deployments	Case for US Overseas Deployment
Protect US homeland from destruction	spread of nuclear weapons	selective, extended deterrence to prevent spread	high cost of low-probability events
Prosperity based on international economic openness	economic nationalism	reduce others' worries about relative gains to preserve stability	hedge bets on account of inconclusive arguments about interdependence
Guarantee access to Persian Gulf oil	near monopoly control by regional hegemon	deter attack and/or conquest of others	simple deterrence
Prevent certain wars	wars between great powers in Europe and Far East; prevent conquest of Israel and South Korea	deter attack and/or conquest of others	additional insurance for low-probability events
Promote democratic institutions and certain humanitarian values abroad, where feasible	other states committing acts of genocide against their own citizens	intervention in other states' internal affairs	humanitarian motives

Source: Robert J. Art, 'A Defensible Defense: America's Grand Strategy after the Cold War', *International Security*, No. 4 (Spring 1991), p. 8 with insignificant modifications of text.

As indicated in the table, Art argues for the primacy of five major interests, from protection of the US homeland to the promotion of democratic governments and overthrow of governments committing mass murder of their citizens. However, he does not consider military power equally useful or appropriate for these objectives. In general, he is skeptical about the ability of the US to intervene militarily in the internal affairs of other states, and about the US capability for imposing regional peace among disputant states throughout the world.[25] Nuclear weapons, according to Art, have severed the connection between the Eurasian balance of power and US security: the only serious threat to US security lies in the spread of nuclear weapons to terrorists or irresponsible Third World heads of state. A case can be made for continued US military presence in the Far East and Europe, in order to support the openness of the economic order among wealthy industrialized nations, and for a military presence in the Middle East/Southwest Asia and in South Korea, in order to maintain access to oil and in order to preserve historical security commitments in that region, including one to Israel.[26]

This assessment of US security in the post-Cold War period, allowing for disagreements on the margin, would not be disputed by many academic or government security studies analysts. More controversial is Art's assessment of threats to US security during the Cold War: they were minimal to non-existent. Nuclear weapons provided absolute security for the American homeland. Moreover, although US policy-makers mixed traditional geo-political logic with nuclear age reasoning to argue for extended nuclear deterrence on behalf of Europe and Japan, US security was not dependent on the success of extended deterrence for those or other states. Nuclear logic invalidated geopolitical logic: the US neither required a Germany and Japan free from Soviet control for the defense of its homeland, nor did it need German and Japanese territory for forward deployments contributory to conventional war fighting against the Soviet Union. As Art explains:

> throughout the Cold War era, the United States could have deterred or defended against any assault on its own territory; it did not need the Germans, the Japanese, or anyone else to do this. It did not have to protect others out of geopolitical logic, even though it may have thought so at the time. It offered protection partly out of a misconception about the continuing relevance of geopolitical logic, but also out of historical memories, concerns for stability and economic openness, and worries about nuclear spread.[27]

Implicit in this argument is an assumption: that domino effects do not matter for states with invulnerable nuclear capabilities. As Robert Jervis has noted, however, the relationship between nuclear weapons and domino effects is two-sided.[28] On the one hand, as Art suggests, the physical importance of dominoes decreased because the Cold War superpowers did not need allies to preserve mutual second-strike capability. On the other hand, nuclear weapons can, and did during the Cold War, increase the psychological importance of allies and of the credibility of commitments to allies.[29] The behavior of the US and the Soviet Union in Cold War confrontations was thought to influence their reputations for protecting allies and vital interests.

Art's analysis of US Cold War security certainly overstates how secure American leaders felt. Even allowing for the exaggerations of office seekers, defense secretaries and think-tanks in the business of defense contracting during the Cold War, even US Presidents and their advisors who were skeptical of pessimistic threat assessments wondered aloud about the stability of nuclear deterrence. They also doubted that traditional geopolitical logic had been totally invalidated by nuclear weapons. As George F. Kennan explained throughout his career, US containment strategy, aimed at keeping selected 'strongpoints' such as industrial Europe out of Soviet hands, was a strategic necessity as well as a moral interest.[30] Nuclear weapons invalidated traditional geopolitical logic only if the US recognized no points on the conflict spectrum between accommodation of Kremlin ambitions and nuclear war. Policy-makers were reluctant to go this far in dissolving the pre-nuclear connection between force and policy.

The Truman administration during the first half of 1950 had already concluded that less rather than more reliance on conventional forces for deterrence and for defense was the prudent policy. This thinking, coalesced within Truman's Policy Planning Staff under the direction of Paul Nitze, led to the drafting of NSC-68, perhaps the most important policy document of the Cold War. Anticipating that the US was more likely to be confronted by piecemeal aggression instead of world war, NSC-68 argued that US policy should be less dependent on nuclear weapons and more on general purpose forces. Although NSC-68 acknowledged that improved nuclear forces would still be necessary for deterrence, a deterrent based exclusively on nuclear superiority would leave the US with 'no better choice than to capitulate or to precipitate a global war'.[31] The same concern, this time about Eisenhower's allegedly excessive dependency upon nuclear weapons, would prompt President Kennedy and Secretary of Defense Robert McNamara to substitute flexible response for massive retaliation.

Although policy-makers at the time were never as confident in nuclear deterrence stability as scholars after the event, Art does call attention to the uniqueness of nuclear weapons. Nuclear weapons did not invalidate pre-nuclear geopolitics, but they did make total war politically unacceptable. And they also made the US both more and less vulnerable than it had been before the Second World War. Nuclear weapons mated to delivery vehicles of intercontinental range ended the invulnerability of the American homeland to enemy destruction: an opposed nuclear superpower would not even have to destroy American forces before laying waste to US cities. On the other hand and as noted earlier, the US was even more invulnerable to enemy invasion and conquest of its national territory than it had been before the invention of nuclear weapons.[32]

Ironically, nuclear stalemate of the Cold War prompted US and allied innovation in high technology, conventional weapons for precision aiming, electronic warfare, surveillance, and command and control. This innovation paid dividends after the Cold War in the successful outcome of Desert Storm. Desert Storm showed that strategic military operations on a theater scale could be conducted without using nuclear weapons. Admittedly, US and allied coalition operations benefited from a favorable diplomatic and political setting for the use of force. Nevertheless, the air–land battle template which crushed Iraq's field forces and command–control systems demonstrated impressive and *usable* military power at an acceptable cost, something that nuclear weapons never provided.

CONCLUSIONS

The Cold War enlarged the size of the peacetime US armed forces and imposed unprecedented requirements for the support of US coercive diplomacy, crisis management and nuclear deterrence. It also led to a reorganized military establishment through which policy-makers sought to impose increasingly greater degrees of centralized control. Although more centralized control over military administration and logistics was generally regarded as contributory to improved strategy, central control over operations was less favorably received among military professionals. Micro-management of operations was resisted by field commanders, and the Goldwater–Nichols reforms created a climate permissive of empowerment for the operational commanders-in-chief, or CINCs, who would actually have to fight a war. Future military professional adjustment will be necessary to a security environment of uncertain threat assessment, high technology weaponization, and military–political stress created by voluntary forces even less integrated into society than now.

NOTES

Parts of this chapter will appear in Sam C. Sarkesian (ed.), *America's Armed Forces* (Westport, CT: Greenwood Press, forthcoming).

1. Seminal studies of US civil–military relations include Samuel P. Huntington, *The Soldier and the State* (Cambridge, MA: Belknap Press/Harvard University Press, 1957); Huntington, *The Common Defense* (New York: Columbia University Press, 1961); Morris Janowitz, *The Professional Soldier: A Social and Political Portrait* (New York: The Free Press, 1961); and Russell F. Weigley, *Towards an American Army: Military Thought from Washington to Marshall* (New York: Columbia University Press, 1962).
2. On security requirements and responses for the pre-Cold War or 'geopolitical' era, see Robert J. Art, 'A Defensible Defense: America's Grand-Strategy after the Cold War', *International Security*, No. 4 (Spring, 1991), pp. 5–53.
3. For example, Cold War conditions posed new problems of inter-service command and control. This is well treated in historical perspective by C. Kenneth Allard, *Command, Control and the Common Defense* (New Haven: Yale University Press, 1990).
4. An expert analysis of US military professionalism in the Cold War years is provided in Sam C. Sarkesian, *Beyond the Battlefield: The New Military Profession* (New York: Pergamon Press, 1981).
5. These developments can be traced in John Lewis Gaddis, *The United States and the Origins of the Cold War, 1941–1947* (New York: Columbia University Press, 1972), esp. pp. 282–352, and Adam Ulam, *The Rivals: America and Russia since World War II* (New York: The Viking Press, 1971).

6. John Lewis Gaddis, *The Long Peace: Inquiries into the History of the Cold War* (New York: Oxford University Press, 1987), p.114.

7. Robert Jervis, *The Meaning of the Nuclear Revolution* (Ithaca, NY: Cornell University Press, 1991), and Lawrence Freedman, *The Evolution of Nuclear Strategy* (New York: St. Martin's Press, 1981).

8. This case is argued in Harry T. Summers, *On Strategy: A Critical Analysis of the Vietnam War* (New York: Dell Publishers, 1982), Ch.1.

9. For an account from the perspective of McNamara's staff, see Alain C. Enthoven and K. Wayne Smith, *How Much Is Enough? Shaping the Defense Program, 1961–1969* (New York: Harper and Row, 1971), esp. pp.117–64. See also William W. Kaufmann, *The McNamara Strategy* (New York: Harper and Row, 1964).

10. Evolution of the NSC is discussed in John Prados, *The Keepers of the Keys; A History of the National Security Council from Truman to Bush* (New York: William Morrow, 1991).

11. For assessments of Goldwater–Nichols, see Robert J. Art, *Strategy and Management in the Post-Cold War Pentagon* (Carlisle, PA: US Army War College, Strategic Studies Institute, 22 June 1992), and Rep. Les Aspin, Chairman and Rep. William Dickenson, US Congress, House Committee on Armed Services, *Defense for a New Era: Lessons of the Persian Gulf War* (Washington, DC: US Government Printing Office, 1992).

12. For a sampling of expert assessments, see Robert J. Art, Vincent Davis and Samuel P. Huntington (eds), *Reorganizing America's Defenses: Leadership in War and Peace* (New York: Pergamon Brassey's, 1985).

13. Art, *Strategy and Management in the Post-Cold War Pentagon*, pp.26–7.

14. A critique of US experience is provided in D. Michael Shafer, *Deadly Paradigms: the Failure of US Counterinsurgency Policy* (Princeton: Princeton University Press, 1988). See also Douglas S. Blaufarb, *The Counterinsurgency Era: US Doctrine and Performance. 1950 to the Present* (New York: Free Press, 1977). For evaluations of Amerian experiences with covert action, see John Prados, *Presidents' Secret Wars: CIA and Pentagon Covert Operations Since World War II* (New York: William Morrow, 1986), and Roy Godson (ed.), *Intelligence Requirements for the 1980s. Vol. 4: Covert Action* (Washington, DC: National Strategy Information Center, 1983). An assessment of the impact of low-intensity conflict on American military professionalism appears in Sarkesian, *Beyond the Battlefield*, Part II, Chs. 4–7.

15. Charles Krauthammer, 'The Unipolar Moment', Ch. 8F in Graham Allison and Gregory F. Treverton (eds), *Rethinking America's Security* (New York: W.W. Norton, 1992), p. 298.

16. For prescriptions about future US grand strategy based on careful appreciation of Cold War experience, see Paul Kennedy, 'American Grand Strategy, Today and Tomorrow: Learning from the European Experience', Ch.10 in Kennedy (ed.), *Grand Strategies in War and Peace* (New Haven: Yale University Press, 1991), pp.167–84.

17. Diverse expert assessments are provided in *Strategic Defense Initiative: What Are the Costs. What Are the Threats?*, Hearings before the Legislation and National Security Subcommittee of the Committee on Government Operations, US House of Representatives, 102nd Congress, 1st session, 16 May and 1 October, 1991.

18. Comparison of the theoretical principle of collective security with the actual practice of it appears in various works by Inis L. Claude, Jr. Most recently, see Claude, 'Collective Security After the Cold War', Ch.1 in Gary L. Guertner (ed.), *Collective Security in Europe and Asia* (Carlisle, Pa: US Army War College, Strategic Studies Institute, March 1992), pp.7–28.

19. What the Gulf War of 1991 portends is explored in Aspin and Dickenson, House Armed Services Committee, *Defense for a New Era*, and Norman Friedman, *Desert Victory: The War for Kuwait* (Annapolis, MD: US Naval Institute Press, 1991), pp.236–60.

20. Robert E. Osgood, 'America's Grand Strategy: Patterns, Problems and Prescriptions', *Naval War College Review*, No.5 (Sept.–Oct. 1983), pp.5–17.

21. Ibid., p.7.

22. Ibid.
23. Art, 'A Defensible Defense', *passim*.
24. Ibid., p.7.
25. Ibid., p.9.
26. Ibid., p.10.
27. Ibid., p.23.
28. Robert Jervis, 'Domino Beliefs and Strategic Behavior', Ch.2 in Robert Jervis and Jack Snyder (eds), *Dominoes and Bandwagons: Strategic Beliefs and Great Power Competition in the Eurasian Rimland* (New York: Oxford University Press, 1991), pp.20–50. It is certainly the case that nuclear weapons combined with bipolarity led some US and Soviet leaders into repeatedly expressed fears of bandwagon and domino effects. The argument finds support in the US Truman Doctrine, developed in the expectation that Western Europe would accommodate Soviet foreign policy demands without any US reaction to the situations in Greece and Turkey, and in the assumptions by US leaders in 1950 that Europe would go neutralist if North Korea was allowed to conquer South Korea. See Deborah Welch Larson, 'Bandwagon Images in American Foreign Policy: Myth or Reality?', Ch.4 in Jervis and Snyder (eds), *Dominoes and Bandwagons*, pp.95–6.
29. Jervis, 'Domino Beliefs and Strategic Behavior', p.39.
30. John Lewis Gaddis, *Strategies of Containment: A Critical Appraisal of American National Security Policy* (New York: Oxford University Press, 1982).
31. NSC-68, cited in Gaddis, *The Long Peace*, p.114.
32. On the unique vulnerability of states in the nuclear age, see John H. Herz, *International Politics in the Atomic Age* (New York: Columbia University Press, 1959).

2

The Paradox of Escalation: A Heterodox View of Cold War Stability

Despite the fact that the Americans and the Soviets signed some significant agreements during the Cold War to reduce arms and to control peacetime and crisis military operations, their policy-makers and military planners waffled on the issue of how any major war, with or without nuclear weapons, would be controlled or limited after it had begun. Neither side could guarantee that escalation from local to general war was *certain*, and neither could provide reassurance that it was *impossible*.[1] Because escalation was neither impossible nor certain, indeterminacy dominated military–strategic calculation and crisis management short of war prevailed. And, because escalation was neither impossible nor certain, there was no logical way to get into a nuclear war or, once in a war, to get out of one. Future potential combatants armed with nuclear weapons will not necessarily be in this favorable twilight between impossible and certain escalation. It follows that states with small and potentially vulnerable nuclear arsenals may be *less* constrained than states with large and survivable nuclear weapons capabilities.

This argument about escalation dynamics as a stabilizing force in Cold War politics is contrary to the conventional academic wisdom that escalation is a corrosive force for crisis or deterrence stability. I make this argument below in several steps. First, the problem that US policy-makers and military planners faced in making the transition from a pre-nuclear world, in which dominating strategies for military victory were possible, to the nuclear world is revisited from the perspective of US strategy-making in the early Cold War years. Second, the implications of these US strategic reconstructions for NATO alliance strategy and politics are considered. The center of gravity in both of these sections is the distance between the perceived necessity for nuclear flexibility of some kind and the impossibility of attaining it, due, according to my arguments in both cases, to the character of escalation dynamics.

Third, US arguments for nuclear flexibility implied a Soviet interest in escalation control which was undemonstrable. Soviet nuclear proclivities could never be known with high confidence, but Soviet military theorists and war plans showed little interest in nuclear bargaining. Escalation which was neither impossible nor certain left too much initiative in the hands of Soviet opponents once conventional war had broken out. Neither certainty-centered nor uncertainty-reliant models of nuclear bargaining impressed the Russians.

The fourth section discusses the problem of escalation control by alliance, illustrated by NATO Cold War decision-making and by comparative examples from the crisis management experience of Europe's great powers immediately before the First World War. I conclude that alliances have even greater difficulty controlling escalation than single states do. The experience of multilateral crisis management in 1914, when crisis management failed, and during the Cold War, when it did not, shows that the logic of alliance and the logic of escalation control are essentially opposed. Alliances emphasize extended deterrence and coupling; escalation control, on the other hand, invites states to consider their separate destinies and military autonomy.

THE PROBLEM OF TRANSITION

Theorists, policy-makers and military technologists, as throughout history, attempted to make a gradual transition from the old world to the new. The line between pre-nuclear thinking and nuclear strategy was not nearly as clear to US policy-makers and strategic thinkers in the early years of the nuclear age as it became later.[2] For example, US leaders during the latter 1940s and early 1950s, on account of the numbers of nuclear weapons available and the anticipated sources of military threat at that time, expected that nuclear weapons could be used in the early stages of a protracted and global war. Such a war would, according to these expectations, be decided ultimately by the mobilization potentials of the two sides. Instead of a classical battle of annihilation in which massive and decisive nuclear strikes might attain a decisive outcome in the initial period of war, US planners during the late 1940s and early 1950s envisioned a complicated war of attrition, of which nuclear exchanges represented the likely first phase.[3] The development of thermonuclear weapons and the proliferation of intercontinental delivery vehicles by the Americans and Soviets forced planners to put these assumptions aside in favor of short war and massive nuclear response, a view transcendant by the time Eisenhower left office.

The development and deployment of plentiful nuclear weapons, and the miniaturization of components which made possible their delivery over large distances by launch vehicles, amounted to a possible technological dethronement of the primacy of politics over strategy. As Robert Gilpin's study of the relationship between international systems and political change noted, the primary source of international systems transformation before the nuclear age was war.[4] Wars were the outcomes of disequilibrium brought about by changes in the distribution of power, prestige and other values favorable to actors dissatisfied with the status quo, and against those supporting the existing order. Although such power transitions could sometimes be managed without war, drastic shifts in the relative power positions among major state actors sooner or later created tension between existing constraints and perceived possibilities which erupted into war. Wars settled at least temporarily the issue of dominance and subordination in the international arena, insofar as the question of postwar pecking order was dependent on territory, wealth, quantity and quality of arms, and other variables customarily used to measure the relative power positions of states.

Nuclear weapons threatened to make these traditional yardsticks of inter-state relative power assessment obsolete, but they did more. After the deployment of fusion bombs the relationship between technological innovation and war planning underwent a fundamental change, in some ways supportive of stable deterrence and status quo politics and in other ways subversive of the existing order in force and policy. As trump cards of the international spectrum of force, nuclear weapons created the potential for devastating first strikes or retaliations against which no defense could be imagined or created for decades, if ever. This appeared to reverse the traditional relationship between offensive and defensive military strategies, in which the making of attacks was thought to be more risk-laden and uncertain of success than the conduct of a successful defense. On the other hand, the speed and lethality of nuclear weapons made offensive technology look more imposing, but not necessarily an offensive *strategy*. Weapons which could be protected from a first strike could be used to execute a retaliation of unprecedented destructiveness against the attacker. Unless the attacker could obtain preclusive protection against retaliation from the victim, the difference between the attacker's and the defender's postwar worlds might be politically and militarily insignificant.

Two kinds of emphases in war planning seemed logical on the basis of this impasse created by the paradoxical primacy of offensive technology and defensive strategy. First, planners could put all their eggs in one basket, emphasizing the certainty of a massive retaliatory response for almost any aggression, including attacks using conventional forces only and those attacks launched against allies protected by a US or Soviet nuclear umbrella. Second, and opposed to the first, planners could emphasize the use of nuclear

43

retaliation in selective doses, including strikes by tactical and theater nuclear forces stationed outside their home territories and by specially tasked strategic nuclear forces aimed at targets in a particular theater of operations. The putative advantage of the first strategy was that it distributed risk more evenly among the protected, non-nuclear members of an alliance and their nuclear protector: massive retaliation was an all or nothing proposition. The alleged advantage of the second strategy was that it provided political leaders with the option to fight war on the installment plan while negotiating to bring it to some conclusion short of total and mutual destruction. Massive retaliation and flexible response also had the vices of their virtues: inflexibility which might freeze leaders into inaction for all but the gravest provocations, in the first case; and seduction into what might be expected to be a small war but which might turn out to be a larger one, in the second case. Accordingly, the Eisenhower administration by its second term had begun to recognize the virtues and vices of both massive and flexible nuclear retaliation, although it produced no actual war plans which placed serious constraints on the geographical scope or societal destructiveness of US retaliatory attacks.[5]

The Kennedy administration inherited this incompletely deconstructed version of the Eisenhower strategy, and was quite dissatisfied with the implications. Although it seemed infeasible to base war plans and force modernization on the assumption of protracted conflict including a nuclear first phase, it also seemed implausible that a strategy for military victory in a short war could be devised with high confidence. Despite an apparent US superiority in numbers of delivery vehicles and warheads during the latter 1950s and early 1960s, US leaders expressed little confidence in the stability of nuclear deterrence and approached the idea of nuclear brinkmanship gingerly. During the Cuban missile crisis and despite a favorable ratio of approximately seventeen to one in deliverable nuclear weapons, President Kennedy pulled back from the invasion of Cuba or the bombing of Soviet missile sites in Cuba, disregarding strong urgings from military and other advisors.[6] Concerned about the danger of escalation which might get out of control during the crisis, Kennedy and his advisors held back their conventional military sword in favor of coercive diplomacy.[7] Instead of seeking military victory below the nuclear threshold which the Soviets were powerless to prevent, Kennedy sought to give Khrushchev a face-saving exit from a pre-established path of mutual confrontation. US nuclear options and war plans were relevant to management of the Cuban missile crisis not because they promised to provide victory at an acceptable cost, but because they created a zone of uncertainty through which Khrushchev and Kennedy were determined not to move.

Although the Kennedy administration would subsequently begin a process of refining US nuclear war plans (SIOPs) with the objective of creating a larger spectrum of military options, neither Kennedy nor his successors could escape the limits placed on strategy by the upper end of the ladder of escalation. Successors to Eisenhower were able to discard the rhetoric of massive retaliation, but not the reality that any feasible plan for US–Soviet nuclear war would of necessity involve massive nuclear responses and unacceptable collateral damage for both sides.[8] Additional refinements to those SIOPs subsequent to those of the Kennedy administration did not change this condition of nuclear rigidity. Accordingly, critics of US nuclear strategy and of NATO nuclear dependency for the deterrence of war in Europe fought a rearguard action to establish credible options short of massive nuclear response, from the 1950s through the 1980s.

The US strategy of massive retaliation and its successor generations of general nuclear response invited dissatisfied analysts and policy makers to borrow from pre-nuclear thinking and from disciplines other than military history and political science. During the 'golden age' of US strategic nuclear theorizing (from the late 1940s until about 1966), operations researchers, social psychologists and economists contributed important new insights into the field of US military strategy.[9] Although these insights revolutionized the way in which the field was conceptualized in academic studies, they provided no consolation to policy-makers and planners who sought ways around the obstinate nuclear technology which obstructed proportionality and discriminate uses of force. It was not only technology that stood in the way of nuclear proportionality as a pathway to the re-establishment of the connection between war and politics in a new version of classical strategy. Politics were even more important; ends became as controversial as means became unyielding. NATO members other than the Americans were never completely sold on the advantages of nuclear flexibility, and in Paris leaders opted for nuclear unilateralism as a guarantee that French national interests would not be hostage to graduated deterrence.[10]

It soon became apparent that the case for flexible nuclear response would be politically controversial in the US policy debate and among NATO allies. Once former Secretary of Defense Robert S. McNamara had abandoned counterforce and damage-limiting strategies in favor of a declaratory emphasis on assured retaliation, classical strategy seemed to have been sold out in favor of nuclear stalemate. McNamara argued that assured destruction described a condition as much as it summarized a preferred policy, although assured destruction was also appealing to him as a metric for establishing minimum force sizes against the more ambitious demands of military services.[11] Counter-arguments against this conversion by McNamara, in con-tradiction to the nuclear strategic utilitarianism of his earlier years, had to argue for nuclear flexibility on grounds of deterrence instead of classical war fighting and victory. Growth in US and Soviet strategic nuclear forces during the 1960s, and McNamara's persistent advocacy in US and alliance policy debates, drove out of the realm of political feasibility a damage-limiting strategy based on offensive force modernization combined with ballistic missile defenses. By the early 1970s, as the conclusion of the SALT I treaty demonstrated, both the Soviet and American leaderships had accepted the anti-classical logic that mutual deterrence could be based on offensive retaliation combined with limited defenses incapable of nationwide pro-tection.[12] The acceptance by both nuclear superpowers of this condition increased the difficulty of US officials in selling nuclear flexibility to a justifiably skeptical European audience.[13]

If SALT codified the death of any feasible search for classical strategy by means of defenses and offenses combined, there was still the possibility that additional military feasibility could be introduced into nuclear strategy by tinkering with offenses alone. The policy innovations from 1974 through the present in US doctrinal guidance for strategic target planning were based on this search for an exit from the apolitical strategic impasse of assured retaliation, judged by the standards of classical strategy. Advocates of flexible nuclear response, from the 1950s through the 1980s, argued from basic premises which constituted neoclassical versions of pre-nuclear thinking applied to nuclear strategy. The term neoclassical is more appropriate for these premises because they acknowledged the futility of traditional war-winning strategies applied to a situation of mutual deterrence. Instead, the neoclassicals attempted to modify assured destruction at the edges by adapt-ing offensive forces to the exigencies of bargaining and coercive diplomacy. Neoclassical reasoning combined psychological arguments about the in-fluence of perceptions on deterrence or escalation control with traditional aspirations for military superiority or favorable outcomes in war.

The neoclassical arguments for nuclear flexibility had two principal varia-tions. The first variation was that, while US officials actually recognized that nuclear war was politically pointless and that nuclear flexibility was of little or no value, for deterrence to work Soviet leaders must also believe those things. It was argued that the Soviet leadership did not share these convictions about the absurdity of nuclear war or about the disvalue of selective nuclear options. Therefore, it followed that the ability to deter a massive Soviet attack against North America did not necessarily deter a lesser provocation, such as an attack on Europe or selective strikes against US territory. Psychologist Steven Kull has referred to arguments of this type as 'greater fool' arguments: US officials acknowledged the futility of nuclear flexibility, but suggested that the possibility of Soviet belief in nuclear flexibility required equivalent US preparedness for similar options.[14]

The second version of neoclassical nuclear flexibility called for the US to improve its offensive forces in order to enforce its will at any level of escalation. Although unprecedented societal destruction could not be avoided in nuclear war, there were, in these views, meaningful distinctions among postwar outcomes, including postwar states of affairs which could be characterized as victory or defeat. The second version of nuclear flexibility sought counterforce capabilities, but not in numbers or in quality sufficient to make possible a credible first strike against Soviet forces. Counterforce capabilities were useful as part of a strategy of bargaining and coercion during war. Although this second form of neoclassicalism groups a diverse congregation into one pulpit, one can discern in retrospect three basic rationales for improving US counterforce offered by those so described.[15] The basic rationales for improved counterforce in this variant of neoclassicalism are: escalation dominance; risk manipulation; and war termination.

Escalation dominance means that one side can establish through favorable exchange ratios, in one or more components of post-attack nuclear forces, a position so superior that the other side is forced to yield to its demands.[16] Escalation dominance is a form of limited nuclear retaliation or warfare. The ability to prevail in a nuclear endurance contest below the level of all-out war is a necessary condition for influencing the wartime behavior of the opponent.[17] In contrast, the manipulation of risk approach does not depend on the ability to prevail at any level of actual nuclear exchange. Manipulation of risk gets both contestants into a competition in brinkmanship and nerve.[18] The purpose of higher levels of destruction is not to impress the opponent with the damage already done, but with the possibility of the unlimited and uncontrollable escalation which might follow. The war termination version of neoclassicalism borrows from escalation dominance and manipulation of risk in order to substitute an attainable political objective short of victory for the unsatisfying dénouement of mutual assured destruction.

Whereas the first of these three varieties of neoclassicalism, escalation dominance, was more relevant in the case of a war which was begun by means of deliberate attack, the other two variations were more appropriate for nuclear wars which resulted from accidents or from inadvertent escalation.[19] The escalation dominance approach presupposed that rational actors would continue their utility-maximizing calculations after nuclear war had already begun. Manipulation of risk and war termination approaches were based on a

47

more skeptical appreciation of rationality in the actual conduct of nuclear war. Manipulation of risk actually depended upon a 'threat that leaves something to chance', as Schelling explained it.[20] A process of nuclear brinkmanship or a two-way competition in risk-taking left open the possibility that both sides would lose control over events, thereby suffering greater than expected or greater than acceptable losses. The possibility of losing control over events was the element which created the shared interest in restraining the level of violence and in moderating political objectives.

War termination theory proved difficult to operationalize in the context of nuclear war, especially the kind of large-scale nuclear war which the US and Soviet arsenals were capable of waging.[21] The implication of war termination theory applied to nuclear war was that some political objective existed which could justify a small war but not a larger one. The theory seemed to suit some situations in which NATO might prefer to use limited nuclear strikes to dissuade further progress in an attack begun by the Warsaw Pact without nuclear weapons. Even in those special situations in which policy-makers, once war had begun, would keep in mind the importance of war termination, grave doubts existed as to the availability of US or Soviet command, control, communications and intelligence (C31) systems adequate to the task.[22]

All three variations of neoclassical arguments for flexible nuclear response were stigmatized by their use in the policy process as ingredients in force-building rationales. In addition, as we shall see below, the Soviets showed little apparent interest in flexible nuclear response, especially in the case of strategic nuclear weapons exploded on Soviet territory. The point is important here too, for the construction of a Soviet adversary determined to exploit any relative counterforce imbalance was all too often perceived by policy-makers as a necessary part of the case for counterforce and nuclear flexibility.[23] While Soviet military doctrine in its politico-military aspects (grand strategy) re-mained essentially defensive and potentially open to the concept of limitation in war, the military-technical level of Soviet military doctrine offered little in the way of encouragement to those US scholars who sought to find Politburo or General Staff interest in war termination or controlled nuclear exchanges.[24]

APPROPRIATE RESPONSES

Advocates of nuclear flexibility asserted a number of premises about the connection between war and politics under a doctrine of assured destruction. In the first of these premises, the strategy of assured destruction was judged to leave the US President with an insufficient number and variety of options for contingencies short of all-out war. Related to this, assured destruction seemed out of proportion to the crime of less than total aggression, which was thought by many defense critics of the 1950s to be more likely to challenge US and NATO interests than total war. Second, the Soviet Union might challenge the threat of massive retaliatory response by defining it as a bluff, pushing at the edges of US and NATO security glacis with conventional war or with assertive crisis management for which the US and its allies might have inadequate or inappropriate responses. Third, although massive retaliatory response was designed in part to reassure NATO Europeans of US resolve to turn any conflict in Europe into a decisive battle for the West as a whole, it also raised their concerns about the possibility of being dragged into undesired war or escalation on American coat-tails. The implications of this continuing tension between European fears of US abandonment and opposite fears of entrapment in wars fought for American interests only, suggested a potential problem of inconsistency. Each of these three major types of problems receives separate attention in the sections that follow.[25]

The first of these sets of questions was the appropriateness of a single and massive nuclear retaliatory response to a wide continuum of possible threats that might be laid down by Moscow or by other sources. The Eisenhower administration itself acknowledged prior to leaving office that massive retaliation was not necessarily going to be the response of choice for all threats to US or allied peace and security. President Eisenhower gave repeated evidence of an ambivalent attitude toward the possible use of nuclear weapons in crises from Korea to Berlin. He refused to rule out the possible use of nuclear weapons in actual warfare, and welcomed the apparent support that the US nuclear arsenal might give to crisis management diplomacy. Eisenhower did not necessarily favor a prompt or massive use of nuclear weapons in response to a crisis in Europe, say over Berlin, but he also wanted to avoid any impression that he would hold back the US nuclear arsenal if the Soviet Union and its allies invaded NATO territory.

The inappropriateness of any US atomic riposte to Soviet aggression in Europe was two-sided, from the standpoint of the Eisenhower administration in its evaluation of Soviet assessments. Although the threat to unleash nuclear war in response to an attack in Europe might seem to pit weapons of mass destruction against weapons of classical strategy, the obverse of this point was equally valid. The weapons of mass destruction, supported by a strategy also suited to massive destruction of social values in addition to military losses inflicted on the opponent, generated the horror and fear of the unknown in the minds of potential aggressors. Since the outcomes of any nuclear war could not be known even within tolerable ranges of uncertainty, the threat of disproportionate response made up in horror what it lacked in symmetry. US leaders in the Eisenhower administration might, according to this logic, have seemed over-dependent on the terroristic aspects of nuclear uncertainty compared with Eisenhower's successors and their preferred strategic analysts. However, the emphasis as between Eisenhower and later planners was more a matter of degree than a difference of kind.[26] Although later nuclear strategic war planners would attempt to build diversity into war fighting options and to establish the force structures necessary to support that diversity, the long march from Eisenhower to Reagan left the US basically dependent on massive retaliatory responses for credible deterrence.

The Kennedy administration, assertive and wanting to place its own stamp on US nuclear strategy, sought to establish the idea of a gradient of options for the deterrence of aggression, and to make available the forces for nuclear and conventional deterrence along a wide spectrum of conflict. From the sub-conventional or low-intensity conflicts to the ultimate spasm exchanges of unlimited nuclear war, the Kennedy planners sought to provide the President with options that were selective and discriminating about the threat being assumed and the objective of the response. In the view of Kennedy defense advisors, a threat based on massive retaliatory response was less than credible as a deterrent for anything other than all-out attack on the US homeland.[27] A wider range of nuclear options would have to be developed, in this view, in order to provide the President with choices between no use and Armageddon. In addition, it followed from this logic of 'flexible response' that more and more competent, conventional war-fighting options would have to be available to commanders and political leaders in order to raise the nuclear threshold and in order to improve the credibility of deterrence. It was also assumed by Kennedy administration planners, somewhat in contradiction to the idea of a fundamental change made in strategy by nuclear weapons, that nuclear weapons could be employed in small doses against restricted targets provided the US or NATO intent to limit the extent of nuclear use was clearly communicated to, and understood by, the adversary.

Involving the adversary in tacit acknowledgment of limited use for limited objectives raised the question of appropriateness of response. The appropriateness of response problem was related to the problem of an adequate spectrum of nuclear and other options. But appropriateness also included a more explicitly political dimension. The ultimate criterion of appropriateness for NATO was whether US choice of a preferred response could generate consensual support within the alliance. The consensus in support of any US response on behalf of NATO might matter more to the object of deterrence, the potential or actual attacker, than the strategically correct choice among finely tuned options from an elaborate menu. Crisis or wartime Soviet bargaining strategy, according to the criterion of appropriateness, would succeed or fail on the strength of NATO alliance cohesion in the face of intimidation and competition in risk-taking through the various stages of crisis or war.

The issue of appropriateness had subtle implications. It had much to do with the European resistance to the US proposal for a Multilateral Force of ships manned by crews of mixed nationality and armed with nuclear weapons. The US proposal was advanced during the Kennedy administration under the assumption that NATO Europeans without their own nuclear forces, especially the Germans, would want some finger on the trigger which might otherwise be pulled by the Americans either too soon or too late. However, the assumption which guided the MLF proposal was misguided in this regard. The German concern was not with the absence of direct, if shared, control over actual nuclear use decisions, but with enlargement of the US appreciation of Germany's singularly vulnerable position in the forward area of NATO's theater defenses. Germany could endure neither a conventional nor a limited nuclear war on its territory without suffering strategic loss, and no guarantees of US or NATO nuclear retaliation against Soviet attackers could be as important as the avoidance of war without surrender of important values.[28]

The MLF was an admittedly complicated response to a deservedly intimidating strategic problem. A plurality of nuclear decision centers might lead to an inappropriate response at the level of policy, grand strategy, or military strategy in a coalition based on democratic societies and consensual development of political aims. At the level of policy, the basic goals and objectives of NATO's member states might be placed into a state of uncertainty by a collective decision mechanism based on operational as well as political multilateralism. In grand strategy, which is the marshalling of all the resources of a state or coalition on behalf of its policy aims, the willingness of leaders in Europe and North America to mobilize for war could be diminished by the temptation for buck-passing implicit in the subdivision of NATO's nuclear trigger. At the third level of analysis, that of military strategy, appropriateness of response might also be compromised by MLF or other multilateral arrangements for implementing nuclear decisions. Crews of mixed nationality opened the door to complexity in the carrying out of NATO commands within the context of an alliance already bedeviled by 'dual hatted' national and alliance commanders (for example the US Commander-in-Chief, Europe who was also Supreme Allied Commander, Europe (CINCEUR AND SACEUR)).

Although MLF did not pass the political test of appropriateness in the long

51

run, it did force the alliance to confront the issue of military appropriateness in another dimension. If a shared nuclear trigger was not to be the basis for ordering weapons of mass destruction into action, then national forces assigned to NATO for the purpose would be the only resort. This reliance upon the forces of states and the decisions of their leaders created a sub-system dominance within NATO nuclear decision-making that favored the Americans, for the obvious reason that the US nuclear arsenal was so much larger than anyone else's and, therefore, constituted the major deterrent against any attack from the Soviet Union. It was De Gaulle's appreciation of this point which contributed to his decision to emphasize France's reliance upon its own nuclear deterrent for its security, despite the apparent absurdity of this posture from the standpoint of the Americans. US leaders objected to a plurality of nuclear decision centers on the grounds that it would detract from alliance deterrent credibility. But in an alliance based on truly national instead of supranational forces, France's position that it was totally self-reliant for its sovereignty and for the protection of its interests from nuclear coercion was as logical as the US fear of mixed signals from multiple decision centers.[29]

That De Gaulle's successors, including the socialist government of President François Mitterrand during the 1980s, have continued to advance French nuclear unilaterism along with a political membership in NATO attests to the appropriateness of the arguments for 'proportional deterrence' which French spokesmen have always made with great cogency. According to the canons of proportional deterrence, the French nuclear deterrent need not threaten an attacker with mutual assured destruction, as is the case for the US deterrent. For the deterrence of any attack against French territory, it sufficed by this logic to threaten any aggressor with the certainty of losses at least equal to the potential gains to be obtained by conquering or obliterating France.[30] The French idea of unilateral, proportionate deterrence was not in keeping with the US definition of an appropriate and proportionate response by NATO, according to the dictates of flexible response strategy formally adopted by the alliance in 1967. The way was clear for NATO to adopt flexible response only on account of the French exceptionalism from NATO's integrated military command after 1966, and by virtue of the diverse interpretations placed on flexible response by European and American leaders.

For US leaders in the Kennedy administration and subsequently, flexible response emphasized the raising of the nuclear threshold in Europe and the improvement of conventional war-fighting capabilities toward that end. Europeans, especially West Germans, were less interested in lengthening the fuse of nuclear first use than they were in making almost automatic the Soviet expectation of nuclear escalation growing out of any conventional war. The objective of raising the nuclear threshold was not totally at variance with the goal of making deterrence more credible, but the two could not be reconciled in quite the manner that US Secretary of Defense Robert S. McNamara and his successors anticipated. The US approach to reconciliation of improved conventional forces for NATO and continuing dependency on prompt nuclear escalation if deterrence failed was to elongate the continuum of nuclear as well as conventional options. If the logic of a wider spectrum of choice applied below the nuclear threshold, according to some variants of flexible response, it ought also to apply above that line of demarcation. Nuclear flexibility would relieve the US President from the dilemma of all or nothing response, a dilemma that Soviet conventional or tactical nuclear forces might seek to impose.

The US version of flexibility extended into the nuclear realm was controversial in Europe from the mid-1960s through the mid-1980s, although the extent of public and parliamentary attentiveness to the relevant force structure and modernization decisions was quite variable. The doctrinal debates about NATO nuclear strategy during that period took place for the most part in the rarefied atmosphere of collegial meetings among experts and leaders. However, the matter of nuclear thresholds and nuclear escalation in Europe became publicly visible again in the early 1980s, pursuant to NATO's decision taken in 1979 for the 'two track' formula of INF modernization and arms control.[31] The Pershing II and cruise missiles scheduled for deployment in NATO Europe were widely criticized by defense analysts and opposition parties in Belgium, Holland, Germany and Great Britain for the very reason that NATO had taken the decision. NATO sought a politically acceptable solution to the problem of coupling the US strategic nuclear deterrent to its theater nuclear and conventional forces deployed in Europe, on the one hand, with the preservation of firebreaks between different levels of warfare in support of flexible response strategy on the other.

The tension between coupling and firebreaks was not only a tension at the military-technical level of NATO doctrine and strategy, but also a problem at the politico-military level where strategy and high politics intersected. For better or worse, the US and its NATO allies had made the decision to initiate deployment of the missiles in December, 1983 and to continue toward full deployment in the absence of any INF agreement between Washington and Moscow, a fundamental test of NATO alliance cohesion. An avalanche of policy propaganda from NATO capitals prior to the taking of the 1979 decision, and again immediately prior to the onset of deployments in 1983, called the deployments of modernized INF a litmus test of NATO's credibility as a military organization in the face of Soviet intimidation.

NATO's choice was based more on politics than it was on strategy, although the two could scarcely be separated in this controversial forum of alliance politicking and deteriorating US–Soviet relations of the early 1980s. The Pershings and GLCMs were defended as useful bargaining chips to be given up in the event of Soviet reductions in their modernized SS-20 mobile IRBM forces. This argument might have passed scrutiny from skeptics, had not the military rationales proffered by government spokesmen in NATO capitals contradicted this arms control logic. Defense ministries from Washington to Brussels offered the rationale of military coupling between US strategic and NATO theater nuclear and conventional weapons. Military experts and some officials in the same countries argued for the opposite military rationale, of additional, intermediate rungs on the ladder of escalation short of total war. Both military rationales, at least partly inconsistent with one another, could not be fully reconciled with the political argument that modernized INF were really bargaining chips slated for the arms control guillotine.

The relationship between coupling and firebreak rationales for inter-mediate range nuclear weapons in Europe provided an example of the military aspect of the political dilemma by which NATO nuclear strategy has always been encumbered. That political dilemma is the contradiction between European fears of abandonment by the US in a moment of crisis or, to the contrary, of entrapment in a hastily derived US decision to involve Western Europe in a conflict that was essentially a US–Soviet bilateral one. The relationship between abandonment and entrapment fears receives more specific and detailed consideration later, as the fourth reason why US and NATO strategy were pushed away from massive retaliation and toward some other variant of nuclear deterrence strategy. The third reason for the shift toward flexible nuclear response given by NATO, and especially by US advocates of flexible nuclear response, was the argument that the Soviet Union might regard the threat of total nuclear war as a bluff. As the Soviet Union improved its capabilities for a conventional offensive in Western Europe from the mid-1960s to the early 1980s, the drift of US analysis of the requirements for credible deterrence in Europe was strongly in the direction of a larger spectrum of nuclear options, including strategic nuclear options, for less than all-out Soviet attacks on the American homeland.

SOVIET STRATEGY

The development of improved Soviet conventional capabilities for war in Europe was a natural outgrowth of the replacement of Party Chairman Khrushchev by Brezhnev and the greater interest of the latter in improving

Soviet and Warsaw Pact conventional forces. In addition, after 1977 Marshal Nikolai Ogarkov, as Chief of the General Staff, pushed even harder than the political leadership for conventional force modernization. Ogarkov's writings, both before and after his tenure at the head of the general staff, expressed skepticism about the military utility of nuclear weapons. The influential Soviet military officer called repeated attention to the future importance of conventional high technology weapons, and he forecast the development of weapons based on 'new physical principles' in the early 1970s.[32] By the usual processes of threat inflation and professional preoccupation in Western defense analytic communities, the relative improvement of Soviet conventional forces in their Western TVD (Theater of Military Action) was taken by NATO pessimists as tantamount to a capability for a conventional first strike. NATO's response to improved Soviet conventional capabilities was not only to reconsider the adequacy of its conventional forces but also to reconsider the relationship between conventional defense and nuclear escalation in its strategy. Whereas flexible response prior to 1979 had been based on the assumption that a Soviet 'conventional option' against Western Europe was precluded by parity in US and Soviet strategic nuclear forces, NATO declaratory policy after 1979 was that a Soviet war-winning strategy had now emerged which required modernized nuclear rungs for NATO between the stages of large-scale conventional and unlimited strategic nuclear war.

The putative Soviet Eurostrategic option for victory short of total war involved both nuclear and conventional aspects, according to the reckoning of NATO's most astute strategic thinkers. The recognition of these two sides of the emerging Soviet theater-strategic option for war in Europe is important, since some very expert foreign and defense ministry spokesmen in Western Europe sounded as if only one or the other side mattered. But NATO was not mainly concerned about a Soviet conventional blitzkrieg without any role for nuclear weapons, or about a surprise nuclear strike against Western Europe after which Moscow would expect a stunned NATO to capitulate. The more serious concern was a conventional war which may not have even been deliberately started, and in the early stages of which NATO faced the possibility of imminent strategic losses without prompt nuclear escalation.[33] In a situation of this type, some NATO strategic planners feared that modernized Soviet theater nuclear forces, especially the intermediate range SS-20s which the Soviets began to deploy in 1977, would deter the US and its NATO allies from prompt nuclear escalation. NATO would have to accept a losing battle for the conventional defense of Western Europe because it lacked any alternative short of unacceptable costly escalation.

The assumption that the Soviet Union could establish such an 'escalation

55

dominance' based on superior theater nuclear forces and conventional forces made sense only if US strategic nuclear forces were somehow separated out of the European deterrence equation. The notion that the US might be deterred from nuclear escalation on account of inferior nuclear firepower ratios at the theater level confused a geographical distinction with a strategic one. The 'theater' level of war, once Soviet and allied Warsaw Pact forces had crossed the inter-German border, was not Europe, but Europe and North America. US forces deployed in Western Europe ensured that American equipment and personnel would be caught up in the forward battle from its earliest days. This would have been a US–Soviet war from the outset in political as well as military terms, and the Soviet recognition of that fact had as much to do with the success of deterrence in Europe during the Cold War as did the balance of conventional or theater nuclear forces in Western and Central Europe.

In addition, from the Soviet standpoint a war in Europe was a total war, for it threatened the survival of the Soviet state even if nuclear escalation never occurred (as improbable as that was). An outbreak of conventional war in Europe which became prolonged would in all likelihood work to the disadvantage of the Soviet Union and in favor of the United States and its allies, whose long-term economic and other mobilization potential exceeded that of the USSR and its allies.[34] Soviet leaders from the 1960s through the 1980s certainly reckoned that a protracted global war would be all too likely to expose the weaknesses of their economic system and military-political base of support in Eastern Europe. As the governments of Eastern Europe tumbled downward or defected from the Warsaw Pact in the aftermath of a stalemated and costly war in Europe, the Soviets would be left with a defense perimeter moving steadily eastward as NATO's gathering strength confronted the remnants of a crumbling empire.[35] The idea that the Soviet Union would view a war in Europe as a 'limited' war with or without the use of nuclear weapons was an idea based on the projection of US flexible response strategy to imaginary Soviet adherents.

If flexible nuclear response was not necessary in order to deter a conventional war winning option, supported by nuclear escalation dominance, against NATO, it was perhaps defensible as a means to avoid holocaust even after strategic nuclear forces had been employed by one or by both sides. The rationale for 'limited strategic options' put forward by National Security Decision Memorandum 242 (NSDM-242, known subsequently as the 'Schlesinger doctrine') in 1974, included the supposition that classical strategy might reappear in the nuclear age even in the foreboding case of US–Soviet strategic nuclear war. The Schlesinger doctrine provided declaratory policy support for trends in US nuclear strategic war planning which had originated in the Kennedy administration search for flexible nuclear and conventional options.[36]

The greater numbers of individually targetable weapons made possible by the MIRV technology and by the continuing modernization of US delivery vehicles created strong inertial pressures for increasing the number of targets in the SIOP, especially those targets which represented Soviet strategic retaliatory forces and command centers which might be attacked promptly.

The Nixon administration and its successors which presided over this drift in nuclear strategic target planning imagined a rung on the ladder of escalation between large-scale theater and global nuclear war. Soviet political and military leaders balked at recognition of such a threshold, and maintained a consistent position against the possibility of limited nuclear war in Europe during the Brezhnev years and subsequently. Expert US analysts suggested that the first uses of nuclear weapons against targets anywhere in Soviet territory might prompt a massive retaliatory use of Soviet nuclear weapons against targets in Europe or in North America.[37] The Soviet definition of a 'strategic' nuclear weapon depended less on the origin of the weapon or on its ownership than on its destination. Weapons aimed at targets within Soviet territory were strategic weapons and would in all likelihood call forth a decisive Soviet military reaction. Although Soviet military planners and theorists apparently recognized the *possibility* that a limited use of nuclear weapons in Europe would not *automatically* lead to general nuclear war, available Soviet military writing and political leaders' statements from the 1960s through the 1980s suggested that Soviet war planning was not based on that assumption as the main variant.[38]

Soviet skepticism about the conduct of limited nuclear war was based on the Soviet Union's own military history and on the strategic culture of its military professionals, party leaders and state officials. Whereas US strategists made the case for flexible nuclear response on the grounds that flexibility introduced the possibility of bargaining and control into war, Soviet military doctrine led naturally to doubts about the possibility of limiting any war which began in Europe. At both the politico-military and military-technical levels of military doctrine, Soviet thinkers in the Cold War years remained skeptical that concepts developed by Western strategists for the scientific management of conflict could be applied to war proper, as opposed to the preparation for war.[39] In this, Soviet military thinkers followed their own interpretations of Clausewitz. At the politico-military level of doctrine, party guidance about the purposes of war suggested that any war in Europe would be a decisive struggle of a global nature, continuing until the demise of capitalism or socialism was assured. At the military-technical level of Soviet military doctrine during the

Cold War years, planners in Moscow doubted that nuclear weapons lent themselves to selective and discriminating use for bargaining in war. Although Soviet theorists acknowledged that nuclear targeting could be selective in order to avoid gratuitous destruction to non-military objectives, Western analysts could find little evidence of Soviet interest in controlled nuclear warfighting for the purpose of war termination and partial victory.

The issue is important on account of the extensive debate in the Western academic literature over the viability of nuclear counterforce strategies. The case for US nuclear counterforce has been presented by US analysts and policy-makers as one resting on improved deterrence and on an improved potential for fighting a nuclear war if deterrence failed. The problem is that these two cases, of improved deterrence and of improved war-fighting capabilities, are positively associated only according to the logic of military marginal utility. According to this logic, changes in the balance between US and Soviet strategic nuclear counterforce capabilities mattered because asymmetries in that balance would lead to coercion of the weaker side by the stronger. Coercion would be possible because the relatively weaker side would have to give way during a crisis confrontation between the two. It would have to give way because it could calculate in advance the expected and unfavorable outcome of any anticipated nuclear exchange.

Opposed to this, the logic of counterforce skeptics argued that in a situation of mutually assured destruction, nuclear flexibility and asymmetries in the strategic nuclear balance mattered little in the calculus of stable deterrence. The logic of marginal utility could not be applied to outcomes of nuclear war in the same way that it had been applied to expected military outcomes by planners prior to the nuclear age. Under pre-nuclear conditions marginal utilities in the military balance mattered in an obvious way; in the hands of skilled commanders marginal military advantages might make the difference between victory and defeat. The basis of nuclear deterrence, on the other hand, was not the calculus of relative military advantage but the obviousness of expected mutual disaster.[40] Of course, basing the stability of mutual deterrence on the inevitability of mutual disaster created discomfort even for advocates of mutual assured destruction.

Advocates of mutual assured destruction were troubled by the use of mutual disaster as the basis of stable deterrence for several reasons. First, the mutual disaster model made no distinction between the justice of the causes of the two sides, nor between the status of attacker and defender. Second, the mutual disaster model committed both sides to early and massive strikes against the vital centers of the opponent's society or to a strategy of delayed retaliation which appalled military advisors and strategic planners. The tension between the military logic of prompt and massive response, as in the traditional artillery duel, and the non-traditional logic of waiting until the last possible moment for massive reprisals in order to control escalation, was apparent in US declaratory policy from the early 1960s through the end of the 1980s. The two realms, as in the medieval status of church and state, could not be completely reconciled in any single policy guidance without inflating the importance of one realm and deflating that of another.

Third, the logic of mutual disaster *at the margin* excluded the divisible character of nuclear deterrence, but nuclear divisibility was required in order to extend the American nuclear umbrella to Western Europe. Denial of this proposition has confounded most expert analyses of the problem of extended nuclear deterrence. Analysts and some policy planners assumed that nuclear flexibility was bad, and nuclear rigidity good, for coupling deterrence of attacks against the American homeland to deterrence of conventional or nuclear attacks against Western Europe. Nuclear rigidity had a deceptive appeal of neatness and simplicity. Having no other options, the US would rapidly escalate to general nuclear response once any war in Europe proceeded beyond its initial period. This logic might convince professors and pundits, but real leaders in a crisis would rapidly resist it. Presidents would want options short of war, and failing that, options short of massive nuclear exchanges in or outside of European or North American territory. The repeated frustration of American Presidents throughout the Cold Wars with the constraints imposed on their crisis management by nuclear weapons, and their rote insistence upon having selective options for nuclear war fighting, make the point.

Selective options for nuclear war fighting were not a basis for war-winning scenarios, however, and Presidents realized this very quickly after having been briefed on the nuclear war plan. Nuclear war was not a shooting gallery. Once a minimum number of nuclear warheads had been exploded on Soviet or American territory, the results of further detonation would be of little interest to political or military leaders. The purpose of selective options was to reassure Presidents and potential opponents that the US deterrent would not be paralyzed in the face of attacks against allies that could not be defeated by conventional forces in place. Counterforce was the offspring of alliance. The implication is not that counterforce was bad for the purpose, as is often argued by US academic strategists. Counterforce was the unavoidable concomitant of alliance commitments backed by nuclear force. Graduated escalation was built into the inevitable geographical and policy differences among NATO allies, and one could not have graduated escalation without counterforce capabilities.

The most common objection to counterforce was its compatibility with first strike strategies.[41] This objection was valid, contingent upon the actual targeting plans for counterforce weapons and the relative survivabilities of the US and Soviet deterrent forces. Counterforce capabilities contributed to first strike instability if either side's second strike capability could be put at risk, especially at prompt risk. In the absence of such vulnerability, as in a M.A.D. condition, counterforce capabilities were at worse superfluous. They might conceivably contribute to arms racing, but if there was no possibility that either side could approximate a first strike capability there was no point to arms racing either. And first strike strategies demanded more than an offensive counterforce capability. They also demanded at least some strategic defenses in order to absorb the retaliatory strike of the defender. In the absence of defenses, no attacker could remove its cities from their hostage condition, and cities which remained as nuclear hostages precluded any first strike advantage for prospective attackers.

In addition, if deterrence failed gradually instead of all at once, nuclear flexibility might be advantageous for bargaining purposes during a crisis or in the early stages of a war. The subject of bargaining with nuclear weapons was complex and controversial. In theory one could posit several ways in which nuclear weapons might be used in a bargaining process. First, they might be part of a competition in risk-taking, in which a psychological duel between opponents was conducted using nuclear exchanges as a backdrop. The purpose of such a duel would be to inflict gradual increments of pain and suffering on the opponent's society. Second, nuclear weapons might be used in bargaining for war termination. The willingness to spare certain targets during retaliatory strikes, such as the command centers for the highest political and military leadership, could create a space within which a cessation of hostilities would be negotiated. Although this second form of use, bargaining for war termination, is related to the first, competition in risk-taking, its basic character is different. Bargaining for war termination assumes that the most important thing about a nuclear war, once it has been started, is the ending of it.[42] Nuclear strikes and re-strikes constitute messages about the terms on which settlement can be obtained. Competition in risk-taking regards the attainment of an advantageous bargaining position as equal in importance to the ending of the fighting. The opponent is to be reminded of the horrible possibility of absolute war and open-ended destruction, not encouraged to consider the most feasible alternatives for war termination. If the bargaining use of nuclear weapons for war termination is to fix the minds of leaders on the character of the postwar world, the purpose of bargaining in risk-taking competition is to remind leaders that the postwar world may be outside the realm of civilization.

These two kinds of nuclear bargaining, for war termination and for competitive risk-taking, share one similarity: their objective is to influence the expectations of enemy leaders about future *uncertainties*. Leaders in a competitive risk-taking or war-termination bargaining process are to be impressed by the unpredictability of further nuclear exchanges and, therefore, by the more attractive alternative of de-escalation. In contrast to risk-taking and war-termination bargaining, another form of nuclear bargaining is designed to affect the opponent's estimate of *certainties*. Additional nuclear strikes destroy more military forces and cause further loss of social and economic values. The *promise* of more destruction to come and the certainty of further suffering is, according to this third model of a nuclear bargaining process, the attribute which gives bargaining power to the employment of nuclear force for political purposes.

Whether nuclear bargaining strategies depended upon certainty or uncertainty was not just an academic exercise, but a matter of some importance for the approach taken to crisis management.[43] Even the choice between 'uncertainty' based models of nuclear crisis or wartime bargaining had important implications. If one assumed that the point of nuclear bargaining was a competition in risk-taking, then it made sense to alert nuclear forces promptly and visibly. The possibility that prompt alerts might provoke the opponent was less important in this model of bargaining than the sending of a message of resolution to defend threatened values. On the other hand, the war or crisis termination model of nuclear bargaining implied the opposite: other things being equal, one would want to limit alerts to the lowest level consistent with survivability of the deterrent. The difference between uncertainty and certainty based models of nuclear bargaining tactics was even greater in this regard than the difference between the two kinds of uncertainty models, although more complicated to explain.

In a 'certainty' model of nuclear bargaining during a process of crisis management, one could take either of two approaches: steadfastness based on high confidence in the survivability of one's deterrent for the purpose of second strike retaliation against value targets, or sang-froid based on equally high confidence that one could achieve a predominant position in the post-attack relationship of second strike forces. The first kind of confidence is usually associated with mutual assured destruction strategies, and the second kind of confidence, with strategies loosely incorporated under the nuclear war fighting label. But there is no necessary logical or empirical association between certainty models of nuclear bargaining and, either confidence in survivability, or confidence in one's capability to destroy targets more efficiently than the opponent can do. Certainty models can be compatible with either kind of confidence in military capabilities. What distinguishes the certainty model of nuclear crisis management or wartime bargaining is its psychological paradigm of influence over the strategy of the opponent. The certainty model, in either passive or active form, asserts that 'no matter what you do to me I can guarantee you that I will do worse to you, or something so bad to you that it is beyond your level of acceptability.'

The nuclear strategy debate in the US during the Cold War years was much preoccupied with the issue whether the Soviets were more impressed by certainty or uncertainty models of nuclear bargaining. As a matter of relative emphasis in this regard, one can contrast the Carter administration 'countervailing' strategy with the 'Schlesinger doctrine' of limited nuclear options.[44] The countervailing strategy called for capabilities in forces and in command systems which left no doubt in the minds of Soviet leaders that their most important values, including their own command posts and control system, would be destroyed. The Schlesinger doctrine embodied in NSDM-242 in 1974, although it called for improved capabilities, was based on the use of early, demonstrative and very limited nuclear attacks to raise uncertainty in the minds of Soviet leaders about the costs of continued fighting.[45] Although the Carter doctrine included uncertainty as a component of its model of crisis and wartime bargaining, it was based on improved capabilities for carrying on a nuclear war even through its extended phases.[46]

ABANDONMENT OR ENTRAPMENT?

The choice between certainty and uncertainty bargaining strategies was in turn related to the fourth major issue raised by critics of massive retaliation: whether the European members of NATO feared abandonment by the US deterrent more than they feared entrapment in a US conflict with the Soviet Union. European members of NATO were not of one mind about these issues, and for US leaders this was the familiar dilemma of choosing between coupling and firebreaks. But coupling and firebreaks were terms appropriate for debates at the military-technical level; NATO's problems were equally serious at the politico-military level. There were three possible solutions to the choice between US nuclear abandonment and entrapment advanced by European political leaders and military analysts during the Cold War years.

The first of these solutions was nuclear dependency. In a condition of nuclear dependency, a state would forgo an independent national nuclear deterrent in favor of reliance upon the US or allied nuclear deterrents. This was the choice more or less imposed on West Germany after it joined NATO in 1955. The same choice was made under less duress by other members of

NATO who lacked either interest in or capability for the development of national nuclear forces. The advantages of nuclear dependency were the cost savings in not having to develop or to deploy one's own forces, and the possible absolution from nuclear strikes directed against one's own territory in the event that war did break out. In the event of any outbreak of war in Europe, nuclear absolution might not have been feasible for West Germany under conditions other than pre-emptive surrender of FRG territory. But for other non-nuclear members of NATO, once conventional deterrence had failed, the possibility of avoiding nuclear strikes against their own capitals or home-based forces was taken very seriously. Norway and Denmark forbade peace-time deployment of NATO nuclear weapons on their soil in order to reduce the likelihood that their countries would become wartime nuclear targets.

An alternative to nuclear dependency was nuclear unilateralism. Nuclear unilateralism implied the development and deployment of a state's own national nuclear force, perhaps independent of the US or NATO nuclear weapons deployed in Europe. The 'softer' form of nuclear unilateralism, as in the case of the British nuclear deterrent, was coordinated with NATO defense planning and remained within the alliance military command framework. The 'harder' form of nuclear unilateralism, as in the French *force de dissuasion*, remained outside the NATO military chain of command and would be activated only if the President of France decided that the vital interests of France made nuclear response necessary. As Edward Kolodziej has shown, France's nuclear unilateralism was not as 'unilateral' as it appeared from Gaullist pronouncements. There was a great deal of cooperation between France and its NATO partners on security matters, including: French connections to NADGE (NATO Air Defense, Ground Environment, an early-warning system); French contributions to the construction of new NATO communications networks; and the participation of French air and naval forces in NATO maneuvers in the Mediterranean in Autumn 1968.[47] The advantage of nuclear unilateralism was that it gave Great Power status to the possessor of an independent national nuclear force, even if the actual force employment planning was coordinated with US or NATO planning. Another advantage of the French and British deterrents was the avoidance of conventional defense expenditures which the political leaderships of those states might otherwise have been pressured to make.

However, the difficulty with British and French nuclear unilateralism was that it was a form of nuclear dependency so long as the US deterrent was the mainstay of dissuasion against any Soviet attack on Western Europe. The British deterrent was immediately implicated in any attack on NATO, and French territory was at imminent risk the moment that Soviet ground forces advanced more than 100 kilometers into West Germany. The idea of nuclear unilateralism was a strategic fiction, and the French admitted as much in their argument that 'independent decision centers' would complicate the plans of any prospective attacker. By this French leaders meant that the Soviet Union might not be able to predict the reactions of three nuclear powers in Western Europe, including one power not subject to NATO command, as well as Moscow could estimate the actions of any one. But the plurality of decision centers only complicated Moscow's estimates if the US deterrent remained secure.[48] And if the US deterrent remained secure, then the only issue of deterrence credibility for the US nuclear umbrella was an issue of will, not of capability.

France was not without advocates of its own version of flexible nuclear response, most notably in the late 1970s and early 1980s. Leading strategic thinkers and prominent political analysts, including Raymond Aron, Michel Tatu and François de Rose, noted that options other than unlimited retaliatory strikes against Soviet cities might increase the credibility of any threatened response to a Soviet attack against French military targets.[49] French General Pierre Hautefeuille outlined a systematic argument for flexible nuclear targeting on the basis of three assumptions, summarizing much of the precedent national debate. First, options other than large anti-city attacks would reduce the probability of self-deterrence prior to the initial decision for nuclear use. Second, additional options would allow the French leadership to retain, after initial nuclear retaliatory strikes, a reserve force for war termination and intra-war deterrence. Third, additional and limited nuclear options would allow for a symmetrical response, should leaders choose to do so, to less than all-out Soviet attacks on French military targets.[50] Notwithstanding some plausible arguments that could be made for nuclear flexibility by French commentators and strategic thinkers, during the 1980s resources did not permit the acquisition of counterforce capabilities and C3 systems necessary to make credible a French version of the McNamara declaratory strategy articulated in 1962 (and later abandoned in favor of assured destruction).

The French debate over nuclear strategy, especially the articulation of a case for flexible nuclear suasion during the latter 1970s, also showed that the argument about whether nuclear technology superseded strategy and imposed a 'M.A.D. world' on military planners was more relevant to the superpowers than it was to medium or small nuclear powers. French nuclear strategic planners could argue for the deterrence of the strong by the weak because the political fate of France could not be decoupled from that of the rest of NATO as easily as French forces could be withdrawn from NATO's military command system. For Soviet leaders who believed that wars were the result of political causes and not spontaneous combustions, the continuing French adherence to NATO's political umbrella meant continued uncertainty about the direction of French nuclear target planning. France could, in theory, choose among the following targeting emphases during the initial period of war: basic anti-cities strategy; extended or 'enlarged' anti-cities strategy, including vital centers of economic and administrative support; and limited counterforce strikes as part of a pre-strategic warning that the aggressor should discontinue his attacks or face further, and more comprehensive, retaliation.[51]

The dilemma of possible US unwillingness to use its nuclear weapons for the defense of Western Europe was that the solution was part of the problem. Nuclear weapons could only liberate Europe at the price of its destruction. If NATO depended solely on nuclear dissuasion, it might be checkmated by US unwillingness to go this far or by European preferences for surrender instead of nuclear destruction. Anticipating this, NATO strategy provided for a sliding scale of alliance commitment to the use of nuclear weapons. War would begin without immediate first use of nuclear forces and with the expectation that conventional war fighting would be tried until it was found wanting. At that point, NATO would take the decision to cross the nuclear threshold in small increments, hoping that the Soviets could be persuaded to cancel their attack and to restore the status quo ante. Further escalation by NATO would be undertaken only if the use of conventional and theater nuclear forces proved inadequate to deter the continuation of fighting or to defeat the attacker in battle.

For this programme of graduated escalation to work, the number of independent decision centers would have to be reduced, preferably to a single center from the US standpoint. If there existed too much 'flex' in flexible nuclear response, the attendant confusion would not permit the Soviet Union to sort out the appropriate signals from the surrounding noise. The control of flexible nuclear response, therefore, implied a condition of nuclear dependency for all those who gathered beneath the US nuclear umbrella. Although once fighting escalated to the level of strategic nuclear warfare the independence of European national deterrents would be irrelevant, their irrelevancy was up for argument below the level of US–Soviet homeland exchanges. Independent national nuclear deterrents, from an alliance command and control standpoint, could lengthen the fuse of gradual nuclear escalation or compress the time between first use and massive exchanges. If, for example, the French were to initiate retaliatory strikes against major Soviet cities in response to the advance of Soviet forces into French territory, the process of graduated escalation would be truncated at once. Even worse, knowing this possibility, Soviet leaders might pre-emptively attack French nuclear forces or escalate sooner instead of later to attacks against North America, on the assumption that general nuclear war had become inevitable.

NATO, like all alliances, was plagued by the trade-off between incentives for coupling of political fates, in order to make deterrence more credible, and opposed incentives for disaggregation of risks, to which all alliances are potentially prone. Since nuclear weapons do not lend themselves very well to disaggregation or extension (the French have always been right about this), planning for flexible nuclear response invites immediate fears of abandonment of the weak by the strong. Therefore, a third option between nuclear unilateralism and nuclear dependency is nuclear risk sharing. Nuclear risk sharing goes against the logic of minimizing the number of independent decision centers. In a nuclear risk-sharing arrangement, a plurality of decision centers is deliberately cobbled together in order to build consensus in support of strategic decisions. Each independent decision center has the capability to veto nuclear use. Such a solution may be taken by the newly independent and former Soviet republics to the problem of controlling inadvertent or accidental nuclear war.

The likelihood that independent centers of decision will contribute to the credibility of alliance decision making for deterrence or crisis management is directly related to the degree of consensus on which the strategies of the various alliance members based. If the members of an alliance are operating on the basis of independently derived strategies with little or no awareness of the strategies of putative allies, the probability of a breakdown of crisis management and a failure of deterrence is increased.[52] Multipolar power systems operating according to the mechanism of balancing among major actors were subject to instability on account of the heterogeneity of actors' deterrent strategies. The groupings of the Triple Alliance and Triple Entente prior to 1914 both suffered from this deficiency in their efforts to avoid war through greater certainty in alliance commitments for deterrence.

For example, British prewar strategy emphasized the avoidance of a generalized continental or world conflict, but placed little emphasis on the prevention of regional crises or outbreaks of war. The British Foreign Secretary was confident that regional crises could remain localized. On the other hand, French leaders after 1912 encouraged Russia to act promptly against any Austrian move to acquire Serbian territory or to deny Serbia its sovereignty. France's ambassador in St. Petersburg exuded confidence that Austria could be forced to back down from any démarche against Serbia by combined French and Russian pressure. Even beyond the expectations of his political masters, Ambassador Paleologue encouraged Russian intransigence in response to Austrian and German moves. Members of the Triple Alliance exhibited similarly dysfunctional behavior based on competing or opposed strategic assessments of the risks of escalation and of their feasible military options should war break out. Austria pushed hard for humiliating concessions from Serbia and refused to accept a conciliatory Serbian reply to Austria's ultimatum of 23 July. On 28 July Austria declared war against Serbia and initiated military action. Austrian obstinacy about the concessions to be had from Serbia and Austria's prompt declaration of war against Belgrade reduced German options for localizing the crisis and thereby preventing the escalation of the crisis into a two-front war for Germany. The Kaiser's seeming assent on 5 July to a harsh line by Austria against Serbia, in the aftermath of the assassination of Wilhelm's friend Archduke Ferdinand, was played back against Germany by Austria to entrap Germany's leaders in a spiral of escalating threats and mobilizations against Russia and France between 25 July and 2 August.[53]

The choices made by leaders during the July crisis of 1914 pertain directly to the problem of a potential trade-off for alliance members between coupling and firebreaks. In turn, the trade-off between coupling and firebreaks provides the military-deterrent aspect of the political impasse between fears of abandonment and fears of entrapment. Leaders during the July crisis feared being abandoned by their fellow travelers as much as they worried about being swept up in a process of escalation. Austria-Hungary wanted reassurance of German backing for her moves against Serbia, and sought to present the remainder of Europe with a *fait accompli* before Germany had a chance to rethink its supporting role. France sought reassurance from Russia that, in the event of war breaking out with a main attack launched by Germany westward through Belgium, Russia would be ready to take the offensive against East Prussia no later than the fifteenth day of its mobilization. France and Russia sought unsuccessfully to obtain advance assurance from England, prior to the eruption of the July crisis and subsequently, that England would take prompt military action against Germany if Germany attacked France allied with Russia. British ambiguity on this point until the very last days of the July crisis may have contributed to Germany's misjudgment that a war against France and Russia could still exclude England as a belligerent.[54]

Success in the conduct of a process of graduated escalation, by an alliance which is potentially subject to the strains of the abandonment – entrapment trade-off, is not necessarily guaranteed if the alliance is an unequal one of one leader and many followers. For most of the Cold War years, the US and the Soviet Union presided over consolidated blocs which precluded their allies from walking too far away from basic guidelines of strategy devised in Washington and Moscow. Despite this greater degree of intra-alliance discipline compared to multipolar systems before 1945, serious disagreements about the very fundamentals of nuclear strategy during the Cold War marked US deliberations with NATO political and military partners. NATO's two-sided mission of military deterrence and the promotion of political détente, pursuant to the Harmel report, ironically contributed to the contradictory fears of entrapment and abandonment. And these fears did not run only in one direction; they also crossed the Atlantic from Washington to Paris, Bonn and London.

American leaders were as eager to obtain European support for their force modernization and arms control initiatives as were Europeans to have a greater say in alliance strategy. Each side feared both abandonment of shared threat perceptions and entrapment in causes not deemed fundamental by its own domestic constituencies. This shows clearly in the intra-NATO tensions over the INF modernization programme agreed to in 1979. INF would support NATO's case for graduated escalation only if a sufficient number of European countries would agree to share the basing of cruise missiles. West Germany had already been singularized by sole possession of Pershing II ballistic missiles. Although having agreed to the INF force modernization proposals favored by the Americans, European members of NATO were more interested, compared to Washington, in the potential for negotiated agreements which would preclude the deployments in part or in toto. INF confronted the European members of NATO with a putative test of alliance solidarity, on the one hand, and with a potential Soviet threat to wreck détente in Europe, on the other. The anti-détente démarches of the Soviet Union were believable because the background music in US–Soviet relations had deteriorated considerably since 1979; by December of 1983, when the deployments were scheduled to begin, the music sounded very much like a funeral dirge.

The case of NATO INF modernization illustrates that alliance solidarity may be hostage to diverse perceptions of strategy if those perceptions include détente and conciliation as part of the context of strategy, as they surely are in the larger political sense of the term. Even in a narrow military-technical sense, the capabilities of Pershing II and GLCM deployed in Western Europe could not be separated from the implicit tension they created between US and European strategic priorities. The INF missiles only made clearer the fact that indivisible risk for alliance partners is a useful propaganda tool; in reality, the risks of alliance membership are never shared equally because the costs of foreseeable military commitments are never going to be distributed equally.

The preceding discussion suggests that alliances will have greater difficulty in managing a process of graduated escalation than a single actor will. This might seem obvious from the standpoint of mathematical logic and decision theory: more participants in a decision process make it more difficult to arrive at a consensus on strategies and priorities. However, the logics of bipolarity and nuclear weapons argue against this seemingly obvious deduction. The stability of a bipolar nuclear world was in part attributed to the restriction in decision latitude imposed upon the lesser by the greater military powers. Because states other than the global superpowers could not formulate their preferred policies and strategies without recognition of a potential US or Soviet veto, it followed that the complexities of alliance aggregation in a multipolar system were replaced by the comparative simplicity of a bipolar world. Nuclear weapons made things even simpler. Classical war-winning strategy was repudiated in favor of deterrence, or the denial of strategy except for the purpose of avoiding war. If nuclear weapons were thought to have driven classical military strategy into a dead end, then bipolarity reinforced a quiescence within the blocs against any outbreak of war between their members which might escalate into a world war. One theorist even argues that bipolarity alone, without nuclear weapons and on the basis of US and Soviet expectations about the costs of any protracted conventional war, was sufficient to discourage resort to war and to preserve deterrence stability during the years of the Cold War.[55]

CRISIS MANAGEMENT, ESCALATION AND ALLIANCES

The argument for the irrelevance of nuclear weapons was one way of restoring classical strategy to the nuclear age. Others noted in case studies of nuclear crisis management, such as the Cuban missile crisis, that nuclear weapons were not irrelevant to the perceptions and crisis management strategies of leaders, but that those weapons were not necessarily the most decisive factors in resolving the crisis.[56] Assessment of the impact of the nuclear revolution on crisis management is complicated by the difficulty in comparing pre-nuclear crises with those taking place after the deployment of large nuclear arsenals. Nuclear weapons made the costs of crisis management failure obviously worse than they had been before, but they also made leaders more reluctant to get into crises. Although the objectives of successful crisis management and crisis avoidance were to some extent interdependent, they were not entirely so. That crisis management and crisis avoidance were only partly congruent can be seen by examining the impact of nuclear weapons on two kinds of deterrence failure, with implications for our earlier discussion of nuclear flexibility.

69

In a situation of general deterrence, states maintain ready forces and military vigilance against the possible resort to war by another state. They exist in a condition of international legal anarchy which, under some conditions, can present perceived security dilemmas to state actors. An acute form of security dilemma is presented by a failure of general deterrence, which is tantamount to the onset of a crisis. On the other hand, the development of a crisis does not guarantee that war will break out. A crisis like a fever may be the sign that is needed by leaders to apply the 'medicine' of conciliation and negotiation in order to avoid war. The potentially beneficial aspects of crisis in this regard are real enough, yet no implication of symmetry is intended between the beneficial and the detrimental attributes of crises. A failure of general deterrence is a precarious state of affairs in which the possibility of war shifts from a state of latency to one of immediacy. Thus a condition of immediate deterrence has supplanted one of general deterrence.[57]

In a condition of immediate deterrence, at least one state is making an explicit threat to attack another unless the second state complies with one or more demands. For example, Austria-Hungary on 23 July 1914 issued an ultimatum to Serbia which contained a number of onerous prescriptions for Serbian compliance. The ultimatum was a clear infringement on Serbian sovereignty and was not acceptable in its entirety, although the Serbian government made every effort to accept most of the provisions of Austria's manifesto.[58] Serbia could not hope to deter Austria-Hungary, given the military inferiority of the former compared to the latter. But Serbia did not count on its own armies to deter Austrian attack and invasion, but on the forces of its offstage ally, Russia. Knowing this, Austria-Hungary counted on support from Germany should Russia come to the defense of Serbia. Assuming that Germany's power would deter Russia, Austria launched its attack on Serbia on 28 July.

This case illustrates the problem that deterrence failures are not all of one kind even during the same crisis. We think today of the 'July crisis' of 1914 as one event, but it had several distinct and important stages from the standpoint of crisis management and deterrence theory. The selection of boundary markers between stages is somewhat arbitrary, depending on the interests of the investigator. One can make a reasonable case for the proposition that general deterrence failed on 23 July (the Austrian ultimatum to Serbia), introducing a crisis and a situation of immediate deterrence. However, there was *not* an immediate outbreak of war among the powers. In fact, there was a hiatus which induced a sense of complacency as more days elapsed between 23 July and 28 July and shooting failed to start. Serge Sazonov, the tempestuous Russian foreign minister who oscillated between moods of optimism and pessimism in preventing war during the month of July, 1914, reacted with extreme despair on 23 July but warmed to the possibility of resolving the crisis without war in the succeeding days until 28 July.[59]

The failure of general deterrence on 23 July opened a window of opportunity for the powers to use assertive crisis management to resolve the crisis without war, but they could not take advantage of this opportunity. The powers in the years immediately prior to the outbreak of the First World War suffered from several delusions which contributed to their mismanagement of the process of escalation during the July crisis. First, they assumed that any regional crisis could be localized, meaning that it could be confined to one region such as the Balkans and prevented from expansion into a wider European war. Second, leaders of the major powers of Europe assumed that the past was prologue: since they had escaped war in earlier crises in the Balkans and in other regions, they would avoid disaster again. Third, it was assumed by military planners of the powers that any war would be short, resulting in a decisive victory for one side instead of a prolonged stalemate. Along with this third assumption of a short, decisive war went its corollary: that governments and their economies were so connected and dependent on uninterrupted commerce across borders that they could not sustain a long war. Therefore, they would of necessity opt for peace.[60]

Taking these assumptions apart, their fallacy is easy to see in hindsight, but the reasons for the fallacious reasoning by leaders in 1914 hold useful lessons for modern students of crisis management and escalation. The first assumption was that the crisis could be localized. The powers had done this in the Balkan crises of 1908 (the so-called Bosnian annexation crisis) and in 1912; in the latter instance, Russia had backed down from support for Serbia after Serbia and Austria had mobilized against one another. However, localization of the 1914 crisis was harder because Russia was no longer willing to back down in any future confrontation between Vienna and Belgrade.

To the contrary, Russia upon learning the news of Austria's ultimatum against Serbia authorized a series of pre-mobilization measures (measures "preparatory to war") throughout the empire and readiness for partial mobilization of the military districts facing Austria-Hungary.[61] Germany, having pledged on 5 July to support Austria against Serbia (including specific reference to assisting Austria should Russia intervene) also failed to emphasize localization of the crisis in its foreign policy until the opportunity had passed. Austria hoped to strike a quick *fait accompli*, against Serbia before Russia had time to think through its options or to mobilize its forces. If Russia did attempt to mobilize against Austria, Vienna counted on the counter-deterrent threat posed by Germany to make Russia back down. Austria therefore favored localization but on very specific terms: the capitulation of Serbia, and these terms were unacceptable to Russia. In addition, localization of the crisis was made more difficult than in 1912 or in 1908 because the sense of commitment on the part of alliance partners within the Triple Alliance and the Triple Entente had hardened to a firmer resolve for war if objectives could not be obtained through diplomacy. Localization of the crisis required that one or more of the powers engage in buck passing, but in fact a pattern of chain ganging obtained during the month of July.[62]

The preceding discussion refers to two kinds of assumptions held by leaders in 1914, assumptions which turned out to be fatally erroneous for the success of crisis management in July. A third set of assumptions had to do with the likely duration of war and the outcome of it. As a result of wishful thinking and other motivated biases, the leaders of France, Germany and Russia for the most part were persuaded that a war in Europe would not, or could not, last long. Each alliance also assumed that in a short war it was bound to emerge victorious. The reasoning of military planners and political leaders in this regard was not necessarily fallacious, before the test bed of actual experience. They reasoned on the basis of selective historical precedent, such as the Franco-Prussian war, that decisive battles of annihilation would be fought within the first few weeks of war. The German Schlieffen plan, although modified in its details after the retirement of Schlieffen from the General Staff, continued to be based on the idea of the massive battle of encirclement by which the German war machine crushed French defenders in a campaign of six weeks or so. France's Plan XVII meanwhile called for the prompt attack of French main forces into German territory, and joint Franco-Russian military planning between 1912 and 1914 contributed to adjustment of Russian plans in favor of a two-pronged, prompt offensive against German forces in East Prussia by the fifteenth day of mobilization (and despite the need for Russian forces to be able to conduct offensives against Austria-Hungary at the same time).[63]

How far these expectations of a short war deviated from reality is now known to readers of history. A sense of the magnitude of personnel losses for Russian, French and German participants can be gained from the estimates made by researchers.[64] A clear sense of the total societal and cultural devastation inflicted by the Great War is more complicated. In addition to personnel losses, the material costs of the war were also very much beyond the expectations of most prewar military planners and political leaders. Lacking the advantage of hindsight, policy-makers at the time might still be faulted for clinging to expectations of a short war in the face of evidence that they could have consulted against that hypothesis. Two factors in particular

TABLE 2.1

INDUSTRIAL POTENTIAL OF GREAT POWERS, 1880–1938
(UNITED KINGDOM = INDEX OF 100 IN 1900)

	1800	1900	1913	1928	1938
Britain	73.3	100	127.2	135	181
US	46.9	127.8	298.1	533	528
Germany	27.4	71.2	137.7	158	214
France	25.1	36.8	57.3	82	74
Russia	24.5	47.5	76.6	72	152
Austria–Hungary	14	25.6	40.7	–	–
Italy	8.1	13.6	22.5	37	46
Japan	7.6	13	25.1	45	88

Source: Paul M. Kennedy, *The Rise and Fall of the Great Powers: Economic Change and Military Conflict from 1500 to 2000* (New York: Random House, 1987), p. 201.

characteristic of the period from 1870–1910 argued against a short war: the growing industrial strength of the major military powers in Europe and of the United States, should the US be drawn into a European war, and the tightening of alliances between 1890 and 1912, guaranteeing a coalition war. Historical experience might therefore have suggested to leaders that combatants with great economic staying power, fighting with the support of allies also holding vast industrial and manpower resources, could not defeat an opposed coalition rapidly. The historian Paul M. Kennedy has estimated the growth of industrial potential among the European and North American powers between 1880 and 1938, using a baseline norm of 100 for total British industrial production in 1900, as shown in Table 2.1.

Although Paul Kennedy was not around to warn leaders that a coalition war among industrializing powers with large armies was almost certain to be prolonged, other experts were. Polish banker Ivan Bloch forecast exactly such a war, and some prewar military thinkers did note that trends in military technology as well as the experience of battle in the latter part of the nineteenth century and early twentieth century favored a defensive stance and a prolonged war of attrition. However, these pessimistic forecasts were not heeded.[65]

If coalition wars are more likely to be prolonged than conflicts limited to two or three opponents, then the crises leading up to coalition wars may be more difficult to bring to a conclusion short of war than other crises. Coalition prewar crises may involve alliance commitments of the kind which make conciliation seem like appeasement. Coalition crises also introduce additional confusion into the policy-making machinery compared to two or three party crises: coordination of foreign policies and of military planning becomes more difficult among more numerous alliance partners. This problem is not only a result of larger numbers of participants in a coalition policy-making process, compared to a one or two party process. The greater complexity of coalition crisis decision-making is also related to the heterogeneity of the actors. The potential for misunderstanding the commitments and motivations of other actors increases as the mixture of their policy-making systems becomes more heterogeneous. For example, the German Chancellor Bethmann-Hollweg was attempting to forestall further Austrian actions against Serbia and to forward a proposal from Britain for mediation of the crisis at the same time that the Chief of the German General Staff, Helmuth von Moltke (the younger), was sending signals to his Austrian counterpart, Conrad von Hotzendorff, to stand firm.[66]

The point about heterogeneity is not irrelevant to bipolar systems, including bipolar systems dominated by nuclear armed states. In the US–Soviet confrontation of the Cold War, US influence over Soviet behavior was very much influenced by the Soviet estimate of the degree to which, on any given issue, NATO could hang together or separately. During De Gaulle's forays against the 'Anglo-Saxon' domination of NATO and against McNamara's version of flexible response, Soviet leaders perceived an opportunity to divide the alliance. On the other hand, the INF modernization decision taken by NATO in 1979 was subsequently supported by the French Socialist government of President Mitterrand. French support for the NATO INF modernization decision was a surprise to some, for two reasons. First, it was thought by some American and European observers that a socialist government which was left-leaning on other issues might favor the arms control facet of NATO's decision at the expense of its modernization aspect. Second, it was feared that the French propensity for go-it-alone nuclearism, based on the rationale of proportional deterrence and national military self-sufficiency, would be inconsistent with a French commitment to graduated deterrence implicit in medium-range missiles.

As it turned out, however, the French perceived Pershing II and cruise missiles as consistent with their own national concepts for the use of nuclear weapons as deterrents, and not as consistent with the more exotic American versions of flexible response or graduated nuclear warfighting. For this the US government deserves some credit, but the greater share of the credit belongs to those French analysts and policy planners who recognized that INF was more of an exercise in political unity building than it was a necessary correction for perceived deficiencies in the spectrum of nuclear deterrence. The French, in other words, rejected the arguments made by former West

74

German Chancellor Helmut Schmidt and others in the latter 1970s: that the intermediate rungs of NATO's ladder of nuclear escalation had to be strengthened against the possibility of Soviet intimidation with the aid of a newly deployed SS-20 IRBM force.[67] The French disinterest in sub-strategic nuclear war, from the American standpoint, offered no barrier to a favorable interpretation of INF modernization in the Elysée Palace or in the Quai d'Orsay so long as the autonomy of France's strategic nuclear *force de dissuasion* was not compromised.

The fact that NATO was sometimes forced to deal with fears of abandonment, and at other times concerns about entrapment, was not a sign of weakness. Both fears were signs of healthy differences of opinion, over very difficult issues of political influence within the alliance on its nuclear strategy. 'Who decides?' was as frequently the issue as 'what is to be decided?' None the less, the relationship between abandonment–entrapment fears and diverse notions of graduated escalation, already discussed in one context, becomes important in the present setting too. The more acute the fears of some alliance partners, especially the more militarily dependent ones, that they will either be abandoned by the less dependent or trapped by the stronger into wider wars, the more controversial become the notions of graduated escalation. When alliance partners are fearful of abandonment or entrapment, simple theories of strategy and gross (instead of fine) increments of escalation work better.

CONCLUSIONS

Stability in the Cold War years was not only the product of survivable forces and diminished expectations for any plausible first strike plan. Equally important, although more fortuitous, was the 'illogical' logic of escalation, from conventional to nuclear war or from limited nuclear war to something worse. Because escalation of either kind was neither impossible nor certain, the concept of a limited nuclear or conventional war in Europe could not be fleshed out with politically realistic scenarios. Certain escalation would have automated deterrence, preventing any war from starting and suppressing risky bargaining tactics as too dangerous. Impossible escalation would have made it safe to fight below the nuclear threshold. Either an 'escalation certain' or an 'escalation impossible' set of expectations in Washington and Moscow would have made traditional sense out of military strategy with nuclear weapons.

If expansion from initial use to ultimate nuclear destruction was certain, then the risks of nuclear war were equally distributed among alliance partners; the first shot at the inter-German border would have been followed by nuclear exchanges between Soviet and American homelands. However, certain expansion left neither the US nor its partners any way out, should leaders decide that a particular war or crisis was not imperative for them. On the other hand, impossible escalation from first use to ultimate destruction meant that NATO had to be prepared for large conventional or theater nuclear war in Europe, which its European members viewed as tantamount to decoupling, weaker deterrence and national suicide in time of war.

If the nether world between impossible or certain escalation forced Cold War nuclear powers to abstain from military adventurism, as I have contended, then the post-Cold War world in which escalation may be certain or impossible for some states will be less stable than was the Cold War. This prognosis does not necessarily forecast an outbreak of nuclear war in the 1990s or soon thereafter, but it does argue for possible conventional war waging without the constraints imposed by Cold War superpower nuclear weapons. Worst of all is the possibility of an outbreak of conventional war, say in Europe or the Middle East, in the expectation that nuclear escalation was not a factor, only to learn in midstream that it actually was. It should not be assumed, therefore, that regional stability can be guaranteed by essentially equivalent force balances. What potential adversaries think about escalation, especially the possibility of nuclear escalation, deserves equally careful consideration in planning for regional security communities.

NOTES

1. Robert Jervis, *The Meaning of the Nuclear Revolution: Statecraft and the Prospect of Armageddon* (Ithaca, NY: Cornell University Press, 1989), p. 80.
2. For interpretations of the nuclear revolution, see Jervis, *The Meaning of the Nuclear Revolution*; Michael Mandelbaum, *The Nuclear Revolution: International Politics Before and After Hiroshima* (Cambridge: Cambridge University Press, 1981); Charles L. Glaser, *Analyzing Strategic Nuclear Policy* (Princeton: Princeton University Press, 1990); and Scott D. Sagan, *Moving Targets: Nuclear Strategy and National Security* (Princeton: Princeton University Press, 1989).
3. Marc Trachtenberg, 'A "Wasting Asset": American Strategy and the Shifting Nuclear Balance, 1949–1954', in Trachtenberg, *History and Strategy* (Princeton: Princeton University Press, 1991), pp. 100–52, esp. pp. 119–20.
4. Robert Gilpin, *War and Change in World Politics* (Cambridge: Cambridge University Press, 1981), pp. 9–14.
5. David Alan Rosenberg, 'US Nuclear War Planning, 1945–1960', Ch. 2 in Desmond Ball and Jeffrey Richelson (eds), *Strategic Nuclear Targeting* (Ithaca, NY: Cornell University Press, 1986), pp. 35–56, esp. pp. 53–5.
6. Graham T. Allison, *Essence of Decision: Explaining the Cuban Missile Crisis* (Boston: Little, Brown, 1971), remains a landmark study. For more recent analyses, see Raymond L. Garthoff, *Reflections on the Cuban Missile Crisis*, rev edn. (Washington, DC: Brookings Institution, 1989); James G. Blight and David A. Welch, *On the Brink: Americans and Soviets Examine the Cuban Missile Crisis* (New York: Hill and Wang, 1989), and McGeorge Bundy, *Danger and Survival: Choices about the Bomb in the First Fifty Years* (New York: Random House, 1988), pp. 391–462.

7. Alexander L. George, David K. Hall and William E. Simons, *The Limits of Coercive Diplomacy: Laos, Cuba, Vietnam* (Boston: Little, Brown, 1971) outlines and applies the concept of coercive diplomacy. Especially pertinent is George's chapter on Cuba.

8. On Kennedy administration nuclear war planning and strategic doctrine, see Janne E. Nolan, *Guardians of the Arsenal: The Politics of Nuclear Strategy* (New York: Basic Books, 1989), pp. 74–88, and Desmond Ball, 'The Development of the SIOP, 1960–1983', in Ball and Richelson (eds), *Strategic Nuclear Targeting*, pp. 57–83, esp. pp. 62–70.

9. Trachtenberg, 'Strategic Thought in America, 1952–1966', in Trachtenberg, *History and Strategy*, pp. 3–46.

10. Edward A. Kolodziej, *French International Policy under De Gaulle and Pompidou: The Politics of Grandeur* (Ithaca, NY: Cornell University Press, 1974), esp. pp. 128–30.

11. Alain C. Enthoven and K. Wayne Smith, *How Much is Enough? Shaping the Defense Program 1961–1969* (New York: Harper and Row, 1971), pp. 207–8.

12. Garthoff, *Deterrence and the Revolution in Soviet Military Doctrine* (Washington, DC: The Brookings Institution, 1990), esp. Ch. 2, p. 34 and *passim*. On the significance of diversity in national styles for nuclear strategy and policy-making, see Colin S. Gray, *Nuclear Strategy and National Style* (Lanham, MD.: Hamilton Press, 1986), *passim*. On the development of Soviet nuclear strategy, see also David Holloway, *The Soviet Union and the Arms Race* (New Haven, CT: Yale University Press, 1983), Chs. 2 and 3.

13. Prominent Soviet military theorists of the early 1970s noted that nuclear weapons provided strategic parity between the US and the Soviet Union, making possible the limitation of any war to the conventional level and preventing Western blackmail of the Soviet Union or its allies through nuclear superiority. See Dale R. Herspring, *The Soviet High Command, 1967–1989: Personalities and Politics* (Princeton, NJ: Princeton University Press, 1990), pp. 84–5. In the 1970s and subsequently, the acceptance of parity allowed a great deal of room for disagreement, as between former Chief of the Soviet General Staff N.V. Ogarkov and his superiors in the early 1980s, on the value of détente and arms control compared to the military buildup of Soviet forces. See Herspring, ibid., pp. 202ff.

14. Steven Kull, *Minds at War: Nuclear Reality and the Inner Conflicts of Defense Policymakers* (New York: Basic Books, 1988).

15. According to Scott Sagan, US arguments for second-strike counterforce have usually fallen into one of three general categories: damage limitation; support extended deterrence; or, deny Soviet war aims. See his discussion in *Moving Targets*, Ch. 2, pp. 72–82. Sagan's discussion notes the arguments in favor of second-strike counterforce but also acknowledges the difficulty of keeping first and second-strike counterforce distinct in the minds of potential adversaries. A more critical view of counterforce appears in Glaser, *Analyzing Strategic Nuclear Policy*, Ch. 7, pp. 207–56.

16. On escalation dominance, see Jervis, *The Illogic of American Nuclear Strategy* (Ithaca, NY: Cornell University Press, 1984), pp. 126–46.

17. See Robert Powell, *Nuclear Deterrence Theory: The Search for Credibility* (Cambridge: Cambridge University Press, 1990), Chs. 2–3.

18. On manipulation of risk, see Thomas C. Schelling, *Arms and Influence* (New Haven, CT: Yale University Press, 1966), pp. 92–125.

19. On accidental or inadvertent war, see Sagan, *Moving Targets*, pp. 135–75.

20. Schelling, *The Strategy of Conflict* (Cambridge, MA: Harvard University Press, 1960), pp. 187–204.

21. Paul Bracken, 'War Termination', Ch. 6 in Ashton B. Carter, John D. Steinbruner and Charles A. Zraket (eds), *Managing Nuclear Operations* (Washington, DC: Brookings Institution, 1987), pp. 197–216.

22. Bracken, ibid., and Stephen J. Cimbala, *Nuclear Endings: Stopping War in Time* (New York: Praeger, 1989).

23. On Soviet expectations as of the middle 1980s in the cases of unexpected strategic surprise attack in peacetime, and of anticipated strategic surprise attack during crisis, see Stephen M.

Meyer, 'Soviet Nuclear Operations', Ch.15 in Carter, Steinbruner and Zraket (eds), *Managing Nuclear Operations*, pp.470–534, esp. pp.476–97 and 497–512. See also Lt. Gen. A.I. Yevseev, 'O nekotorykh tendentsiyakh v izmenii soderzhaniya i kharaktera nachal'nogo perioda voiny', *Voenno-istoricheskii zhurnal*, No.II (November, 1985), pp.10–20; Meyer, 'Soviet Perspectives on the Paths to Nuclear War', Ch.7 in Graham T. Allison, Albert Carnesale and Joseph S. Nye, Jr. (eds), *Hawks, Doves and Owls* (New York: W.W. Norton, 1985), pp.167–205; William T. Lee, 'Soviet Nuclear Targeting', Ch.4 in Ball and Richelson (eds), *Strategic Nuclear Targeting*, pp.84–108; Edward L. Warner III, *Soviet Concepts and Capabilities for Limited Nuclear War: What We Know and How We Know It* (Santa Monica, CA: RAND Corporation, February 1989); Marshal N.V. Ogarkov, *Vsegda v gotovnosti k zashchite Otechestva* (Moscow: Voyenizdat, 1982), p.16; Ogarkov, *Istoriya uchit bditel'nosti* (Moscow: Voyenizdat, 1985), pp.89–90; and M.A. Gareev, *M.V. Frunze: Voennyi teoretik* (Moscow: Voyenizdat, 1985), translated and published by Pergamon-Brassey's in English (New York, 1988), esp. pp.213–14. It would be superfluous to note that all of this underwent significant restructuring under Gorbachev, even before the abortive coup of 18–21 August 1991 and the official decommunization of the armed forces.

24. For recent evidence of Soviet views on controlling and possibly terminating a major war, see Garthoff, *Deterrence and the Revolution in Soviet Military Doctrine*, Ch.5, and Garthoff, 'New Soviet Thinking on Conflict Initiation, Control and Termination', Ch.2 in Stephen J. Cimbala and Sidney R. Waldman (eds), *Controlling and Ending Conflict* (Westport, CT: Greenwood Press, 1992), pp.65–94.

25. Valuable discussions of pertinent NATO strategy issues can be found in Gregory F. Treverton, *Making the Alliance Work: The United States and Western Europe* (Ithaca, NY: Cornell University Press, 1985), esp. Chs. 2 and 3; Josef Joffe, *The Limited Partnership: Europe, the United States and the Burdens of Alliance* (Cambridge, MA: Ballinger, 1987); and Kurt Gottfried and Paul Bracken (eds), *Reforging European Security: From Confrontation to Cooperation* (Boulder, CO: Westview Press, 1990).

26. On Eisenhower strategy, see David Alan Rosenberg, 'US Nuclear War Planning, 1945–60,' Ch. 2 in Ball and Richelson (eds), *Strategic Nuclear Targeting*, pp.35–56.

27. William W. Kaufmann, *The McNamara Strategy* (New York: Harper and Row, 1964).

28. David N. Schwartz, *NATO's Nuclear Dilemmas* (Washington, DC: The Brookings Institution, 1983), pp.82–135 covers the MLF debate and its strategic implications for NATO.

29. For relevant documents and commentaries on the development of French nuclear weapons and Gaullist strategy, see *L'Aventure de la Bombe: De Gaulle et la Dissuasion Nucléaire (1958–1969)* (Paris: Librairie Plon, 1985).

30. Pierre Gallois, *The Balance of Terror: Strategy for the Nuclear Age* (Boston: Houghton Mifflin, 1961), translated by Richard Howard. See also Gallois, 'La dissuasion du faible au fort,' in *L'Aventure de la Bombe*, pp.165–74.

31. Schwartz, *NATO's Nuclear Dilemmas*, pp.193–252.

32. Herspring, *The Soviet High Command, 1967–1989*, contains an excellent discussion of Ogarkov's contributions to Soviet military thought: see especially, pp.174–6. Ogarkov's interesting analysis of the Reagan–Weinberger defense strategy offered in *Vsegda*, pp.15–17, warns of a US strategy of 'direct confrontation', of which the two major subconcepts are (according to Ogarkov) 'geographical escalation' and 'active countermeasures'. Noting US and NATO plans for limited or 'Eurostrategic' nuclear war but dismissing the possibility of confining nuclear war within any limited 'framework', Ogarkov deduces that the US concept of 'geographical escalation' is a main component of a strategy for fighting on a global scale using conventional forces only.

33. For a discussion of European escalation scenarios applicable to the mid-1980s, see Fen Osler Hampsen, 'Escalation in Europe', Ch.4 in Allison, Carnesale and Nye (eds), *Hawks, Doves and Owls*, pp.80–114.

34. P.H. Vigor, *Soviet Blitzkrieg Theory* (New York: St. Martin's Press, 1983).

35. This in fact came to pass in peacetime at the end of the 1980s. See Charles Gati, *The Bloc that*

Failed: Soviet–East European Relations in Transition (Bloomington: Indiana University Press, 1990).

36. For background to NSDM-242, see Ball, 'US Strategic Forces: How Would They Be Used?', *International Security*, No. 3 (1982/83), in Steven E. Miller (ed), *Strategy and Nuclear Deterrence* (Princeton, NJ: Princeton University Press, 1984), pp. 215–44; and Ball, *The Evolution of United States Strategic Policy since 1945: Doctrine, Military Technical Innovation and Force Structure*, Reference Paper No. 164 (Canberra: Strategic and Defense Studies Centre, Research School of Pacific Studies, Australian National University, Jan. 1989).

37. Meyer, 'Soviet Perspectives on the Paths to Nuclear War.'

38. Notra Trulock III, 'Soviet Perspectives on Limited Nuclear War', Ch. 3 in Fred S. Hoffman, Albert Wohlstetter and David S. Yost (eds), *Swords and Shields* (Lexington, MA: Lexington Books, 1987), pp. 53–86, and Warner, *Soviet Concepts and Capabilities for Limited Nuclear War.*

39. Ball, *Soviet Strategic Planning and the Control of Nuclear War*, Reference Paper No. 109 (Canberra: Research School of Pacific Studies, Australian National University, Nov. 1983); Garthoff, 'Soviet Perceptions of Western Strategic Thought and Doctrine', Ch. 4 in Gregory Flynn (ed.), *Soviet Military Doctrine and Western Policy* (London: Routledge, 1989), pp. 197–328.

40. Or, in the French variant, guaranteeing to any aggressor a loss at least commensurate with the value of defeating or destroying France. See Gallois, 'La dissuasion du faible au fort'.

41. This issue is discussed in Sagan, *Moving Targets*, Ch. 3.

42. For theory and case studies on war termination, see Fred Charles Ikle, *Every War Must End* (New York: Columbia University Press, 1971), and Paul Pillar, *Negotiating Peace: War Termination as a Bargaining Process* (Princeton, NJ: Princeton University Press, 1983).

43. An assessment of the social science literature on crisis management is provided in Ole R. Holsti, 'Crisis Decision Making', Ch. 1 in Philip E. Tetlock *et al.* (eds), *Behavior, Society and Nuclear War*, Vol. I (New York: Oxford University Press, 1989), pp. 8–84. See also Richard Ned Lebow, *Nuclear Crisis Management: A Dangerous Illusion* (Ithaca, NY: Cornell University Press, 1987).

44. On Carter doctrine, see Walter Slocombe, 'The Countervailing Strategy', in Miller (ed) *Strategy and Nuclear Deterrence*, pp. 245–54, and Jervis, *The Logic of American Nuclear Strategy*, passim.

45. Secretary of Defense James R. Schlesinger, Press Conference, 10 Jan. 1974, excerpts in *Survival*, Vol. XVI, No. 2 (March/April, 1974), pp. 86–90.

46. That Soviet strategists and policy-makers remained equally skeptical of the Schlesinger doctrine and of the Carter countervailing strategy approaches to limited nuclear war is noted in Fritz W. Ermarth, 'Contrasts in American and Soviet Strategic Thought', Ch. 3 in Derek Leebaert (ed.), *Soviet Military Thinking* (London: Allen & Unwin, 1981), pp. 50–72. For Soviet proclivities in non-strategic war, see also, in the same volume, Nathan Leites, 'The Soviet Style of War', Ch. 7, esp. pp. 190, 194.

47. Kolodziej, *French International Policy under De Gaulle and Pompidou*, p. 143.

48. This and other aspects of French nuclear deterrent strategy are very well explained in David S. Yost, *France's Deterrent Posture and Security in Europe*, Parts I and II, Adelphi Papers No. 194 and 195 (Winter 1984/85), esp. Part I, p. 41.

49. Relevant citations appear in Yost, *France's Deterrent Posture and Security in Europe*, Part I, p. 41.

50. Ibid.

51. John J. Hyland III notes that growth of the numbers of warheads deployed on the French SSBN/SLBM force by the mid-1990s will provide the capability for increased flexibility in targeting. By 1992 France will be capable of maintaining at sea or on patrol about 290 warheads and 160 EMT, offering the possibility of multiple retaliatory strikes. See Hyland, 'Potential Impact of French Nuclear Modernization on French Force Employment', Ch. 5 in Robbin F. Laird (ed.), *French Security Policy* (Boulder, CO: Westview Press, 1986), pp. 75–

80, esp. p. 76. See also, in the same volume, Robbin Laird, 'The French Strategic Dilemma', Ch. 6, pp. 81–104 for a discussion of French strategic options, esp. pp. 97–100 on the options for expanding the roles of its independent nuclear force.

52. Interesting historical examples are provided by the behavior of European powers during the age of Louis XIV and Frederick the Great. See Theodore Ropp, *War in the Modern World* (Durham, NC: Duke University Press, 1959), pp. 24–35.

53. Laurence Lafore, *The Long Fuse: An Interpretation of the Origins of World War I* (Philadelphia: J.P. Lippincott, 1965), pp. 196–7 notes that British domestic political and constitutional factors precluded a definite peacetime military commitment to support France against Germany. This did not preclude extensive consultations and joint war planning between the two armed forces' general staffs, however, including British planning assumptions that the British navy would protect the French channel ports and that the British would place an army on the continent soon after any German attack against France. The British General Staff was established in 1904 within the War Office as its department for strategic planning. In 1904 and 1905, the General Staff and the War Office used the Committee of Imperial Defence (CID), established in 1902, as a forum to redirect British defense planning away from its Central Asian–Imperial focus on the defense of India and toward a more Euro-centered planning focus, centered on Germany as a potential adversary. See J. McDermott, 'The Revolution in British Military Thinking from the Boer War to the Moroccan Crisis', Ch. 4 in Paul M. Kennedy (ed.), *The War Plans of the Great Powers, 1880–1914* (London: Allen & Unwin, 1979), pp. 99–117. On the hesitations of Sir Edward Grey, British Foreign Minister, during the July crisis and his reluctance to make a firm statement to Germany dissuading any German optimism about British neutrality in a European war, see Luigi Albertini, *The Origins of the War of 1914*, translated and edited by Isabella M. Massey, Vol. II (Oxford: Oxford University Press, 1953), pp. 514–15.

54. For pertinent details, see Sidney Bradshaw Fay, *The Origins of the World War*, Vol. II (New York: Free Press, 1966), Chs. V–IX; L.C.F. Turner, *Origins of the First World War* (New York: W.W. Norton, 1970), Chs. 4–6; Turner, 'The Significance of the Schlieffen Plan', Ch. 9 in Kennedy (ed.), *The War Plans of the Great Powers*, pp. 199–221; I.I. Rostunov, *Istoriya pervoi mirovoi voiny, 1914–1918*, Vol. I (Moscow: Izdatel'stva 'Nauka', 1975), esp. pp. 185–205 and map insert, pp. 192–3; and Iurii Danilov, *La Russie dans la Guerre Mondiale (1914–1917)* (Paris: Payot, 1927), esp. pp. 121–32.

55. John Mueller, 'The Essential Irrelevance of Nuclear Weapons: Stability in the Postwar World', *International Security*, No. 2 (Fall, 1988), reprinted in Sean M. Lynn-Jones, Steven E. Miller and Stephen Van Evera (eds), *Nuclear Diplomacy and Crisis Management* (Princeton, NJ: Princeton University Press, 1990), pp. 3–27. Mueller's interesting argument would be stronger but for the assumed logical connection between two propositions: that conventional deterrence was adequate to forestall the outbreak of global war after the Second World War; and, that nuclear weapons were, therefore, irrelevant to deterrence of war between the superpowers. The connection dissolves because the logics of nuclear and conventional deterrence operate differently. The logic of nuclear deterrence depends upon the manipulation of risk and uncertainty, whereas conventional deterrence operates by creating the near certainty of defeat in battle.

56. Trachtenberg, *History and Strategy*, Ch. 6, pp. 235–60.

57. For this distinction, see Patrick M. Morgan, *Deterrence: A Conceptual Analysis*, 2nd edn (Beverly Hills, CA: Sage, 1983), pp. 27–78.

58. Albertini, *The Origins of the War of 1914*, Vol. II, pp. 358–60.

59. Fay, *The Origins of the World War*, II, p. 308.

60. For a résumé of these factors, see Geoffrey Blainey, *The Causes of War* (New York: Free Press, 1973), pp. 35–56.

61. The character and significance of Russian 'measures preparatory to war' are described in Fay, *The Origins of the World War*, II, pp. 313–21.

62. Buck passing refers to avoidance of a state's share of the responsibility for deterrence or

defense preparedness, and chain ganging means that states are willing to align their security and defense commitments to those of other states even at some risk. For expansion, see Thomas J. Christensen and Jack Snyder, 'Chain gangs and passed bucks: predicting alliance patterns in multipolarity', *International Organization*, No.2 (Spring, 1990), pp.137–68. Christensen and Snyder use the metaphors of chain ganging and buck passing to describe two fundamental sources of destabilization in balance of power systems. Related to their arguments is the discussion of this by Kenneth N. Waltz, *Theory of International Politics* (Reading, MA: Addison-Wesley, 1979), and George H. Quester, *Offense and Defense in the International System* (New York: John Wiley & Sons, 1977).

63. On French strategy, see S.R. Williamson, 'Joffre Reshapes French Strategy, 1911–1913', Ch. 6 in Kennedy (ed.), *The War Plans of the Great Powers, 1880–1914*, pp.133–54; and Douglas Porch, 'The French Army in the First World War', Ch.6 in Allan R. Millett and Williamson Murray (eds), *Military Effectiveness, Vol. 1: The First World War* (London: Unwin Hyman, 1988), pp.190–228, esp. pp.200–1. On German strategy, see Turner, *Origins of the First World War*, pp.62–4; Turner, 'The Significance of the Schlieffen Plan'; Holger H. Herwig, 'The Dynamics of Necessity: German Military Policy during the First World War', Ch. 3 in Millett and Murray (eds), *Military Effectiveness, Vol. 1*, pp.80–115; A.J.P. Taylor, *The Struggle for Mastery in Europe, 1848–1918* (Oxford: Clarendon Press, 1954), pp.528–9; and Ropp, *War in the Modern World*, pp.204–9.

64. For pertinent estimates, see Lt. Gen. N.N. Golovin, *The Russian Army in the First World War* (New Haven: Yale University Press, 1931), republished by Archon Books (1969), p.94. Golovin estimates Russian total losses (killed in battle, died of wounds and wounded) at 5,500,000; French, at 3,900,000; and German, at 6,055,000. As percentages of these states' total mobilized forces, Russian losses amounted to 35.5 per cent; French, to 47 per cent; and German, to 55 per cent.

65. Excerpts from Bloch's prescient *The Future of War and Its Economic and Political Relations: Is War Now Impossible?* (Boston: 1903) appear in Ropp, *War in the Modern World*, pp.201–2.

66. Fay, *The Origins of the World War*, II, pp.506–14, esp. pp.507–58.

67. Schwartz, *NATO's Nuclear Dilemmas*, pp.214–16.

3

Defensive Strategy and Military Choices: Russia and Europe after the Cold War

The interest of theorists and planners in post-Cold War Europe in non-offensive defense is motivated by the desire to create a durable security community from the Atlantic to the Urals. Offensive military doctrines and forces poised for surprise attack reduce leaders' confidence in the stability of the status quo. It follows that arms control should be used not only to reduce the size of potentially opposed forces in the region, but also to diminish the expectation of insecurity based on defenses vulnerable to surprise attack in the initial period of war. Non-offensive defense *policies* are open to either form of military *strategy*. There is no necessary contradiction between a state's unwillingness to prepare for attack until it feels imminent threat, on the one hand, and its insistence on pre-emption once it does feel threatened. Nuclear weapons deployed in Europe during the Cold War, combined with US and Soviet security guarantees to allies, forced pre-emption-prone strategies on states whose policies, without superpower involvement, would have permitted less provocative stances.

The end of the Cold War and the repolarization of European politics creates the opportunity for states formerly without strategic discretion to choose between strategies of annihilation and strategies of attrition. De-nuclearization of the continent would offer even more elbow room for strategic selection. However, even in that hopeful event the choices are not simple, and the trade-offs between attrition and annihilation strategies are never as obvious before the fact of war as they are afterward. The following discussion considers some of the dilemmas and options facing Europe's future planners on the basis of past experience with grand strategic choice. Non-offensive defense is a viable strategy for states and coalitions under some conditions, but even strategies fully innocent of pre-emption and surprise attack motives must cope with the eventual need to destroy or numb the forces of an attacker. The study is especially mindful of the strategic dilemmas of imperial Russia and its successor the Soviet Union, which will continue to challenge the post-Soviet planners in Moscow, and therefore, in the rest of Europe also.

STRATEGIES, DOCTRINES AND POLICY CHOICES

The development of non-offensive defenses is not a new topic for Europeans. European strategic thinkers and others dissatisfied with the military postures of the Cold War years studied various alternatives for individual or coalition defenses based on territorial self-defense or on other concepts excluding surprise attack and large-scale conventional offensives.[1] The 'solutions' to regional stability offered by superpower extended deterrence and offensively poised conventional forces did not commend themselves especially to the non-aligned states of northern Europe. Even NATO member states produced leading advocates of non-offensive defenses, and some US and European analysts were willing to endorse non-military, in addition to non-offensive, defenses as the basis of regional security. The development of interest in non-offensive defenses was significant not only as an alternative to the super-power-oriented bloc politics of the Cold War. Non-offensive defense also offered an alternative to those states that sought to transcend Cold War military postures but distrusted supranational solutions, in the form of politically powerful multilateral institutions. States such as Sweden and Switzerland offered different forms of non-offensive defense while reserving to themselves the right to decide when and where their forces would be committed to battle.

During the Cold War, the idea that members of NATO or the Warsaw Pact might turn to non-offensive defenses contradicted preferred NATO and Soviet planning guidance. It was all very well for the Swiss, for example, to plan for territorial homeland defenses on the assumption that Switzerland might escape direct attack or invasion. However, this solution would not do for those states whose territory would certainly be violated by invaders once war began on the Central Front that separated NATO and Pact forces. The vulnerability of much of Germany to a Soviet strategy of rapid penetration and encirclement of vital areas seemed also to diminish the credibility of non-offensive defenses for states bound to NATO and close to the Cold War firing lines. Finally, the presence of US and allied NATO nuclear weapons of various ranges deployed within the probable area of battle almost guaranteed levels of destruction which would preclude the effectiveness of any defensive strategy based on attrition, which non-offensive defense schemes often were.[2]

Other political obstacles both domestic and foreign seemed to stand in the way of major actors, such as France or Germany, adopting non-offensive defense concepts as the basis for national defense or for their contributions to coalition defense. These political obstacles included the possibility that, faced with NATO Europeans adopting self-oriented non-offensive strategies beneath the alliance umbrella, the US might return to fortress America and allow Europeans to non-offensively defend themselves into surrender.

Regardless of the pros and cons of non-offensive defense as seen from the Cold War perspective, the future European environment may be more conducive to the implementation of non-threatening defensive alignments and reduced security dilemmas. The security dilemma is a construct that refers to the propensity for one state's search for greater security to cause another state to feel more insecure, on account of being threatened by the first state.[3] States' intentions in force building or in mobilizations may be benign and not, in their own minds, designed to destabilize the existing equilibrium in a particular region or in the system as a whole. However, the stability of any particular balance of power among states is determined by their perceptions of one another's intentions as much as by the 'reality' of state intentions that an objective observer might describe. The security dilemma suggests that there is a significant difference, for the inferences that leaders will draw about the probable intentions of potential adversaries, between those force deployments and modernizations which appear preparatory to attack, compared with those which appear to have been motivated by defensive, that is, self-protective goals.

Doctrinal Choice

The difference between forward-leaning or offensively-oriented and rearward-looking or defensive conventional force postures is not always obvious. More than the counting of men and arms is required. Some concept of the opponent's operational doctrine, or maxims for the conduct of battle should deterrence fail, is a necessary supplement to weapons and troop inventories if states are to draw accurate conclusions about the intentions of others. Intentions cannot be separated from capabilities: the capabilities that a state thinks it has will influence its definition of acceptable policy and war aims. Capabilities will also affect bargaining strategies during a crisis or in peacetime. The fact that the United States had apparent nuclear superiority relative to the Soviet Union during the Cuban missile crisis was an important part of the context for decision-making by President John F. Kennedy and his advisors.

States may choose to adopt a defensively-oriented strategy, or circum-

84

stances may force one on them. Stalin was incapable of pre-empting Hitler between 1939 and 1941. The Soviet leader therefore sought to placate Hitler while he bought time to improve Soviet defensive capabilities. Even improved capabilities would not have substituted for lack of good intelligence about the German Army's style of war.[4] Despite premonitory information from the conduct of the German campaigns in Poland in 1939 and against France in 1940, Soviet forces were insufficiently prepared mentally as well as physically to combat the *blitzkrieg* strategy designed by Hitler's generals. France offered an example of a state which based its strategy on the offensive before the First World War, with apparent lack of success. Between the World Wars French planning, cognizant of First World War experience, based its strategy for future war on a defensively-oriented concept based around the Maginot line and other fortifications. The concept was a not unreasonable extrapolation of First World War experience into a future war, but it was proved wrong. The Germans simply went over and around the line, striking at the heart of France by concentrating their main force through the Ardennes. Although the defensively oriented concept was not necessarily a bad theoretical basis for French prewar planning, it demanded a better system for command and control and improved capabilities for timely reinforcement of threatened sectors. These capabilities could not be improved in the midst of the pounding administered to French defenders by German tactical fighters and armored spearheads.[5]

The German Schlieffen plan for the First World War has also been subjected to retroactive criticism which faults the plan excessively. The plan, or rather Schlieffen's various drafts of it, provided for a strategy of annihilation, striking a decisive blow against the French armies through a massive encircling movement executed by the right wing of advancing German forces. The strategy has been criticized for being offensively-oriented to excess, whereas the French strategy up to the Second World War has been criticized for overemphasis on the defensive.[6] However, both strategic concepts were influenced by the perceived constraints of domestic and foreign policy. Expectations about alliance commitments or defections, military organizational biases and institutional role perceptions, and intelligence appreciations of probable enemy strategy all figured in the German offensive First World War and the French defensive Second World War conceptual frameworks for military planning. That the armed forces attached to those concepts proved inadequate in battle does not necessarily prove that the concepts were flawed, only that neither First World War Germany nor Second World War France could field forces which would guarantee the successful enactment of their preferred concepts once pitted against the strategy and forces of the opponent.

Other examples could be summoned to show, as well as these two cases do, that the relational quality of war precludes a valid assessment of prewar plans based on postwar outcomes. Good plans can fail badly, and bad plans can succeed against the odds. In the Second World War the Germans fought on the western and eastern fronts with much greater operational and tactical efficiency than did any of their opponents. The efficiency was expended in a lost cause, for want of adequate grand strategy. Hitler's grand strategy allowed the formation of a decisive winning coalition against Germany. Hitler strategy was the antithesis of Bismarck strategy in the nineteenth century, which isolated potential enemies of Germany from one another in a variety of short-term agreements. Because Bismarck was able to keep Germany's most competent potential adversaries from making common cause, the armed forces of the German General Staff did not have to rely on a strategy as offensively biased as the Schlieffen plan.[7] The departure of Bismarck left uncertain political guidance to the German General Staff, which filled the vacuum with a war plan that seemed to satisfy operational requirements, if not grand strategic ones.

Annihilation versus Attrition

The Russian military theorist and Soviet professor A.A. Svechin grouped strategies into two general categories: strategies of annihilation and strategies of attrition.[8] Svechin adopted these categories from the German historian Hans Delbruck, although Svechin's family of attrition strategies was rather an extended one.[9] Almost all strategies other than ones predicated on great battles of annihilation were included in the category of attrition. But the distinction remained useful for Svechin and for other theorists. A strategy of annihilation or destruction required an 'extraordinary victory' based on one operation or on several coordinate operations with the goal of 'the complete disorganization of the enemy's manpower and its complete destruction, splitting every link between his intact fragments and capturing communications that are most important for the armed forces rather than the country as a whole'.[10]

In contrast to a strategy of annihilation or destruction, a strategy of attrition involves the creation of a protracted military stalemate, often on several fronts, in order to wear down the opponent's military strength and to weaken his resolve to continue fighting. According to Svechin, the 'weary path of a strategy of attrition, which leads to the expenditure of much greater resources than a short destructive strike aimed at the heart of the enemy, is in general chosen only when a war cannot be ended by a single blow'.[11] Offsetting its lack of promise for a rapid and decisive victory, an attrition strategy favored a defender with superior mobilization potential and economic resources. Svechin's analysis of the Soviet condition in the early 1920s, relative to the military and economic potential of Soviet enemies, was that a strategy of attrition based on large territory and superior mobilization potential was preferable for Russia to a strategy betting everything on prompt offensives.[12] For Russians, a strategy of attrition, however improvised it was, prevailed against Bonaparte's invasion in 1812. Napoleon's campaign of annihilation, like Hitler's, came to nothing against the vastness of Russia and the inability of invaders since the reign of Peter the Great to subject the vital areas of western Russia to hostile control.

A strategy of attrition is risky for a small state without allies facing a large invader. A rapid campaign of annihilation will appeal to the larger state.[13] However, the Finns, much to the disappointment of Stalin, executed a strategy of delay and denial in 1939 and 1940 before the Soviets were forced to throw overwhelming forces against them. One might argue for this example that the Soviet strategy was not one of annihilation of Finland's military power or political system, but a strategy of limited aim to induce Finnish cession of strategic territory for the defense of Leningrad. Stalin obtained this objective at the price of military institutional and party embarrassment. Finnish resistance revealed not only the tenacity of that state's outnumbered armed forces and the improvisational skills of Marshal Mannerheim, but also the lackluster preparedness of Soviet commanders for the larger war which was eventually coming. Stalin's purge trials were paid for on the shores of Lake Ladoga, and later in larger coin on the western front.

Soviet lack of preparedness for Hitler's invasion is well known, although Soviet sources are not agreed on the reasons for it. The best known Soviet critiques of Stalin's political decision-making, related to Soviet preparedness for the German invasion, are unsparing of the dictator and his advisors, including his military ones. A large Soviet literature devoted to the topic of the 'initial period of war' attempted to unravel the reasons for the nearly decisive defeats inflicted on Soviet border and other forces in the early months of Hitler's attack.[14] During the period of *glasnost'* set in motion by Gorbachev, 'new thinkers' among Soviet military writers asserted along with highly regarded authors from the General Staff that, prior to *Barbarossa*, the Soviet armed forces lacked an adequate concept for conducting defensive operations on a strategic scale.[15]

If the point about the lack of sufficient awareness of the need for strategic defense in the initial period is fairly taken, it provides a perspective which loses none of its relevance for the Russian military planner of the 1990s and beyond.

The western borders of Russia, after the separation of the Baltic republics from Soviet control, are now even closer to Moscow and St. Petersburg than they were on 22 June 1941. A strategically defensive military posture for the Russian armed forces would be a logical derivative of the widely discussed concepts of 'defensive sufficiency' and 'reasonable sufficiency.'[16] The Russian armed forces, if not tied down policing border and ethnic disputes in the remaining republics of the former Soviet Union would present, with or without nuclear weapons, a formidable challenge to any invader from the west. Democratization of the states on the western border of Russia makes it even less likely that a forward-leaning Russian military strategy, based on annihilation instead of attrition, will be necessary. Svechin's argument that an attrition oriented strategy was preferable for a state with Russia's territorial vastness and underdeveloped economy resonates with strategic prescience more than half a century later.

On the other hand, the broad strategic choice between annihilation and attrition applied mostly to total wars among great powers. Future challenges to Russian security might come from less than great power border states with designs on Russian or other Commonwealth territory. Inter-ethnic and regional conflicts within the Russian Federation or between Russians and other nationals outside of Russia might spill over into interstate war. For example, separatist and Russian nationalist sentiment have combined to produce conflict in the trans-Dniester region of Moldova for several years: this conflict had the potential to involve Russia, Ukraine and Romania in military actions during some of its more active phases in 1992.[17] Inter-ethnic nationalism and separatism are certainly forces which must be contained if the Commonwealth and Russia are to survive. For Russian defense planners, the worst-case situation is not only the problem of inter-ethnic containment and regional strife, but also the potential combination of these with foreign invasion. For that reason the broad choice between offensively or defensively-oriented strategic military options remains highly pertinent.

Ideal Types of Strategy

In his study *Conventional Deterrence,* John Mearsheimer sets out three ideal types of strategy: attrition; blitzkrieg, another expression for a strategy of annihilation; and a strategy of limited aim.[18] The strategy of limited aim describes a campaign more than it does a war, but it is a useful collective for those military operations which have as their motive the accomplishment of improved positions for postwar bargaining or very restricted territorial gains. For major wars involving large arms of service in more than a single theater of operations, the dichotomy between attrition and annihilation strategies holds up well. Mearsheimer's contribution to the distinction includes his pointing away from the meaningless distinction alleged to exist between attrition and 'maneuver' strategies; maneuver is more appropriately characterized as an ability which armies must have under either an attrition or annihilation strategy.

In a study of Germany's pre-First World War grand strategy, Dennis Showalter argued that the conceptual framework for German military planning prior to the First World War could be characterized as one of total war for limited aims.[19] This seemingly paradoxical appraisal he drew from his analysis of German policy and strategy in the Franco-Prussian war and from subsequent strategic planning by the German General Staff under the direction of Helmuth von Moltke (the elder). Moltke's military strategy after German unification ruled out the likelihood that Germany could inflict total defeat on the field forces of France and Russia simultaneously or sequentially. He envisioned an offensive–defensive strategy on two fronts which would present to either France or Russia an impossible scenario for victory in battle, so the better to deter them individually or jointly. The German General Staff departed from this planning guidance under Schlieffen when political conditions, absent Bismarck, changed for the worse. However, even the Schlieffen plan in its various incarnations, as described by Ritter and other experts, did not necessarily entail the annihilation of Germany's opponents on all fronts, or the complete destruction of France's field forces. Instead, the prompt surrender of many of France's intact forces once they had been encircled and Paris besieged was the preferred outcome of the western campaign as envisioned by Schlieffen and his successor, von Moltke (the younger).

Historians have correctly noted that pre-First World War military planners mistakenly foresaw a short war, and that the actual war of attrition that resulted was poorly planned for. The First World War illustrates the complexity of the issue of attrition versus annihilation in several directions. As Michael Howard has noted, neither Germany nor Britain in the First World War had as a preferred war aim the total elimination of the opponent from the group of major powers on the world stage.[20] Each sought to inflict military losses on the other in order to change its intentions and imperial reach, but neither entered the war with the intent to remake the internal regime of the loser or to destroy fully its capacity for national self-defense. Military technology dictated on the western front a prolonged war of attrition, as did the alliance entanglements which discouraged defections from the carnage by any single state despite its growing losses. The First World War became a war of attrition unexpectedly, shattering prewar plans based on short war assumptions and destroying societies and governments which rested shakily on that premise.

Types of Attrition

If it is correct that a strategy of annihilation can support a defensive grand strategy of marginal adjustment to the status quo, can a strategy of attrition be used in support of the maximum political objective of total conquest and defeat of opposed armed forces and regimes? The strategy employed by the Union in the American Civil War exhausted the manpower and resources of Confederate armed forces and laid waste to the social and economic structure which supported those armed forces. Grant's Wilderness and Cold Harbor campaigns were archetypal examples of attrition, but his victory at Vicksburg exploited the opportunities for maneuver and surprise which the larger theater of operations in the west made possible. Vicksburg is among many campaigns which give the impression that battles fought over large territories involve more opportunity for maneuver and for an offensive thrust which strikes a decisive blow against the unprepared defender. However, the choice of attrition or annihilation strategy is not dictated only by the geographical extent of the fighting. US strategy against Japan and Germany in the Second World War was basically a strategy of attrition, crushing the opponents under the endless stream of logistics and fresh personnel supplied by the world's strongest economy.

Attrition strategies are distinguished from annihilation and other rapid victory strategies by their assumption that war will be protracted and un-avoidably costly. Because war is assumed to involve more than one important phase, attrition strategies for fighting on land can be based on defenses which are assumed impenetrable and immediately repelling, or on those which are designed for flexible absorption of attackers and gradual expulsion of the attacker from the defender's territory. The French Maginot line was thought to be impregnable, and in fact the Germans did not plan to overrun it, but to circumvent it. An interesting 'thought experiment' is what would have happened had the Maginot line been extended to cover the entirety of the French and Belgian vulnerable fronts. In any event, the French strategy was to wear out German attackers who fruitlessly threw their forces against the Maginot line. This first and stalemated phase of the war was to be followed by a protracted counteroffensive into Germany using the combined armies of Britain and France. It was envisioned by French planners that this process of counteroffensive against Germany would require great losses on both sides and consume great quantities of societal resources. Therefore, total mobili-zation capacity for a war of long duration was judged to be more significant

90

than the capability for counterattacks and counteroffensives in the initial period of war. The French defensive concept was a logical one for the war which France hoped to fight, but not for the kind of war which the German armed forces launched in May 1940.[21]

Russia's war planning in the late nineteenth and early twentieth century was bedeviled by the emotional attachment of some quarters to the fortresses in western Russia (Congress Poland). Some Russians had a 'Maginot' mentality about these fortresses, which were obsolete and in danger of being overrun in the early stages of any attack eastward by Germany. Symbols of Russian commitment to forward defense of the outer reaches of the empire, the fortresses became the subjects of fierce controversy among General Staff defense planners, war ministers and various other actors in the Tsarist policy-making process. Among the partisans for preserving the fortresses at any cost were the 'Grand Dukes' who interfered repeatedly in military planning and personnel issues. The costs of maintaining the fortresses diverted Russian military resources which would almost certainly have been better used. As critics had predicted, in the event of war the fortifications were quickly reduced by the modern field artillery which was brought to bear against them, and they contributed nothing to retarding the devastating thrusts of German offensives in 1915.[22]

Although Russian pre-First World War fortifications and French Maginot line defenses proved inadequate given the technologies and strategies which defeated them, neither French nor Russian emphasis on defense in the initial period of a major war was illogical. Each sought to take advantage of its perceived strengths and to offset its apparent weaknesses. For Russia in 1914, planners recognized that Germany might make its main thrust eastward against Russia or westward against France. If the main German attack were eastward against Russia, plan 'G' would mobilize and deploy the greater part of Russia's ready forces against Germany, leaving a comparatively smaller force deployed against Austria. If, as was thought to be more likely by the Russian and French general staffs, the bulk of Germany's forces were initially directed westward against France, then the greater share of Russia's already mobilized defenses would be deployed against Austria (Plan 'A').[23] Mobilization plans called for significant deployments in both directions, and for prompt offensives against both Austria and Germany with the aim of rapidly transferring the conduct of battle onto enemy territory.[24] However, Russian General Staff pessimists doubted whether prompt offensives against Germany in East Prussia would be successful and recognized that any two-front war would almost certainly strain the total fighting capacity and resources of the empire.

French military leaders between the World Wars recognized that any strategy for prompt offensives against Germany would be doubtful of success. Although they were aware of the necessity for mechanization and motorization of the armed forces to keep pace with the technology of their probable enemies, French armed forces planners did not adjust their theory of war to take the extreme possibilities for exploiting this technology into account. Neither did the German General Staff, in the main. But faced with Hitler's insistent demands for a victory strategy without a war of attrition that would bleed Germany into economic stasis, innovators in the Wehrmacht proposed the attack through the Ardennes, which disrupted French command and control and defeated French field armies. The French theory of war was logical on the basis of the First World War experience and on the assumption that 'normal' usage would be made of newly mechanized and modernized forces on both sides.

Offensive strategies can pay large dividends if the attacker catches an unprepared defender or if the attacker's strategy is superior to that of the defender. On the other hand, to take the offensive is to gamble that Clausewitz's friction or Machiavelli's *fortuna* will work in your favor and against your opponent. Military analyst Trevor N. Dupuy studied 42 selected battles from 1805 to 1973, including the most significant campaigns fought in Western Europe in that space of approximately one and a half centuries.[25] Of these 42 battles, 28 attackers and 14 defenders were successful. Twelve of 13 numerically inferior attackers succeeded. In addition, 24 victors were numerically *inferior*, and only 18 numerically superior, to their opponents. Dupuy's summary of some of those battles, including the force sizes and attacker/defender outcomes, is presented in Table 3.1.

Russian Second World War strategy was based on attrition in the initial period of the war against Germany. How much this was a matter of choice, as opposed to necessity, is still a subject of debate among Soviet historians. Soviet armed forces eventually regrouped from their initially disastrous campaigns, reconstituted powerful offensive forces, and launched successful campaigns of annihilation against German defenders on the Eastern front.[26] A delaying strategy forced upon an underprepared or outperformed defender is not necessarily a strategy of attrition. Thus the strategy employed by Fabius Maximus against Hannibal in 217 B.C. was improvised under duress. It succeeded in denying to the attacker a decisive battle of annihilation, so it accomplished one denial aim which is a necessary, but insufficient, condition for fulfilling the requirements of a strategy of attrition.[27] An attrition strategy, properly conceived, seeks to wear out the war-making capacity and military tenacity of the attacker, not just to buy time for the defender to regroup. Some

92

TABLE 3.1

OUTCOMES FOR ATTACKERS AND DEFENDERS IN SELECTED BATTLES, 1805–1973
(VICTORIOUS SIDE IN CAPITAL LETTERS)

Battle	Date	Attacker	Force	Defender	Force
Austerlitz	1805	FRENCH	75,000	Allies	89,000
Auerstadt	1806	Prussians	50,000	FRENCH	30,000
Borodino	1812	FRENCH	130,000	Russians	120,000
Dresden	1813	FRENCH	100,000	Allies	150,000
Leipzig	1813	ALLIES	300,000	French	180,000
Ligny	1815	FRENCH	77,000	Prussians	83,000
Waterloo	1815	*ALLIES	129,000	*French	72,000
Buena Vista	1847	Mexicans	16,000	US	16,000
Cerro Gordo	1847	US	8,500	Mexicans	12,000
Shiloh	1862	Confederates	40,335	UNION	62,642
Antietam	1862	Union	80,000	CONFEDERATES	45,000
Fredericksburg	1862	Union	106,000	CONFEDERATES	77,500
Chancellorsville	1863	Union	161,000	CONFEDERATES	57,352
Gettysburg	1863	Confederates	75,000	UNION	88,289
Chattanooga	1863	UNION	56,359	Confederates	46,165
Cold Harbor	1864	Union	107,907	CONFEDERATES	63,797
Koenniggratz	1866	PRUSSIA	220,000	Austria	215,000
Sedan	1870	PRUSSIA	190,000	French	110,000
Frontiers	1914	GERMANY	1,200,000	Allies	1,390,000
Tannenberg	1914	GERMANY	187,000	Russia	160,000
Marne	1914	*ALLIES	1,200,000	*Germany	900,000
Masurian Lakes	1914	GERMANY	288,600	Russia	273,000
Champagne II	1914	French	500,000	GERMANY	190,000
Gorlice–Tarnow	1915	GERMANY	175,000	Russia	300,000
Arras	1917	British	276,000	GERMANY	120,000
Aisne II (Nivelle)	1917	French	1,000,000	GERMANY	480,000
Meuse–Argonne	1918	US	600,000	Germany	380,000

(Continued overleaf)

93

(*Table 3.1 continued*)

Flanders	1940	GERMANY	2,500,000	Allies	3,000,000
Crete	1941	GERMANY	20,000	Anglo-Greek	41,000
Barbarossa (Group Kliest)	1941	GERMANY	132,000	Soviet Union	150,000
Malaya	1941–42	JAPAN	60,000	Britain	130,000
El Alamein	1942	BRITAIN	177,000	Axis	93,000
Stalingrad	1942	SOVIET UNION	1,000,000	Germany	800,000
** Kursk–Oboyan	1943	Germany	62,000	Soviet Union	90,000
Anzio (US 45th Inf. Div.)	1944	Germany	41,974	US	20,496
Velletri (US 1st Armored Divis.)	1944	United States	14,620	GERMANY	12,327
Metz (US XX Corps)	1944	United States	60,794	GERMANY	39,580
Ardennes (US 4th Inf. Div.)	1944	GERMANY	10,000	United States	8,634
Iwo Jima	1945	US	68,000	Japan	22,000
Sinai, Six Day War	1967	ISRAEL	54,993	Egypt	100,000
West Bank, Six Day War	1967	ISRAEL	45,650	Jordan	43,300
Golan, Six Day War	1967	ISRAEL	40,450	Syria	60,000

* Where both sides were attacking, attacker–defender designations refer to their final dispositions or posture (for example, Waterloo and Marne).
** The Battle of Kursk was actually a major Soviet victory and a turning point in the war against Germany. The reference in the above table is only to one aspect of that battle, the German 48th Panzer Corps sector for the first seven days of battle and before the arrival of a new Soviet army group.
Source: Adapted with abridgement from Trevor N. Dupuy, *Numbers, Predictions and War: Using History to Evaluate Combat Factors and Predict the Outcome of Battles* (Indianapolis: Bobbs-Merrill, 1979), pp. 14–15.

recipes for 'mobile defense' on NATO's central front, and other mobile defense schemes proposed as part of non-offensive defense postures in Cold War Europe, elided this distinction between a true strategy of attrition and any mobile defense.

A strategy of attrition requires a reasonably large territory relative to the forces attempting to seize and capture it, a relative balance of forces not too lopsided in favor of the attacker, and a capacity for reconstitution of losses by the defender to replace armies, fleets and tactical air forces lost in the initial period of war. The Swiss do not possess a lot of territory, but they have territory which is difficult for invaders to hold and to occupy. Russia's historic disadvantage in making an attrition strategy work was the open access to the vitals of its country provided by endless plains and steppes. A parade of invaders from east and west drove Muscovy to expand until the Tsars had more secure borders, which, in the event, added to the insecurity of their neighbors, including the Turks, the Japanese, and the Germans, among others. One of the difficulties with proposals for a delaying or attrition-oriented strategy for the defense of West Germany from 1945 to 1990 was the lack of territorial breadth in that country relative to the ranges of modern Soviet weapons and to the presumed speed of any Warsaw Pact offensive in Central Europe. Subtraction of France from the NATO military command structure only added difficulty to any plan for a delaying and denial-oriented defense of the FRG without a prompt counteroffensive into Eastern Europe.

Types of Annihilation

Just as there are multiple variations of an attrition strategy as dictated by geography, climate, numbers of forces on the opposed sides and so forth, so are there also many variations of offensively oriented 'annihilation' strategies. In modern times, a decisive campaign of annihilation may be directed, primarily, against the enemy's armies, government or people at large. However, most conquerors have preferred to subjugate defeated populations rather than to exterminate them, since the extraction of economic wealth from the defeated state usually requires at least some cooperation from its remaining citizens. And even if directed at the opponent's government, a strategy of annihilation does not necessarily require the physical destruction of that government. It suffices to get that government to call off its armed forces from further resistance to the inevitable. A considerable risk for a strategy of annihilation directed against the enemy's government is that it may work too well. If the enemy has significant field forces remaining to carry on the fight and the government dissolves before effectively commanding those forces to

95

stand down, the formal surrender by the loser may be followed by a protracted campaign of resistance without official approval. Proponents of a strategy of annihilation need to keep in mind that tactical defeat, tactical surrender and strategic surrender are different realities. Tactical defeat implies that the field forces are no longer capable of putting up effective resistance to the opponent's armed forces. Tactical surrender occurs when the condition of tactical defeat is officially acknowledged by military commanders. Strategic surrender occurs when one government capitulates to another, officially renouncing its war aims and, on occasion, its very existence.[28]

For the most part, strategies of annihilation have been directed against the field forces of the opponent. The assumption has been that once they have been defeated, terms can be imposed at will on the loser's government and population. It follows from this that advocates of a strategy of attrition will seek to trade space for time and remove many of their forces away from their borders and into the interior of their country. For example, from the time of the Franco-Prussian war until the outbreak of the First World War, the relative proportion of Russian forces stationed near the western frontier in Tsarist Poland, relative to the number of active and reserve formations located in the interior of the empire, was a matter under constant review by the General Staff and War Ministry.[29]

From Obruchev through Danilov, Russian war planners faced the problem that the Polish salient provided both a danger and an opportunity. If the Austrians and the Germans could coordinate their efforts and mount a combined offensive from East Prussia and Galicia, the encirclement and crushing of Russian forces in Congress Poland might deal to the Tsar a decisive blow. Among other things, a wave of rebellion for independence might be let loose among Poles. However, the Polish salient also allowed Russia extra time in the event of a war against Germany. Provided that the forces sacrificed in the initial period of war could be replaced with other effectives capable of maintaining a provisional defensive cordon around the vitals of interior Russia, reserves could eventually retake the lost territories after the German offensive had reached its culminating point. The expectation that Russian armies would, if attacked from the west, simply retreat into their interior, denying the enemy a victorious strategy of annihilation, was one reason why von Moltke (the elder) eventually decided in favor of an offensive defense in two directions as the basis for General Staff war planning.

For most of the nineteenth and twentieth centuries, strategies of attrition have not appealed to professional military planners, nor to the apostles of daring operational art. Blitzkrieg became a twentieth-century synonym for the rapid and decisive defeat of opposed forces by artful maneuvering of armored and tactical air forces. Blitz strategies certainly offer more glamour than sitz, and they may make possible victory at a lower cost than would an extended and brutal campaign of slaughter. However, not all annihilation strategies are blitzkriegs: blitzkrieg is a strategy for the disruption of an enemy's command and control system more than it is a strategy for the physical destruction of his armies. Annihilation strategies, including those based on blitzkrieg operations, accept maximum risk for maximum gain. If they fail, they are apt to fail badly. Hitler's strategy in 1940 defeated France but not England. England's survival until America entered the war ensured Hitler's eventual defeat. Japan's attack against Pearl Harbor was designed to inflict a stunning operational blow which would induce American strategic pessimism against an all-out war on Hirohito's empire, and in favor of a *modus vivendi* with Japanese imperialism in the Far East. This misestimate of US tenacity cost Japan its empire and regime.

A New Threat Environment

The Cold War threat of a Soviet campaign of annihilation, by means of a theater-strategic offensive against NATO Europe dissolved along with the Warsaw Pact and the Soviet Union. The Russian Federation seems almost driven toward a strategy of non-offensive defense in some form, if non-offensive defense means any strategy which is more attrition- than annihilation-oriented. However, it may be a mistake to suppose that Russia will evolve a strategy of attrition without a very competent counteroffensive component.[30] Faced with reunited Germans, free Poles, and liberated Baltic republics, Russia's western frontier poses serious potential vulnerabilities as nuclear weapons inventories are drawn down to token levels or eliminated entirely. Therefore, the Russians could maintain a residual nuclear force of 2,000–3,000, nuclear charges and long-range delivery vehicles, no longer directed against America but instead devoted to deterrence of any territorial revisionism against their western, southern and eastern borders. Nuclear weapons in a bipolar world were the principal components of offensively oriented strategies of annihilation. In the Europe after Cold War, nuclear weapons may be the weapons of last resort which provide the ultimate power of attrition to dissuade against any temptation to strategies of annihilation.

If the strategy of Russia evolves in this direction, toward a conventional and nuclear force posture which is rearward-regarding instead of forward-leaning, Russian military power could serve as a bulwark of stability on the Eurasian continent. This evolutionary trend in Russian military power would merely return Russian military planners to the decision context faced by their general staffs in the latter part of the nineteenth and early twentieth centuries. A multipolar power system which allowed for flexibility of alignment, and for the separation of peripheral wars from central European conflicts, created a favorable political and military context for defensively oriented strategies of attrition instead of offensively oriented campaigns of annihilation. As alliances became more committing and mobilization timetables more rigid in the years immediately preceding the outbreak of war, speed and weight of blow in the initial period of war received more emphasis from military planners than did the capacity for sustainability and reconstitution. As it turned out in the First World War, sustainability counted for more, and Russia's premature and ill-prepared offensives against Germany cost her dearly in the early stages of fighting.

For current and future US and European defense planners, one lesson of nineteenth and twentieth century experience is that attrition or reconstitution strategies must be based on the potential to bring to bear superior maritime power and industrial war potential if things go badly in the first weeks or months of war. A strategy of attrition by means of reconstitution presupposes that the defender has the superior industrial, technological and social potential to defeat any combination of adversaries which may assemble from the outset of war to its dénouement. Reconstitution also assumes that the industrial and post-industrial base for rebuilding forces can be kept from enemy hands. If reconstituted rather than ready US forces, excluding nuclear weapons, become the overseas guarantors of peace and stability for Europe, then a novel experiment in the nuclear age is being tried: extended deterrence conveyed by means of delayed rather than prompt retaliation.

The credible threat of attrition as a deterrent has not been thoroughly studied, nor fully tested in crisis management. Crisis management in the nuclear age, under the umbrella of US–Soviet nuclear pre-eminence, has mostly been about the avoidance of surprise attack and pre-emption through deliberate or inadvertent escalation. Future crisis management in a more denuclearized world may need to place greater reliance on the credible threat of escalation by attrition: facing potential disturbers of the peace with protracted coalition warfare which would exhaust their resources and slowly destroy their armies. The strategy of deterrence by threat of attrition, short of nuclear escalation, should certainly be among the salient military-strategic menu items for US military planners. The US homeland faces no serious threat of military invasion, and continued friendship with post-Soviet Russia eliminates the problem of large-scale nuclear attack. As the world's only conventional military superpower, the US can rely on mobilization and reconstitution for global or major regional war, with a saving remnant of forward presence and rapid response forces available to it and to NATO for contingencies short of major war. One could argue that US experience in Desert Storm has been misread by those who assume that the victorious campaign against Iraq was a textbook campaign of annihilation. The Iraqi field forces and command and control infrastructure were certainly subjected to rapid and decisive strikes once war had broken out. However, the rapid operational victories of January and February 1991 were made possible only after an uninterrupted buildup of five months, *subsequent* to almost a decade of the most extensive peacetime modernization of US armed forces during the Cold War years.[31]

If attrition-based strategies are to serve as tools of crisis management in Moscow, Russia must estimate correctly how any future war might begin. With regard to the timing of mobilization and concentration of forces, Soviet and other major power twentieth century war planners have essentially assumed one of four possible cases:

1. most or all of the major powers' forces are mobilized and concentrated before the outbreak of war;
2. partial mobilization of major power forces before war begins, with completion of mobilization thereafter;
3. one-state attacks to attain operational–tactical advantage while its opponents are still mobilizing and concentrating;
4. one-state attacks to achieve strategic surprise before opponents can mobilize and concentrate.[32]

Soviet military planning during the 1920s was essentially based on variations 1 and 2, above, and during the 1930s assumptions vacillated between numbers 2 and 3. Germany's blitzkrieg into the western USSR in 1941 represented the most memorable example of variation 4 for the Soviet armed forces, and perhaps will rise in significance for future Russian ones. The ultimately destructive form of variation 4, successful strategic surprise in the initial period of war, would be a nuclear surprise attack on an unprepared defender whose retaliatory power was pre-emptively destroyed. Mutual assured destruction turns this form of strategic surprise into a self-defeating proposition.[33]

Defensive strategic models for conventional deterrence, in addition to those proposed by Kokoshin and Larionov, surfaced during the Gorbachev era military policy and strategy discussions. One new model was based on a publication in 1989 of the alleged defensive plan for the group of Soviet occupation forces in Germany, designed in 1946.[34] Of more relevance to future Russian defensive strategies within a multipolar system are models based on Soviet experiences and planning during the 1920s and 1930s. One model recreates the assumptions of the international setting during most of the 1920s and until 1935, arguing for some similarities between then and now. This model includes newly independent East European states bordering Germany and Russia and a militarily constrained but potentially stronger Germany in the center of Europe.[35] A second model based on analogies with earlier multipolar systems is based on Soviet strategy from about 1935 to 1941. Soviet planners during this period were faced with the need to develop, within the context of a politically defensive grand strategy and while facing a growing threat perception, a military strategy which would provide for larger and more capable armed forces and a more mature system for accomplishing the transition from peace to war.[36]

Despite last-minute efforts which were impeded by doctrinal confusion, delayed force rebuilding and truncated strategic rethinking, Stalin's war planners were the victims of his decision for non-provocation over pre-paredness. Insufficiently prepared for fighting in the initial period of war on the defensive, Soviet planners also failed to perceive the rudiments of Hitler strategy designed to inflict strategically as well as operationally and tactically decisive blows in the initial weeks and months of war. However, Hitler equally underestimated Soviet resources and resilience. Despite some misgivings among military traditionalists, Napoleon's experience in Russia shows that attrition strategies can impose a terrible price on the loser of a protracted campaign.

Soviet Army counteroffensive operations during the Second World War demonstrated that forces equal or inferior to the opponent in numbers of personnel and equipment could launch counterattacks from the defensive and obtain objectives of strategic or operational-strategic importance.[37] The preparation of Army counteroffensive operations by Soviet planners was characterized by three attributes. First, counteroffensives were organized in parallel with defensive operations. Second, the attacker usually had the initiative and superiority in equipment and personnel. Third, the time available for armies and other formations for transition from defensive to offensive forms of war was very limited. Table 3.2 summarizes some of the more important Army level counteroffensives conducted by the Soviet armed forces during their battles against the Wehrmacht on the Eastern front.

It should be appreciated how far the ratios shown in Table 3.2 are removed from the more favorable ratios of Soviet to enemy forces which are preferred

100

TABLE 3.2

SELECTED SOVIET ARMY COUNTEROFFENSIVE OPERATIONS, SECOND WORLD WAR:
PERSONNEL AND EQUIPMENT RATIOS

Name	Front	Army	Date began	Personnel	Tanks and SP artillery	Guns and mortars
CO at Rostov	Southern	9th	17 Nov. 1941	2.4:1	1:2.4	1.6:1
CO at Tikhvin	Leningrad	54th	3 Dec. 1941	1.1:1	1:7	1.2:1
Klin–Solnechnogorsk Offensive	Western	16th	7 Dec. 1941	1.2:1	1:1.2	1.7:1
Tula Offensive	Western	50th	8 Dec. 1941	1.2:1	1:1.2	1.3:1
Klin–Solnechnogorsk Offensive	Western	5th	11 Dec. 1941	1.2:1	1.4:1	1.5:1
Kotelnikovo Offensive	Stalingrad	51st	26 Dec. 1942	1.5:1	1.1:1	1:1.5
Orel Offensive	Central	13th	15 July 1943	1.6:1	1.1:1	2.4:1
Front CO on Belgorod/Kharkov Axis	Voronezh	6th Gds	20 July 1943	2.8:1	1.4:1	13:1
Zhitomir/Berdichev CO	1st Ukrainian	60th	26 Dec. 1943	2.1:1	2.6:1	1.5:1
East Pomeranian Offensive	1st Belorussian	61st	1 Mar. 1945	2.5:1	1:1.2	10:1
Vienna Offensive	3rd Ukrainian	26th	20 Mar. 1945	1.6:1	2.2:1	2.3:1

Source: Compiled from USSR TsAMO (Central Archives of the Ministry of Defense), in Colonel Y.F. Yashin, Cand. Hist. Sci., docent, and
Lieutenant Colonel V.I. Kuznetsov, 'Army Counteroffensive Operations: (Historical Experience)', *Voennaya mysl'*, No.1 (Jan. 1992),
pp. 26–34, **JPRS**-92-UMT-006-L, p.16.

for well-prepared offensive operations. From mid-1943 onward, as German forces on the Eastern front lost the initiative and were forced to fight more frequently on the defensive, the ability of the Germans to fight on the operational and tactical defensive improved through bitter experience. Thus Soviet leaders who planned major offensive campaigns in the third and conclusive period of the Great Patriotic War had to assume that decisive breakthroughs of a prepared defense could only be accomplished by superior numbers of personnel and by fire superiority in the attacked sectors. By early 1944 the state of Soviet force regroupment permitted their commanders to plan for the exploitation of force and fire superiority, as evident in Table 3.3 showing selected offensive operations during that final period.

Attrition strategies and other varieties of non-offensive defense are non-offensive only to the degree that they abjure reliance on pre-emptive or too-prompt offensives as decisive moves. Attrition neither precludes a robust counteroffensive nor prohibits the eventual grinding down of opposed forces and the occupation and reconstruction of their governments. Europeans big and small could do worse in the next century than to emphasize attrition as a way station toward a deterrent, crisis and arms race stable repolarization. The landpower of Russia and the seapower and economic strength of America, working at common purposes, could support the global status quo by means of attrition-oriented military planning which would be conducive to arms reductions between the Atlantic and the Urals. The possibility of such benign outcomes in conventional arms control is intertwined, however, with the fate of nuclear weapons and the decisions about nuclear strategy in the new Europe.

NUCLEAR WEAPONS AND THE EVOLUTION OF COLD WAR SOVIET STRATEGY: FROM STALEMATE TO SUFFICIENCY

Nuclear weapons not only increased the destruction that armed forces could do. They also exploded pre-nuclear understandings of military strategy. Before nuclear weapons it was almost always the case that the vital works and population of a state would be secure until its armed forces had been destroyed or its government surrendered in the expectation of imminent destruction. Nuclear weapons could leapfrog the defensive glacis of oceanic and land barriers between antagonistic states. Once they had been mated to delivery vehicles of intercontinental range, they created the potential for prompt and massive destruction of enemy forces, industry, and command systems. Since no defenses against nuclear weapons offered more than token

TABLE 3.3

RATIOS OF SOVIET TO GERMAN PERSONNEL AND EQUIPMENT
Selected Offensive Operations, 1944–45

Operation	Dates	Men	Artillery	Tanks/SP guns	Aircraft
Korsun–Shevchenkovskiy	24 Jan.–17 Feb. 1944	1.5:1	2.0:1	2.2:1	0.8:1
Belorussia	23 June–29 Aug. 1944	2.0:1	3.8:1	5.8:1	3.9:1
L'vov–Sandomir	13 July–29 Aug. 1944	1.2:1	2.6:1	2.3:1	4.6:1
Iasi–Kishinev	20 Aug.–29 Aug. 1944	1.4:1	2.1:1	4.6:1	2.7:1
East Prussia	13 Jan.–3 Feb. 1945	2.1:1	3.1:1*	5.5:1	4.0:1
Visla–Oder	12 Jan.–3 Feb. 1945	3.9:1/ 4.2:1**	6.0:1	5.5:1/ 8.0:1**	8.0:1
Berlin	16 Apr.–8 May 1945	2.5:1	4.0:1	4.2:1	2.0:1

* Excludes rocket launchers and anti-aircraft guns.
** The higher figures are German estimates; the lower, Russian.

Source: C.J. Dick, *The Operational Employment of Soviet Armour in the Great Patriotic War* (Sandhurst, UK: Soviet Studies Research Centre, RMA Sandhurst, Oct. 1988), p.38. See also B.V. Panov, *et al.*, *Istoriya voennogo iskusstya* (Moscow: Voenizdat, 1984), JPRS–UMA–85–009–L, 21 March 1985, p.308 on Visla–Oder and p.323 on Berlin operations. On East Prussian operations, see also V.A. Matsulenko, *Operatsii i boi na okruzhenie* (Moscow: Voenizat, 1983), JPRS–UMA–84–019–L, 28 Sept. 1984, pp.166–7.

protection during the Cold War years, it became necessary for US and Soviet leaders to guarantee security by means of the potential for devastating retaliatory strikes with survivable offensive weapons.

The existence of mutual second strike capability, a fact of life if not a desirable endpoint for some influential Americans and Soviets, required by the middle to late 1960s a reappraisal of the relationship between nuclear weapons and regional deterrence in US and NATO strategy. US relative advantage in strategic nuclear weapons could no longer be used as a means of 'extending' deterrence based on the threat of deliberate nuclear retaliation against conventional attack. Although the US could still engage in a competition in risk-taking and compete with the Soviet Union in nuclear 'manipulation of risk' on the brink of war, actual crisis management could not guarantee that leaders would step up to the brink in controllable increments.[38] The cost-benefit model of nuclear crisis management was judged to have worked successfully in favor of the United States in the Cuban missile crisis. However, the unfolding of the crisis represented a serious misjudgment by the Soviet leadership of US perceived vital interests, and it occurred when the US had an overwhelming superiority in strategic nuclear weapons.[39]

After Cuba 1962 mainstream US and Soviet strategic thinking drifted away from optimism about the use of nuclear weapons in combat or about the reliability of nuclear weapons for coercive diplomacy.[40] After having attained virtual strategic nuclear parity by the end of the 1960s, Soviet leaders were ready to acknowledge in arms control negotiations that a condition of mutual deterrence existed between the nuclear superpowers.[41] This condition was both reassuring and perturbing to military planners and to political leaders. On the one hand, a stable stasis in strategic nuclear deterrence meant that neither side would be tempted in a crisis to hasty escalation or inadvertent pre-emption. On the other hand, either the Americans or the Soviets might fear that the perimeter of their strategic reach was in danger of encroachment by conventional or unconventional war which remained well below the nuclear threshold. In short, too much parity was too 'crisis stable', and too much crisis stability led to the stability–instability paradox that nuclear disutility could open the door to conventional war.

The stability–instability paradox did not lead from nuclear stasis to conventional war between the superpowers or their allies in Europe, for both political and military reasons. Nixon and Brezhnev sought political and military détente in order to accomplish a number of global objectives, including the use by each side of its relationship with China as a mechanism for balancing its triangular interests.[42] The 1970s witnessed the development of a multipolar political and economic world system while the global deterrent system remained locked into a duopoly. This contrast between military stasis and political-economic fluidity in interstate relations was apparent during the success of the OPEC oil embargo in 1973 against the US and other supporters of Israel. The nuclear weapons of the United States and of the Soviet Union provided neither side with leverage sufficient to prevent the outbreak of war in October 1973 between their allies in the Middle East, a war which resulted in a US–Soviet diplomatic confrontation supported by unilateral Soviet threats of military intervention and a responsive US global military alert.

Supremacy of Defensive Strategy

The military impasse created by US and Soviet nuclear weapons meant that offensive technology had made supreme for the time being a defensive military strategy. The point bears repetition, for it was misexplained in many US policy debates. Offensive nuclear weapons were more competent than strategic defensive weapons during the Cold War years. Therefore, for each side it became rational to rely on second strike retaliation, a defensive strategy, instead of first strike pre-emption, an offensive strategy.[43] Taken alone, offensive force technologies such as multiple warheads and improved accuracies might have encouraged first strike fears. But those force improvements were offset by the improved survivability of defending forces; the survivability of sea-based forces against detection and pre-emptive destruction was almost absolute, and US naval officials claimed absolute undetectability for American SSBNs.

Nuclear weapons made possible a battle of annihilation only against a non-nuclear power or against a power which lacked a second strike capability. Against a power which had survivable nuclear forces sufficient to destroy the attacker's society, a campaign of nuclear annihilation was self-defeating. Theorists and planners sought in futility to define ways around this impasse. It was argued that the Soviet Union might carry out a limited strategic attack against one portion of the US retaliatory force, say ICBMs. The US President would then be faced with a choice between retaliation, certain to be followed by the destruction of many American cities, or capitulation. Another scenario posited various ways by which a carefully orchestrated Soviet nuclear attack could decapitate the US command and control system, precluding retaliation according to the fine-grained details laid down in prewar US plans.

These hypothetical counterforce and counter-command attacks which Soviet leaders were thought to be capable of launching were more works of art than they were serious planning guidance.[44] The idea that even in the more intrepid Khrushchev years Soviet leaders would have launched a 'try and see'

105

limited nuclear attack against the American homeland was inconsistent with historical Soviet experience and with Soviet expectations that such a war must escalate into a decisive conflict between capitalism and socialism. While Soviet leaders throughout the Cold War gave ritualistic expression to the superiority of their system even in the awful event of nuclear conflict, their leaders especially after 1970 acknowledged that the outcomes of any general nuclear war would be off the baseline by which previous military victories and defeats had been determined.

That nuclear weapons had established the supremacy of the defensive over the offensive did not mean that those weapons favored a strategy of attrition instead of a campaign of annihilation. Some Soviet and US strategists of the Cold War years offered attrition strategy versions of nuclear wars, in which 'post attack' surviving forces slugged it out while citizens in North America and in the Soviet Union huddled together in civil defense shelters. In the Soviet version of the Khrushchev years, exchanges of nuclear weapons would be followed by global war involving all the armies, fleets and air forces of the various capitalist and socialist powers until one side capitulated. US notions of protracted nuclear war gained favor in the Carter administration, whose PD-59 strategic nuclear employment policy envisioned forces and command systems which could endure for weeks or months after a major nuclear attack.[45]

Excluding Limited Nuclear War

However, the bulk of informed US academic and government analysis suggested that neither a protracted nor a limited nuclear war could be fought with available US and Soviet nuclear forces at any time after the arrival of mutual second strike capability in the latter sixties, and in all probability not even earlier.[46] The collateral damage attending counterforce attacks on US or Soviet strategic nuclear forces, and the sensitivity of vital nodes in the US nuclear command and control system to prompt destruction, made a controlled nuclear war out of reach for serious planning purposes.[47] And without the ability to maintain continuous control over wartime force employment and to bring about war termination, leaders and planners would be at the mercy of a randomly disconnected military machine of which they were the reluctant servants, not the masters.

US and Soviet leaders were unable to contemplate limited nuclear war for different reasons. US planners could not make the case on technical grounds that: command and control systems were subtle enough to make fine distinctions between light and heavy attacks; that reciprocal communications between wartime leaderships would remain sufficiently clear to make possible orderly war termination; or, that even with partial defenses and improved command systems, expected outcomes of nuclear wars fought by US and Soviet strategic nuclear forces could be kept within acceptable economic and social ranges. For the Soviet leadership, the dilemma was to explain how nuclear weapons made nuclear war an infeasible way of spreading communism, while still allowing for the connection between any war and state policy prescribed by Lenin, as adapted from Clausewitz.[48] It was clear that the uncontrollable effects of any large nuclear exchange would make the preservation of 'policy' as Lenin had understood it impossible, for policy control would vanish with the demise of the state and society. Soviet leaders, from the time of Brezhnev's 'Tula' speech in 1977 through the end of the Gorbachev era, acknowledged the self-evident disconnection of nuclear war from policy.[49]

Since a strategy of selective annihilation was beyond the capabilities of US and Soviet planners and of little apparent interest to the Soviet military leadership, it followed that only massive pre-emption accompanied by preclusive defenses would give one side the option for a rapid and decisive victory in nuclear war. No such defenses were in prospect during the Cold War years, and the Bush administration has jettisoned the Reagan policy objective of providing comprehensive societal protection by means of ballistic missile and other strategic defenses. Precluding wars of annihilation or attrition fought with nuclear weapons returned the search for relative military advantage to conventional forces. The stability–instability paradox was feared to permit the nuclear threshold to operate as a sealant. Below that threshold, either NATO or the Warsaw Pact might contemplate a war-winning scenario by denying the other side its capability for nuclear escalation, or by intimidating it against escalation with the credible threat of counter-escalation.

Threat Assessment in the 1960s and 1970s

US defense analysts therefore were concerned during the 1980s about the possibility of a Soviet theater-strategic offensive against NATO Europe, based on conventional war fighting supported by nuclear deterrence. Soviet conventional force improvements had made possible by the early 1980s, according to NATO assessments, a multi-front attack in the Western TVD (theater of military actions) which might isolate continental Europe from US immediate reinforcement and deny to NATO the opportunity for theater nuclear escalation.[50] We now know that Soviet assessments were not so sanguine. Michael MccGwire's careful reconstruction of the major shifts in Soviet strategic thinking during the Cold War years shows that the 'seventies

107

strategy' elevated the avoidance of world war as a major policy objective, compared to the strategy of the 1960s.[51]

US efforts to convince NATO in favor of 'flexible response' strategy and McNamara's shift to assured destruction in US nuclear declaratory policy contributed to Soviet reassessment in 1966 of the likelihood that any world war would inevitably go nuclear. Improving Soviet strategic nuclear forces might deter US nuclear escalation even in the event that NATO was being defeated in Europe. Therefore, it followed that a two-phase war was possible: a first phase in which NATO forces might be defeated in Europe, after which the US would still be capable of fighting; and, a second phase, a protracted global war the outcome of which was unpredictable.[52] The Soviet doctrinal shift was reassuring from the standpoint of crisis stability and arms race stability. The rethinking of the 1960s implies a 1970s strategy which would be less dependent on strategic nuclear pre-emption, compared to launch on warning or second strike ride out. It also implied less Soviet dependency on first use of tactical nuclear weapons in Europe.

However, the strategy of the 1970s, compared with that of the 1960s, which had been formulated under Khrushchev, did not fully resolve the problem of how to defeat NATO in Europe without nuclear weapons. A blitz attack against NATO theater nuclear forces and command systems could not be guaranteed to eliminate NATO's capability for nuclear first use, with the attendant risks of escalation to eventual war between the American and Soviet homelands. Second, Soviet planners never fully resolved whether, in the first phase of such a two-phased war, they were to rely more on NATO paralysis in decision-making or on the nearly complete destruction of NATO's nuclear inventory in Europe. If the latter, a major air offensive against NATO's qualitatively superior forces had to be carried out on a theater-wide basis before NATO forces became fully alerted.

These may be among the reasons why the strategy of the 1970s was the *preferred* option for any war between East and West, while Soviet planners nevertheless prepared for the possibility that the strategy might fail. NATO might forestall the conventional blitz with its conventional defenses, placing on the Soviet leadership the burden of nuclear first use. Or, the Soviet conventional offensive might succeed in the first phase, followed not by temporary armistice and a US buildup for a return to Europe, but by American escalation to strategic nuclear war. Thus, from the military standpoint, the transition to the preferred strategy of the 1970s did not preclude the need to be able to implement that of the 1960s, if necessary.[53] Table 3.4 summarizes aspects of the strategies during the 1960s and 1970s, with regard to Soviet doctrine on the nature of world war.

During the period 1979–82, emphasis in Soviet military thinking began to shift toward defensive operations in Europe. Numerous General Staff studies and important military conferences in the early 1980s attested to the growing interest in defensive combat operations, as did some nine articles on the subject appearing in *Voennaya mysl'* between August 1979 and July 1984.[54] Two authoritative editions of Reznichenko's *Taktika* each devoted a separate chapter to defensive operations under modern conditions of combined arms combat.[55] In 1985, Deputy Chief of the General Staff M.A. Gareev noted that in the 1960s and 1970s (variants of the 'sixties strategy' as described by MccGwire), Soviet military writers tended to assume that war 'under all circumstances' would be waged with nuclear weapons.[56] Battles fought with conventional weapons only would be brief episodes, in this view. Gareev

TABLE 3.4

COMPARISON OF SOVIET DOCTRINES ON WORLD WAR: THE 1960s AND 1970s

Aspect	1960s	1970s
Nature of World War:		
Military	Inevitably nuclear; strikes on Soviet territory unavoidable	Not necessarily nuclear; strikes on Soviet homeland not inevitable
Political	Decisive struggle between social systems	Vital campaign in the larger struggle between systems
Primary Military Objectives:		
Survival of USSR	Preserve socialist system	Avoid nuclear destruction of USSR
Defeat of enemy	Destroy capitalist system	Seriously weaken the capitalist system

Source: Adapted from Michael MccGwire, *Perestroika and Soviet National Security* (Washington, DC: Brookings Institution, 1991), p.25, and MccGwire, *Military Objectives in Soviet Foreign Policy* (Washington, DC: Brookings Institution, 1987), p.45.

argued that this judgment needed to be reconsidered in view of NATO's conventional force modernization, and he made special note of NATO's 'highly accurate, guided weapons which in terms of effectiveness are close to low-power nuclear weapons'.[57] Therefore, according to Gareev, 'as is assumed in the West', there will be a greater opportunity to carry on 'a comparatively long war employing conventional weapons and primarily new types of high-precision weapons'.[58]

The Defensive in the 1980s

The acknowledgment of the possibility of a prolonged conventional phase to fighting in Europe was part of a broader perspective on the role of the defensive in Soviet military strategy and operational art during the 1980s. It was not immediately obvious that this was so. Gareev anticipated many of the problems that later advocates of greater Soviet attention to the strategic defensive would have to confront. On the one hand, he noted that Soviet military planning for the outbreak of war on 22 June 1941 had been inadequate. Soviet leaders had expected that the initial period of the war would be like that of past wars, especially the First World War, in which the main force engagements were preceded by an extended period of skirmishing between covering forces deployed near the border. However, border forces were not properly prepared for the kind of offensive which Hitler was about to lay on them. Forces deployed forward in the border districts lacked proper command and control, appropriately echeloned formations, and adequate mobilization resources in order to respond to the shock waves of the early phases of Hitler's operation *Barbarossa*.[59] Many Soviet historians had shared that assessment of their nation's military preparedness for some time.[60]

On the other hand, this presented a dilemma for planners of the future, given the capabilities of conventional high technology weapons. The traditional remedy for surprise attack had been to anticipate the enemy attack and to pre-empt. This might not be possible under modern conditions: the effort to anticipate and forestall enemy surprise attack might itself provoke the attack. Gareev indicated sensitivity to this problem by noting that all necessary forces and means to ward off surprise attack under modern conditions could not necessarily be deployed by the Soviet armed forces in the period preceding the outbreak of a war. The effort to carry out all necessary measures of mobilization ahead of time was theoretically correct, according to Gareev, but in practice it ignored the complexity of the task and was 'reminiscent of the demand of a fire chief that his team arrive at the fire an hour before it starts'.[61]

Even if practical, early strategic deployment of forces prior to the outbreak of war is not always feasible from the standpoint of political considerations, according to Gareev, 'regardless of all the benefits of this in purely military terms'.[62] Mobilization, not to mention the entire range of measures related to strategic deployment of the Soviet armed forces, 'has always been considered tantamount to a state of war and it is very difficult to achieve a return from it back to a peacetime status'.[63] This acknowledgment that a mobilization which is too successfully carried out at the military-technical level may bring about a war which the political leadership seeks to avoid is consistent with the drift of Soviet military doctrine during the 1980s, and very much in contrast to the emphases of the mid-1970s.[64] Undoubtedly one reason for Gareev's explicit warning about the relationship between mobilization and provocation was his reading of the Soviet political leadership and its drift toward greater interest in political as opposed to military measures for resolving East–West differences. Gorbachev, of course, would later make this primacy of political measures for conflict resolution his stock in trade.

Another reason why Gareev would have been inclined to point specifically to the problem of pre-emption was that, despite his and his General Staff colleagues' awareness of the improvements in NATO and Soviet conventional military forces over the past decade or so, nuclear weapons remained in the picture. The possibility of nuclear escalation could not be excluded from a war which began with conventional pre-emption. Conventional pre-emption might be motivated by an expectation by one side that the other side favored a war-winning strategy without resorting to nuclear weapons and had high confidence in that strategy. Therefore, in the language of US strategists, deterrence by denial with conventional forces could not be neatly separated in Europe from deterrence by threat of punishment with nuclear forces. Writing on the subject of the changing contents and character of the initial period of war in 1985, Lieutenant General Yevseev noted that 'the initial period of a future nuclear-rocket war may be the fundamental and decisive period which in large measure predetermines the further development of armed conflict, and in certain conditions the outcome of the war'.[65] Gareev acknowledged the inescapable relationship between conventional deterrence and the threat of nuclear escalation by noting that a world war might start with the use of conventional weapons only, but broaden into a nuclear war. Any nuclear missile attack on the Soviet Union or other countries of the socialist common-wealth would call forth a destructive retaliatory strike. Under those con-ditions, the 'role of the initial period of war will increase further' and this may be 'the main and decisive period which largely predetermines the outcome of the war'.[66]

Gorbachev and the Risk of War

From the politico-military as well as the military-technical standpoint, there-fore, movement toward a more explicitly defensive Soviet doctrine and force posture required that the perceived dangers of pre-emption and of nuclear escalation be tamed. Gorbachev could not accomplish this without help from the West. The US–Soviet strategic nuclear balance was actually quite stable in 1985 when Gorbachev assumed the post of General Secretary. The Soviet leader could not suggest with plausibility that either side's vulnerability to first strike might tempt the other into pre-emptive attack during a crisis or conventional war. Therefore, Gorbachev and his new thinkers had to stress instead the possibility of inadvertent nuclear war or escalation. This was part of a new nuclear defensivism which marked an important turn in the Soviet

111

doctrinal road. Whereas previous Soviet military literature had for the most part discussed the problem of accidental nuclear war as something that the *West* might permit to happen, now it was acknowledged as a problem for both sides. Moreover, and related to the concession that even the Soviet Union might suffer from an un-Marxist nuclear inadvertency, Gorbachev pressed home the point that political, not military, means had to be used in the nuclear age to resolve outstanding differences between the blocs.[67] In his book *Perestroika: New Thinking for Our Country and the World*, he argued that, for nuclear or major conventional war, politics had been disconnected from the use of arms to resolve political differences: 'Clausewitz's dictum that war is the continuation of policy only by different means, which was classical in his time, has now grown hopelessly out of date'.[68]

Gorbachev, with the support of the military leadership restructured to his taste between 1985 and 1987, began to equate the destructiveness of modern conventional war with that of nuclear war. In *Perestroika*, which was widely circulated in the West, Gorbachev contended that 'military technology has developed to such an extent that even a non-nuclear war would now be comparable with a nuclear war in its destructive effect'.[69] It is doubtful that Gorbachev or his advisors believed this as a scientific statement. The assessment was designed to play a political role in future debates over Soviet force structure, defense expenditures and war-fighting strategy. Only if conventional war could be equated with nuclear war could the priority of avoiding world war altogether be asserted as a fundamental policy objective which *constrained* further modernization of the armed forces. Chief of the Soviet Armed Forces General Staff Marshal Sergei Akhromeev indicated in an article in May 1987 the willingness of the professional military leadership to subscribe to the asserted symmetry between the effects of nuclear and large-scale conventional war. Akhromeev, emphasizing that the Soviet Union now rejected the use of armed force as a means of resolving political disputes, added that allied socialist states 'proceed from the premise that under present-day conditions neither nuclear nor conventional war must in any circumstances be allowed; it must not be unleashed'.[70] Defense Minister Dmitri Yazov, in a book published in 1987, also commingled the unacceptability of nuclear and large-scale conventional war, offering two reasons: first, conventional war could escalate into nuclear exchanges; and, second, modern, high-accuracy conventional weapons approached nuclear weapons in their lethality.[71]

By positioning his military leadership in favor of an acknowledgment that large-scale conventional warfare could be as devastating as nuclear, Gorbachev had deprived them of the second of two Cold War justifications for high defense budgets and extensive military modernization. The first justification had been the threat of nuclear war: of a global battle of annihilation. The second, after the attainment of nuclear-strategic parity by the Soviet armed forces, was the possibility of war in Europe, with its probable expansion into global war, fought without nuclear weapons. The second scenario was the global war of attrition. The Soviet Armed Forces General Staff turned to the second scenario after nuclear parity deprived them of the first. One of the most articulate and visible spokesmen for this second rationale and the threat assessment on which it was based had been Marshal Nikolai V. Ogarkov, Chief of the General Staff from January 1977 to September 1984.

Combined Arms and Restrained Budgets

Ogarkov sought to develop a more efficient combined arms strategy for the Soviet armed forces which would adapt to trends in politics and in technology. The political trends included lower defense budgets under Brezhnev than Ogarkov felt necessary, and the unavoidable destructiveness of a world war fought with nuclear weapons. In addition, Ogarkov was forced to accept the SALT arms control regime and its ceilings on the modernization of Soviet strategic nuclear forces. The technological trends involved the promise of new conventional arms technologies and the potential damage they could do to Soviet war planning if the USSR fell drastically behind the West on this issue. Both politics and technology thus pushed Ogarkov toward advocacy for conventional force modernization and preparedness for general war, with or without nuclear weapons. Ogarkov did not rule out the possibility of nuclear escalation from large-scale or small conventional war. But his writings even before the 1980s emphasized the development of effective fighting forces below the nuclear threshold.[72]

During the early 1980s Ogarkov became more explicit about his view that modern conditions had changed drastically since the end of the Second World War, and that these changes would have to be taken into account in future force and strategic planning. For example, in *Always in Readiness to Defend the Fatherland*, Ogarkov noted that a 'profound revolution' was taking place in connection with the development of thermonuclear weapons, of electronics, of weapons based on new physical principles, and of 'extensive qualitative improvement of conventional weapons'.[73] During the Second World War, the Soviet Armed Forces had conducted the front operation as the major form of military action on an operational scale. But in a number of instances in the later stages of that war, operations conducted over several fronts simultaneously were required. These operations over groups of fronts provided, according to Ogarkov, a foretaste of the speed, mobility and comprehensiveness which combined arms warfare would require under modern conditions. The 'principal operation' in contemporary war would be, according to Ogarkov, the 'strategic operation in a theater of military actions'.[74]

Ogarkov's preferred war-fighting strategy below the nuclear threshold and on the basis of simultaneous operations over many fronts drew upon a rich tradition of Soviet military thought, including the works of innovative thinkers who developed the concepts for deep battle and operations in depth during the 1920s and 1930s.[75] And the resource dilemma he posed to his political masters was not new from the standpoint of Russian history. Russian military and economic planning required that leaders in the 1870s, 1880s and 1890s make hard choices between short-term military investment and long-term economic modernization. Improving the economy and the potential mobilization base for future war was the priority of influential economic ministers such as Sergei Witte. On the other hand, heads of the armed forces were focussed on preparedness for the shorter term in which politicians might commit their forces to battle. The crunch between investment for industry or current expenditures for military personnel and equipment carried over into the operational and tactical planning debates within the General Staff about how far west Russia could reliably defend its frontier against German or Austrian attack. It also extended into debates about the extent to which the flag and forces to defend it would follow adventurers and investors in the Far East.[76] Russian resource constraints dictated less reliance on a strategy for hasty attack than Russia's French allies on the eve of the First World War had hoped, prompting French subventions of Russian railway construction after 1910.[77]

Ogarkov's vision that nuclear weapons had increased in quantity and effectiveness to the point at which they neutralized themselves as instruments of combat was by 1984 not atypical thinking for Soviet military and political leaders. Yet Ogarkov went further than most in extending this military – technical insight 'upward' to its politico-military implications, and 'downward' to its implications for troop control and force modernization. Its politico-military implications were that the US and NATO, maintaining political aims hostile to the USSR, would seek to exploit these revolutionary developments in military affairs for unilateral advantage. The 'downward' implications of Ogarkov's insight were that lagging modernization and insufficient military resources would place Soviet and allied armed forces at the mercy of NATO high-technology weapons and US AirLand battle strategy.

Russian Military Doctrine and the 1990s

In May, 1992 the General Staff of the newly nationalized Russian armed forces published a draft military doctrine. This draft doctrine carried over from the Gorbachev era the following declaratory policies: of rejecting war or threat of war as a means of attaining policy objectives; of adherence to the principle of inviolability of existing state borders; of pledging not to be the first to use nuclear or other weapons of mass destruction; and, of setting the prevention of war as the principal goal of security policy.[78] The draft doctrine avers that the immediate threat of a world nuclear war and conventional war has been considerably reduced. However, political, economic, religious and other contradictions that can lead to wars still exist, and Russia foresees the following sources of 'military danger':

(1) striving of some states or coalitions of states to dominate the world community or selected regions, and their insistence upon resolving disputes by force;
(2) the presence of 'powerful groupings of armed forces' in a number of states or coalitions of states and the continued basing of those armed forces near the Russian border;
(3) the 'instability of the military–political situation' resulting from some states continuing to build to higher levels their military potential, and the proliferation of nuclear and other weapons of mass destruction;
(4) efforts to use political and economic pressure or other means of blackmail against Russia.[79]

Specifically identified as potentially 'serious' sources of conflict between Russia and other states are violations of the rights of Russian citizens and 'persons who identify themselves with Russia ethnically and culturally in the former USSR republics'.[80] Two additional passages relative to the future relationship between offensive or defensive proclivities in Russian defense policy or military planning bear directly on the issue of escalation. First, Russia, according to the draft military doctrine, will view the introduction of foreign troops into the territory of neighboring states, or a buildup of foreign military forces on Russia's borders, as a 'direct security threat'. Second, if any aggressor unleashes a war, the purposeful destruction of strategic nuclear forces, nuclear power installations and other 'potentially dangerous installations' by conventional or other means 'will be taken as a transition to the use of weapons of mass destruction'.[81]

The intention to cooperate with other members of the Commonwealth of Independent States, with regional actors such as NATO and CSCE, and with universal actors (the United Nations) toward the prevention of war is stated as a primary Russian policy objective in the draft doctrine. Russian armed forces have the following strategic missions:

(1) deterrence of potential enemy aggression;
(2) repelling of a surprise aviation–missile attack and defense of main administrative–political and industrial centers and other important state institutions;
(3) infliction of retaliatory strikes on the aggressor to bring a halt to his actions, to disrupt his capability for the restoration of his armed forces, and to weaken his military–economic potential;
(4) repelling of any invasion from the land, sea or air while holding the most important territorial districts of the country and routing the invading groups of the enemy;
(5) liquidating the consequences of aggression and restoration of the prewar border positions; and
(6) frustration of any new attempt at the renewal of aggression.[82]

Sufficiency of defense according to the draft doctrine of May 1992 requires that strategic forces be adequate to guarantee deterrence of any nuclear attack against Russia and allied CIS states. Strategic forces should also be capable of performing retaliatory combat missions in the event of war. General purpose forces (in Russia *Sil obshchego naznacheniya* or 'forces of general designation') should guarantee the 'reliable defense of Russia' but should not be of sufficient power to permit a surprise attack or large-scale offensive against another state.[83] In order to repel aggression, Russian armed forces will be required to perform timely forward movement and maneuver of mobile reserves, strategic deployment and mobilization of all army and navy forces, and other measures to shift Russia from a peacetime to a war footing. Toward this end, Russian Armed Forces include the following components:

(1) *permanent readiness forces* of limited number deployed in potential theaters of military operations in order to immediately repel local attacks;
(2) *mobile reserves*, or rapid reaction forces, which can be transported to any region in a short time; together with the permanent readiness forces, these forces should be capable of defeating aggression on a medium scale;
(3) *strategic reserves*, which are formed during a period of threat and during war in order to conduct military operations on a large scale.[84]

In the event of an outbreak of war among member states of the Commonwealth or within the Russian Federation, Russia considers it a 'paramount task' to achieve a cessation of fighting and a settlement of the conflict by political and diplomatic means. In 'exceptional' conditions when other methods have been tried and failed, military force can be employed for the 're-establishment and maintenance of peace'.[85] The main goal of the Russian armed forces in other wars will be to defend Russian sovereignty and territorial integrity along with the sovereignty and territory of allied Common-wealth states.[86] A large-scale conventional war may grow out of a local war by escalation, and the initial period would be decisive in any war of this type. In the initial period of a possible future large-scale conventional war, according to the draft doctrine, enemy invasion may begin not on land but in 'air and sea space'.[87] The initial period of this type of war will be characterized by the involvement of large groupings of air, air defense, naval and assault landing groupings in order to disrupt strategic deployment, to disorganize command and control, and to disengage individual members of the Commonwealth of Independent States from the war.[88] It can be expected that an aggressor in this type of war would use precision weapons and electronic warfare in order to destroy military and economic targets 'to a great depth'.[89]

The mention of attacking military and economic targets at great depth with precision weapons supported by electronic warfare is an obvious reflection on the Gulf War of 1991 by the General Staff. Apparently they have drawn the conclusion that strategic aims can be accomplished with conventional, high-technology weapons in the initial period of war. NATO never found it necessary to apply this template of modernized conventional arms and information systems against the Warsaw Pact, but the US and allied coalition forces did apply it with some success against Iraq in 1991.[90] The accomplish-ment of strategic aims in the initial period of a war against a major adversary and without nuclear weapons is now a present reality, based on the experience of the Gulf War of 1991. Iraq had significant strategic depth, modern weapons and communications systems, and heavily fortified positions to deter any attacker. Coalition advantages included isolation of the Iraqis from any sanctuary, lack of militarily significant allied support for the Iraqi cause, and the successful application of technologies for precision aiming and electronic warfare in the context of Desert Storm.

The draft doctrine expectation that the objective of fighting is to restore the status quo allows for the possibility of conflict resolution short of a decisive counteroffensive. Neither is a counteroffensive into enemy territory specifi-cally precluded. The reduced expectation of large-scale conventional warfare compared to the Cold War years is a logical outgrowth of the political transformations in the former Soviet Union and in Eastern Europe, and of the likelihood that US, and Russian interests will not necessarily clash outside of Europe to the extent that US–Soviet interests frequently did. The assump-tion that the treatment of Russian nationals in other republics or the treatment of persons who identify with Russian culture is a Russian security interest opens the door to some expansive definitions of Russian self-interest. The potential for military involvement, pursuant to this very inclusive definition of interest, looms large, although uncertain of specifics.

The draft Russian military doctrine of May 1992 also explicitly endorses the participation of Russian and CIS military forces in international peace-keeping missions under multinational auspices, for example, as authorized by the United Nations. Whereas Cold War conflicts between the US and the Soviet Union dictated that their forces should be kept apart from UN peacekeeping contingents, future US–Russian political entente is more permissive of successful collective security using American or Soviet forces. US officials from the Central Intelligence Agency have already begun con-ferences with their Russian counterparts who now preside over a politically correct KGB, at least in its public face. Legislative oversight over Russian armed forces and security services, and a reorganized Russian defense and security decision-making process, make possible, although not certain, gradual transition toward democratically accountable coercive forces in both domestic and foreign policy. Given continuation of the favorable trends in defense and foreign intelligence decision-making of 1992, US–Russian security cooperation could provide a framework within which Europeans between the Atlantic and the Urals could work out new security regimes of enduring stability.

CONCLUSION

Not all of Russia's past and present defense choices can be squeezed into the dichotomous selection of an attrition or an annihilation strategy. But that dichotomy does call our attention to important decisions about grand strategy made by Tsars and Party Chairmen of the past, with implications for the future. Russia, bereft of communism and reverting to the status of a 'mere' great power in a potentially multipolar system, must decide whether to base strategic planning on short and offensively-oriented campaigns with defensive phases, or on basically defensive operations containing a necessary com-ponent of counterattack. Events may not give Russia forever to choose, as the forces of nationalism and economic backwardness threaten the cohesion of its army and polity.

As the Russians must choose, so must the remainder of Europe. NATO's formerly American dependent allies in Europe have more options, including the option of disconnecting their defense from the US altogether. They might do this in favor of a European pillar within NATO, by using the Western

European Union as a military arm of a politically united European community. Or, former European members of NATO may choose to go it alone, replacing allied defense with autarchic security. Whether together or separately, the former NATO allies of the US, along with the newly independent states of East and Central Europe, must choose between forward leaning and rearward regarding military force capabilities and doctrines. It is not so obvious that peace and stability will follow from a pandemic rush to defensive doctrines, although there is no harm in that result per se. More important is whether actors dissatisfied with the European political status quo undertake to develop new capabilities for surprise attack and large scale offensives.

NOTES

I am most grateful to Charles Dick, Director, Soviet Studies Research Centre, Royal Military Academy Sandhurst; Stephen Shenfield, Brown University; and Tim Sanz, Foreign Military Studies, US Army Command and General Staff College, Fort Leavenworth, Kansas, for comments on earlier drafts and suggestions about source materials. They are not responsible for any arguments or opinions herein. This chapter includes material from 'Security in Europe after the Cold War, Part II', *European Security*, Vol. 2, No. 3 (Autumn, 1993), pp. 365–99, and 'Nonoffensive Defense and Strategic Choices: Russia and Europe after the Cold War', *Slavic Military Studies*, Vol. 6, No. 2 (June 1993), pp. 166–202.

1. See, for example, Horst Afheldt, 'New Policies, New Fears', *Bulletin of the Atomic Scientists*, Sept. 1988, pp. 24–8, and John Grin and Lutz Unterseher, 'The Spiderweb Defense', *Bulletin of the Atomic Scientists*, Sept. 1988, pp. 28–30. According to Stephen J. Flanagan, there are four basic types of non-offensive defense concepts: area defense; wide-area covering defenses; the fire barrier; and integrated and interactive forward defense. See Flanagan, *NATO's Conventional Defenses* (Cambridge, MA: Ballinger Publishing, 1988), Ch. 7, esp. pp. 110–20; Andreas von Bulow, 'Defensive Entanglement: An Alternative Strategy for NATO', in Andrew J. Pierre (ed.), *The Conventional Defense of Europe: New Technologies and New Strategies* (New York: Council on Foreign Relations, 1986), pp. 112–52; and Von Bulow, 'O nesposobnosti k napadeniyu' (On the Impossibility of Attack), *Kommunist*, No. 7 (May 1989), pp. 122–5.
2. A critique of conventional deterrence strategies, including territorial self-defense schemes, in the context of their viability in a NATO–Warsaw Pact war scenario is provided in Josef Joffe, *The Limited Partnership: Europe, the United States and the Burdens of Alliance* (Cambridge, MA: Ballinger Publishing, 1987), pp. 148–65.
3. Robert Jervis, 'Cooperation under the Security Dilemma', *World Politics*, No. 2 (Jan. 1978), pp. 167–86, in Robert J. Art and Robert Jervis (eds), *International Politics: Anarchy, Force, Political Economy and Decision Making* (New York: Harper Collins, 1985), pp. 86–101, esp. p. 88.
4. Soviet intelligence appreciation failures in this regard are noted in John Erickson, 'Threat Identification and Strategic Appraisal by the Soviet Union, 1930–1941', Ch. 13 in Ernest R. May (ed.), *Knowing One's Enemies: Intelligence Assessment before the Two World Wars* (Princeton, NJ: Princeton University Press, 1984), pp. 375–423.
5. Douglas Porch, 'Arms and Alliances: French Grand Strategy and Policy in 1914 and 1940', Ch. 8 in Paul Kennedy (ed.), *Grand Strategies in War and Peace* (New Haven, CT: Yale University Press, 1991), pp. 125–44, and Eliot A. Cohen and John Gooch, *Military Misfor-*

tunes: The Anatomy of Failure in War (New York: The Free Press, 1990), pp. 197–230.

6. The definitive study of the Schlieffen plan is Gerhard Ritter, *The Schlieffen Plan: Critique of a Myth* (London: Oswald Wolff, 1958), which includes the text of Schlieffen's great memorandum of Dec. 1905, pp. 134–47. See also A.J.P. Taylor, *War by Time-Table: How the First World War Began* (New York: American Heritage, 1969), pp. 25–8, and Holger H. Herwig, 'The Dynamics of Necessity: German Military Planning during the First World War', Ch. 3 in Allan R. Millett and Williamson Murray (eds), *Military Effectiveness. Vol. 1: The First World War* (Boston: Unwin Hyman, 1988), pp. 80–115.

7. Ritter, *The Schlieffen Plan*, p. 21.

8. Aleksandr A. Svechin, *Strategiva* (Strategy), Second Edition (Voennyi Vestnik, 1927), translated into English and edited by Kent D. Lee (Minneapolis, MN: East View Publications, 1991), esp. pp. 239–56. See also, in the same volume, introductory and interpretive essays by A.A. Kokoshin and V.V. Larionov, V.N. Lobov, and Jacob W. Kipp.

9. On Delbruck, see Gordon A. Craig, 'Delbruck: The Military Historian', Ch. II in Edward Mead Earle (ed.), *Makers of Modern Strategy: Military Thought from Machiavelli to Hitler* (Princeton, NJ: Princeton University Press, 1943), pp. 260–86.

10. Svechin, *Strategiia* (Strategy), p. 241.

11. Ibid., p. 247. Of course, there can be campaigns of annihilation within a general war of attrition, as discussed in the text further on. Soviet military historical studies of the Manchurian campaign against Japan in 1945 emphasized the point.

12. For which views Svechin was roundly chastised by Red Commanders. See M. Tukhachevskii, 'Protiv reaktsionnykh teorii na voenno-nauchnom fronte (kritika strategicheskikh i voenno-istoricheskikh vzgliadov Prof. Svechina)' (Against Reactionary Theories on the Military-Scientific Front: A Critique of the Strategic and Military-Historical Views of Professor Svechin), *Problemy marksizma*, no. 8–9 (1931), pp. 187–209. Recent scholarship on Svechin has been more flattering, especially during the Gorbachev era and subsequent to renewed interest in Russian research institutes in strategic defense. See, for example, A.A. Kokoshin, 'A.A. Svechin: O voine i politike' (A.A. Svechin: On War and Politics), *Mezhdunarodnaia zhizn'*, No. 10 (Oct. 1988), pp. 133–42.

13. P.H. Vigor, *Soviet Blitzkrieg Theory* (New York: St. Martin's Press, 1983), p. 147 and *passim*.

14. S.P. Ivanov, *Nachal'nyi period voiny* (The Initial Period of War) (Moscow: Voyenizdat, 1974); Lt. Gen. A.I. Yevseev, 'O nekotorykh tendentsiyakh izmenii soderzhaniia i kharaktera nachal'nogo perioda voiny' (On Certain Tendencies in the Changing Content and Character of the Initial Period of War), *Voenno-istoricheskii zhurnal* (Military-Historical Journal), No. 11 (Nov. 1985), pp. 10–20; Lt. Gen. M.M. Kir'yan, 'Nachal'nyi period Velikoi Otechestvennoi Voiny' (The Initial Period of the Great Patriotic War), *Voenno-istoricheskii zhurnal*, No. 6 (June 1988), pp. 11–17; Maj. Gen. M. Cherednichenko, 'O nachal'nom periode Velikoi Otechestvennoi voiny' (On the Initial Period of the Great Patriotic War), *Voenno-istoricheskii zhurnal*, No. 4 (1961), pp. 28–35. Recent literature is well traced in Richard H. Phillips, *Soviet Military Debate on the Initial Period of War: Characteristics and Implications* (Cambridge, MA: Center for International Studies, MIT, Nov. 1989). For historical perspective see Jacob W. Kipp, *Barbarossa. Soviet Covering Forces and the Initial Period of War: Military History and AirLand Battle* (Ft. Leavenworth, KS: Soviet Army Studies Office, undated).

15. Andrei Kokoshin and Valentin Larionov, 'Kurskaia bitva v svete sovremennoi oboronitel'noi doktriny' (The Battle of Kursk in View of Contemporary Defensive Doctrine), *Mirovaia ekonomika i mezhdunarodnye otnosheniia* (World Economy and International Relations), No. 8 (1987), pp. 32–40. Excerpts from debates among Soviet historians about the reponsibility for failures attendant on *Barbarossa* are included in A.M. Nekrich, *22 June 1941* (Moscow: 'Nauka', 1965), translated in Vladimir Petrov (ed.) *June 22 1941: Soviet Historians and the German Ivasion* (Columbia, SC: University of South Carolina Press, 1968).

16. For a discussion of reasonable sufficiency, see L. Semeiko, 'Razumnaya dostatochnost' – put' k nadezhnomy miru' (Reasonable Sufficiency – Path to Reliable Peace), *Kommunist*, No. 7 (May 1989), pp. 112–21. The concept of reasonable sufficiency was first promulgated

at the 27th Party Congress of the CPSU. Variable approaches to stability with different mixes of offensive and defensive conventional force postures are outlined very schematically in Kokoshin and Larionov, 'Protivostoianiia sil obshchego naznacheniia v kontekste obespecheniia strategicheskoi stabil'nosti' (The Counterpositioning of Conventional Forces in the Context of Guaranteeing Strategic Stability), *Mirovaya ekonomika i mezhdunarodnye otnosheniya*, No. 6 (1988), pp. 23–31. Examination of the Kokoshin–Larionov and other past and possible future approaches to Soviet or Russian defensivism is provided in Col. David M. Glantz, *Soviet Military Strategy after CFE: Historical Models and Future Prospects* (Ft. Leavenworth, KS: Soviet Army Studies Office, January 1990).

17. For perspective and additional information on this issue, see Stephen R. Bowers, 'Ethnic conflict in the "Soviet" Commonwealth', *Low Intensity Conflict and Law Enforcement*, No. 1 (Summer, 1992), pp. 42–56.

18. John J. Mearsheimer, *Conventional Deterrence* (Ithaca, NY: Cornell University Press, 1983), Ch. 2.

19. Dennis E. Showalter, 'Total War for Limited Objectives: An Interpretation of German Grand Strategy', Ch. 7 in Kennedy (ed.), *Grand Strategies in War and Peace*, pp. 105–24.

20. Michael Howard, 'Europe on the Eve of the First World War', Ch. 7 in Howard, *The Lessons of History* (New Haven, CT: Yale University Press, 1991), pp. 113–26. See also Howard, 'British Grand Strategy in World War', in Kennedy (ed.), *Grand Strategies in War and Peace*, pp. 31–42.

21. On the interwar doctrine and planning of French armed forces, see Robert A. Doughty, 'The French Armed Forces, 1918–40', Ch. 2 in Allan R. Millet and Williamson Murray (eds), *Military Effectiveness: Vol. II* (London: Unwin Hyman, 1988), pp. 39–69. On the reasons for French failure in 1940, see Eliot Cohen and John Gooch (eds), *Military Misfortunes: The Anatomy of Failure in War* (New York: The Free Press, 1990), pp. 197–230.

22. Yuri Danilov, *La Russie dans la Guerre Mondiale (1914–1917)* (Paris: Payot, 1927) expresses the exasperation of General Staff war planners over the fortresses issue.

23. Rostunov, *Istoriya pervoi mirovoi voiny*, Vol. 1, pp. 196–7, and Danilov, *La Russie dans la Guerre Mondiale*.

24. Rostunov, *Istoriya pervoi mirovoi voiny*, Vol. 1, pp. 196–7.

25. Col. T.N. Dupuy, *Numbers, Predictions and War: Using History to Evaluate Combat Factors and Predict the Outcome of Battles* (Indianapolis: Bobbs-Merrill, 1979), pp. 12–15.

26. Svechin warned in the second edition of *Strategy* that 'a strategy of attrition in no way renounces in principle the destruction of enemy personnel as a goal of an operation. But in this it sees only a part of the mission of the armed front rather than the entire mission'. *Strategy*, p. 246.

27. Brian Caven, *The Punic Wars* (London: Weidenfeld & Nicolson, 1980), p. 127.

28. For these distinctions, see Paul Kecskemeti, *Strategic Surrender: The Politics of Victory and Defeat* (Stanford, CA: Stanford University Press, 1958); p. 11 notes that a series of tactical surrenders may lead to strategic surrender. Strategic surrender concerns 'not merely the belligerent role of military units' but the 'maintenance of belligerency itself'.

29. I.I. Rustunov, *Russkii front pervoi mirovoi voiny* (Moscow: 'Nauka' Publishing House, 1976), esp. pp. 64–6. See also Rostunov, *Istoriya pervoi mirovoi voiny, 1914–1918*, Vol. 1 (Moscow: 'Nauka' Publishing House, 1975), pp. 176–84 on Russian military doctrine from the Franco-Prussian war until the First World War. On the implications of Russian pre-First World War manpower policy for its military strategy, see Lt. Gen. N.N. Golovin, *The Russian Army in the World War* (New Haven, CT: Yale University Press, 1931), reissued by Archon Books, 1969.

30. Rostunov, *Istoriya pervoi mirovoi voiny, 1914–1918*, pp. 176–84 notes that Russian military theory in the late nineteenth and early twentieth centuries acknowledged the likelihood that future war could involve coalitions of states, be protracted, and depend as much on the economic and social resources of the country as on the fighting power of combat forces. Nevertheless, Russian tactical and operational art during this period had a decidedly offensive cast, emphasizing wide-ranging maneuver battles and the advantages of taking the

initiative.

31. One could argue that the Reagan modernization was record-setting even for strategic nuclear forces, in addition to the obvious precedent setting pace for general purpose forces. Although the McNamara years represented a period of active force posture growth in numbers of missile launchers and in the configuration of the basic strategic nuclear triad, McNamara retired many bomber and air defense forces and canceled other proposed strategic offensive forces, including the B-70 bomber, the Snark cruise missile, and the Skybolt air-launched ballistic missile. During the Reagan years the US supported modernization programs for two ICBMs and two bombers, and the modernized systems were more expensive per unit (and presumably more capable) than their predecessors. For relevant cost estimates, see Kevin N. Lewis, *Historical US Force Structure Trends: A Primer* (Santa Monica, CA: RAND Corporation, July 1989), pp. 46–9.

32. These typologies are explained in David M. Glantz, 'Future Directions in Soviet Military Strategy', Ch. 8 in John Hemsley (ed.), *The Lost Empire: Perceptions of Soviet Policy Shifts in the 1990s* (New York: Brassey's, 1991), pp. 123–44, esp. p. 137.

33. A point eventually acknowledged by Soviet military theorists in the Brezhnev years, most emphatically during the late 1970s and early 1980s. Ironically, this was at the very time that some critics of US strategy argued that it was deficient for lack of counterforce competency and war-fighting/war-survival capability, allegedly hallmarks of Soviet military doctrine and strategy. For comments on these variations as applied to the 1920s and 1930s, see Glantz, 'Future Directions in Soviet Military Strategy', p. 137.

34. Glantz, *Soviet Military Strategy after CFE*.

35. Glantz, 'Future Directions in Soviet Military Strategy', p. 127.

36. Ibid., p. 128.

37. Col V.F. Yashin and Lt Col V.I. Kuznetsov, 'Army Counteroffensive Operations: Historical Experience', *Voennaya mysl'*, No. 1 (Jan. 1992), pp. 26–34, JPRS–92–UMT–006–L, 14 May 1992, pp. 15–20.

38. The phrase is Thomas Schelling's. See Schelling, *Arms and Influence* (New Haven: Yale University Press, 1966).

39. The literature on the Cuban missile crisis is now quite extensive. An early classic is Graham T. Allison, *Essence of Decision: Explaining the Cuban Missile Crisis* (Boston: Little, Brown, 1971). More recent and important studies include McGeorge Bundy and James G. Blight, 'October 27, 1962: Transcripts of the Meetings of the ExComm', *International Security*, No. 3 (Winter, 1987–88), pp. 30–92; Raymond L. Garthoff, *Reflections on the Cuban Missile Crisis*, second edition (Washington, DC: Brookings Institution, 1989), and James G. Blight and David A. Welch, *On the Brink; Americans and Soviets Reexamine the Cuban Missile Crisis* (New York: Hill and Wang, 1989).

40. Alexander L. George discusses the coercive aspects of the Cuban missile crisis in 'The Cuban Missile Crisis: 1962', in Alexander L. George, David K. Hall and William E. Simons, *The Limits of Coercive Diplomacy* (Boston: Little, Brown, 1971), pp. 86–143.

41. The transition can be traced in the development of authoritative Soviet military doctrine from the early 1960s until the middle 1970s, when the acceptance of mutual deterrence and the inadmissibility of victory in nuclear war were constituents of party policy. Compare, for the Khrushchev years, V.D. Sokolovskii, *Voennaya Strategiya* (Military Strategy) (Moscow: Voyenizdat, 1962), and materials taught at the Voroshilov Academy of the Soviet Armed Forces General Staff in the 1970s, edited and translated with commentary in Ghulam Dastagir Wardak (compiler), and Graham Hall Turbiville, Jr. (general editor), *The Voroshilov Lectures: Materials from the Soviet General Staff Academy*, Vol. I (Washington, DC: National Defense University Press, 1989).

42. Adam B. Ulam, *Dangerous Relations: The Soviet Union in World Politics, 1970–1982* (New York: Oxford University Press, 1983), pp. 39–82.

43. For a discussion of the distinction between offensive and defensive weapons as applied to nuclear forces, see Lynn Eden, 'Introduction: Contours of the Nuclear Controversy',

pp. 1–36 in Lynn Eden and Steven E. Miller (eds), *Nuclear Arguments: Understanding the Strategic Nuclear Arms and Arms Control Debates* (Ithaca, NY: Cornell University Press, 1989), pp. 1–36, esp. p. 1, fn. 1.

44. Benjamin S. Lambeth, 'Uncertainties for the Soviet War Planner', *International Security*, No. 3 (Winter, 1982–83), reprinted in Sean Lynn-Jones, Steven E. Miller and Stephen Van Evera (eds), *Soviet Military Policy* (Cambridge, MA: MIT Press, 1989), pp. 347–74.

45. For a résumé and critique of various Cold War models of strategic nuclear exchange, see Michael Salman, Kevin J. Sullivan and Stephen Van Evera, 'Analysis or Propaganda? Measuring American Strategic Nuclear Capability, 1969–88', Ch. 3 in Eden and Miller (eds), *Nuclear Arguments: Understanding the Strategic Nuclear Arms and Arms Control Debates*, pp. 172–244. A critique of US 'countervailing' strategy during the Carter years and of highly counterforce-competent US nuclear doctrines is provided in Robert Jervis, *The Illogic of American Nuclear Strategy* (Ithaca, NY: Cornell University Press, 1984).

46. Richard K. Betts, *Nuclear Blackmail and Nuclear Balance* (Washington, DC: Brookings Institution, 1987), Ch. 4, pp. 144–71 discusses the nuclear balance as perceived by policy-makers in the so-called Golden Age of US nuclear superiority.

47. On the vulnerability of command and control systems, see Bruce G. Blair, *Strategic Command and Control: Redefining the Nuclear Threat* (Washington, DC: Brookings Institution, 1985); Desmond Ball, *Can Nuclear War Be Controlled?*, Adelphi Papers No. 169 (London: International Institute for Strategic Studies, Autumn, 1981); and Paul Bracken, *The Command and Control of Nuclear Forces* (New Haven: Yale University Press, 1983). On the collateral damage attending any nuclear attacks during the Cold War years, see Office of Technology Assessment, *The Effects of Nuclear War* (Washington, DC: US Government Printing Office, 1979).

48. Soviet efforts to explain this conundrum in military theory, between the political absurdity of any particular nuclear war and the ontological connection between even nuclear wars and politics, are illustrated in B. Byely, *et al.*, *Marxism–Leninism on War and Army* (Moscow: Progress Publishers, 1972), US Air Force Soviet Military Thought Series. See also Stephen J. Cimbala, 'Separating Nuclear War from Politics: Implications of Change in Soviet Perspective'; *Arms Control*, No. 1 (May 1991), pp. 35–71.

49. Raymond L. Garthoff, *Détente and Confrontation: American–Soviet Relations from Nixon to Reagan* (Washington, DC: Brookings Institution, 1985), esp. pp. 777–9. See also Garthoff, 'Soviet Perceptions of Western Strategic Thought and Doctrine', Ch. 4 in Gregory Flynn (ed.), *Soviet Military Doctrine and Western Policy* (London: Routledge, 1989), pp. 197–328, and Garthoff, *Deterrence and the Revolution in Soviet Military Doctrine* (Washington, DC: Brookings Institution, 1991). However, a lively debate continued among Soviet military and political analysts on this issue, even into the Gorbachev years. See, for example, Daniil Proektor, 'Politics, Clausewitz and Victory in Nuclear War', *International Affairs* (English edition), No. 5 (1988), pp. 74–80, and Nikolai Grachev, 'Nuclear War and Its Conse-quences', *International Affairs*, No. 3 (1988), pp. 91–4. See also Vitaliy Zhurkin, Sergei Karaganov and Andrei Kortunov, 'Vyzovy bezopasnosti – starye i novye' (Challenges to Security: Old and New), *Kommunist*, No. 1 (1988), pp. 42–50 for the views of important 'new thinkers' under Gorbachev.

50. John G. Hines and Phillip A. Peterson, 'The Warsaw Pact Strategic Offensive: the OMG in Context', *International Defense Review* (Oct. 1983), pp. 1391–5 and Christopher N. Donnelly, 'Soviet Operational Concepts in the 1980', in *Strengthening Conventional Deterrence in Europe: Proposals for the 1980s*, Report of the European Security Study (New York: St. Martin's Press, 1983), pp. 105–36 explored the risks attending Soviet planning scenarios of this type.

51. Michael MccGwire, *Military Objectives in Soviet Foreign Policy* (Washington, DC: Brookings Institution, 1987).

52. MccGwire, *Perestroika and Soviet National Security* (Washington, DC: Brookings Institution, 1991), esp. pp. 25–7. MccGwire was original in noticing that the discussions by Admiral Sergei Gorshkov, Commander-in-Chief of the Soviet Navy, of naval operations in the

Second World War only made sense in the context of a policy debate then going on about the role of the Soviet navy in the second phase of a world war.

53. MccGwire, *Perestroika*, pp. 27–8. According to MccGwire, the strategy of the 1970s probably became fully operational in 1976, although it had been based on doctrinal developments for which 1966 was the turning point.

54. Ibid., p. 37, attributed to Raymond Garthoff, personal communication.

55. V.G. Reznichenko, *et al.*, *Taktika* (Tactics) (Moscow: Voenizdat, 1984), Reznichenko *et al.*, *Taktika* (Moscow: Voenizdat, 1987).

56. M.A. Gareev, *M.V. Frunze: Military Theorist* (New York: Pergamon Brassey's, 1988), in English, p. 216. The original edition appeared in 1985.

57. Ibid.

58. Ibid. In the 1987 edition of Reznichenko *et al.*, *Taktika*, high-precision weapons are defined to include reconnaissance–strike and reconnaissance–fire complexes; automated systems for fire control; anti-tank rocket complexes; self-directed missiles for field artillery; guided rockets of various classes; anti-radiolocation rockets (presumably radar-seeking missiles); and guided aerial bombs and cluster bombs (p. 24).

59. Ibid., p. 209.

60. See A.M. Nekrich, *1941 22 Iyunya* (22 June 1941) (Moscow: 1965), translated in Vladimir Petrov, '*June 22, 1941': Soviet Historians and the German Invasion* (Columbia, SC: University of South Carolina Press, 1968), pp. 24–245. According to Lt. Gen. M.M. Kir'yan, large-scale deployment of the Soviet armed forces only began after the Second World War had actually broken out. In 1939 the Soviet ground forces had 98 divisions; by spring of 1941, 303 divisions, including 170 divisions and two brigades in the border military districts of the western Soviet Union. M.M. Kir'yan, 'Nachal'nyi period Velikoi Otechestvennoi Voiny', pp. 13–14. See additional references to this literature in note 14.

61. Gareev, *M.V. Frunze*, p. 218.

62. Ibid.

63. Ibid.

64. For example, see the Voroshilov lecture materials, Vol. I, section on strategic deployment of the armed forces.

65. Yevseev, 'O nekotorykh tendentsiyakh', p. 17. Professional Soviet views of the initial period of a nuclear strategic war continued to emphasize that such a war would be decisive and catastrophic throughout the Cold War. See Stephen M. Meyer, 'Soviet Nuclear Operations', Ch. 15 in Ashton B. Carter, John D. Steinbruner and Charles A. Zraket (eds), *Managing Nuclear Operations* (Washington, DC: Brookings Institution, 1987), pp. 470–534.

66. Gareev, *M.V. Frunze*, p. 214.

67. This was the hallmark in many ways of Gorbachev's politico-military redefinition of Soviet security requirements, for it opened the door to reduced levels of military preparedness and diminished threat perceptions of the US and NATO. For military reactions, see Dale R. Herspring, *The Soviet High Command, 1967–1989: Personalities and Politics* (Princeton, NJ: Princeton University Press, 1990), Chs 7 and 8.

68. Mikhail Gorbachev, *Perestroika; New Thinking for Our Country and the World* (New York: Harper and Row, 1987), p. 141.

69. Gorbachev, *Perestroika*, p. 141. Also cited in Herspring, *The Soviet High Command*, p. 231.

70. Akhromeev, 'Velikaia pobeda i uroki istorii' (The Great Victory and the Lessons of History), *Novyi mir*, No. 5 (1985), p. 19, cited in Herspring, *The Soviet High Command*, p. 231.

71. D.T. Yazov, *Na strazhe sotsializma i mira* (On Guard over Socialism and Peace) (Moscow: Voenizdat, 1987), p. 31, cited in Herspring, *The Soviet High Command*, p. 231.

72. Herspring, *The Soviet High Command*, Chs. 5–6 covers the impact and perspective of Ogarkov. I am also grateful to Mary FitzGerald for the opportunity to read several of her draft papers on this topic. Ogarkov's writings are noted extensively in FitzGerald, *Marshal Ogarkov on Modern War: 1977–1985* (Alexandria, VA: Hudson Institute, March 1986).

73. N.V. Ogarkov, *Vsegda v gotovnosti k zashchite Otechestva* (Moscow: Voenizdat, 1982), p. 31. See

also Ogarkov, *Istoriya uchit bditel'nosti* (History Teaches Vigilance) (Moscow: Voenizdat, 1985), p.41.

74. Ibid., pp.34–5.
75. G. Isserson, 'Razvitie teorii sovetskogo operativnogo iskusstva v 30-e gody' (The Development of the Theory of Soviet Operational Art in the 1930s), *Voenno-istoricheskii zhurnal*, No.1 (Jan. 1965), pp.36–46, in Harold S. Orenstein (ed.), *Selected Readings in the History of Soviet Operational Art* (Ft. Leavenworth, KS: Combined Arms Center, Soviet Army Studies Office, 1 May 1990), pp.29–46. See also M.N. Tukhachevskii, *Izbrannye proizvedeniya* (Selected Works), Vol.I (Moscow: Voenizdat, 1964); and other works of his pertinent to his view of future offensive and defensive warfare: 'Novye voprosy voyny' (New Problems in Warfare), *Voenno-istoricheskii zhurnal*, No.2 (1962), pp.73–7; *National and Class Strategy* (Rostov-on-Don, 1920), mimeo; and *Voprosy vysshego komandovaniya* (Problems of Higher Command) (Moscow: Gosvoenizdat, 1924).
76. For an overview of important trends in these years, see Walter Pintner, 'Russian Military Thought: The Western Model and the Shadow of Suvorov', Ch.13 in Peter Paret (ed.), *Makers of Modern Strategy: From Machiavelli to the Nuclear Age* (Princeton, NJ: Princeton University Press, 1986), pp.354–75. Especially important are the reforms carried out under Dmitrii Miliutin, Russian War Minister from 1861 to 1881. See Forrest A. Miller, *Dmitrii Miliutin and the Reform Era in Russia* (Nashville, TN: published 1968).
77. Russian economic backwardness relative to the great powers of Europe in the late nineteenth century has often been noted, and sometimes overstated. Equally problematical was the percentage of Russia's growing economy devoted to military expenditure. Thus, although the Russian state budget grew approximately 93 per cent from 1900 to 1913, Russia's per capita income in 1913 was only 27 per cent of the English per capita income. Relative to the British, about 50 per cent more of an average Russian's income was used by the state for current defense expenditure. See D.C.B. Lieven, *Russia and the Origins of the First World War* (New York: St. Martin's Press, 1983), pp.12–13.
78. *Osnovy voennoi doktriny Rossii (Proekt)* (Fundamentals of Russian Military Doctrine (Draft), *Voennaya mysl'*, Special Edition, May 1992, pp.3–9.
79. Draft Russian military doctrine, *Voennaya mysl'*, pp.3–4.
80. Ibid., p.4.
81. Ibid.
82. Ibid., p.7.
83. Ibid., p.8.
84. Ibid., pp.8–9.
85. Ibid., p.5.
86. Much depends on the character of the Russian armed forces and their relationship with the armed forces of other republics. Many developments are uncertain at this writing. For expert assessments, see Richard F. Staar, *The New Russian Armed Forces: Preparing for War or Peace?* (Stanford, CA: Hoover Institution, 1992), and Jacob Kipp, 'The Uncertain Future of the Soviet Military, From Coup to Commonwealth', *European Security*, No.2 (Summer, 1992), pp.207–38. The future of the Russian armed forces as well as the armed forces of other republics is bound up with the larger question of political federalism in the aftermath of Soviet disintegration. For perspectives pertinent to military issues, see Stephan Kux, *Soviet Federalism: A Comparative Perspective* (New York: Institute for East-West Security Studies, Occasional Paper Series, 1990).
87. Draft Russian military doctrine, p.5.
88. Ibid.
89. Ibid., pp.5–6.
90. For details, see Norman Friedman, *Desert Victory: The War for Kuwait* (Annapolis, MD: Naval Institute Press, 1991).

4

European Security after the Cold War

Entering into the post-Cold War world, policy-makers in Europe and in North America find that the uncertainties of freedom have replaced the certainty of stable pacification. Leaders now can choose, and, therefore, they can choose badly. Three issues make clear the importance of logical strategic choice in post-Cold War Europe: the potential re-establishment of a multi-polar power system in Europe; the dilemmas of denuclearization and greater dependency on conventional deterrence for crisis management and war avoidance; and, the potential development of truly defensive military doctrines and force postures from the Atlantic to the Urals.

In this chapter the implications of Europe's repolarization for its leading state and non-state actors in security matters are considered. A return to the multipolarity of the years immediately preceding the Second World War is improbable: Europe's security *problématique* has changed too much and possible responses are too different to expect that future security dilemmas will be clones of those which plagued Europe between the world wars. Second, the implications of projected US military strategy for European and global security are discussed, emphasizing its implications for the future of deterrence. Future US strategy will be more dependent upon conventional deterrence to cover the entire conflict spectrum. While this makes future *Desert Storms* potentially manageable and lesser conventional contingency operations feasible, the nuclear and low-intensity conflict ends of the spectrum may create off-line strategic perturbations. Third, two ideal-typical constructs are developed to discuss the relationship between Europe's per-ceived security dilemmas and the reliance by states upon offensive or defen-sive military postures for deterrence and defense. Application of these ideal types to historical experience and to future prospects for the European security community supports guarded optimism about the credibility of non-offensive defense in Europe, notwithstanding uncertainty about the future of Russia and its armed forces.

126

REPOLARIZATION

Repolarization of the European political and military landscape returns Europe to its pre-Second World War status as a multipolar power system. However, the multipolar system after the Cold War cannot duplicate exactly the system that preceded 1945 and which fell into ruins as a result of the Second World War. The new multipolarity will be different from the older one for several reasons.[1] First, nuclear weapons cannot be disinvented. Even if all the states of Europe somehow agreed to discard their existing nuclear arsenals, the knowledge of how to make nuclear weapons would remain available to scientists and technicians throughout the developed world.

Second, the multipolar system of the eighteenth and nineteenth centuries did not avoid war. It used war to preserve the essential variables of the system, primarily the rights of the major powers, in a status of greater or lesser dynamic equilibrium. This was a dynamic equilibrium subject to much erosion at the edges and uncertainty as to the growth and decline of relative power positions. In the twentieth century the United States was forced to intervene in Europe with its armed forces in order to rescue a faltering balance of power from aspiring hegemons. The future multipolar balance of power, unlike the ones of the past, cannot rely on war as a cheap means by which the strong restrain those who aspire to join the majors club. Nuclear and high-technology weapons make even small wars unacceptably costly for developed societies. And those blunderbuss weapons will be of limited value in deterring and coercing non-state actors who engage in small wars within and across state borders.

Repolarization of the European continent after the Cold War also differs from previously established multipolar power systems in another way. Before the Second World War, the essential action in the global balance of power was in Europe. Although US and Japanese military power threatened the primacy of European states in the world order as a whole, Europe between the world wars was still the most important potential tinderbox for armed conflict among major powers. Subsequent to the Cold War, Europe is no longer necessarily the focus of any successful balance of power system based on shifting alignments and multilateral security. A balance of power could still be maintained in Europe while terribly destabilizing developments overtook the status quo powers in Asia, the Middle East or elsewhere outside of Europe. Although stability in Europe may be a necessary condition for world peace after the Cold War, it is far from a sufficient condition.

Another difference between emerging multipolarity and traditional multipolarity in Europe is that estimates of future power will be based much more on the power of state-supported trade, finance capital, investments and other

127

non-military aspects of power compared to the nineteenth and early twentieth centuries.[2] Military power after the Cold War is less important because of the end of rivalry between the US and Russia. It is also less important now than formerly because the West has a large political stake in the establishment of free market capitalism and democratic political forms in the former Soviet Union. An atmosphere of threat will diminish, not enhance, the receptivity of Russia and other republics in the CIS for Western aid, technology and training.

Repolarization of Europe after the Cold War, and its apparent destination in some new kind of multipolarity, also differs from older multipolarity in the character of the relationship between state and non-state actors now, compared to then. Non-state actors had little or no significance between the world wars, especially in the area of peace and security. Following the Cold War, non-state actors such as the Conference on Security and Cooperation in Europe (CSCE), the European Community (EC), the Western European Union (WEU), and the North Atlantic Cooperation Council recently formed to include NATO and former Warsaw Pact states within a single consultative framework, will have to play a significant role in reducing the risk of war or crisis leading to war. Experience in this century and earlier has taught leaders that a broader definition of security community in Europe must be accompanied by trans-national institutions that establish their own political legitimacy for the performance of certain functions on behalf of states. While not usurping the fundamental powers of states, trans-national institutions such as the EC and WEU would build on the policy concurrency of states to formulate regimes favorable to the avoidance of war and crisis in Europe.

The concept of a regime is a useful way of gaining insight into some aspects of Cold War politics that seem illogical or inexplicable otherwise. A regime is a cluster of norms, expectations and assumptions about appropriate behavior by which states resolve their differences within a designated issue area.[3] Regimes exist in arms control, international finance, civil aviation, and in other issues that affect states within and beyond Europe. Although mostly informal, regimes may usefully be supported by formal agreements such as arms limitation treaties. The SALT and START agreements between the US and the Soviet Union, for example, concretized norms and expectations already established by the two powers through years of crisis management and arms race experience. These norms included the notion of avoiding any direct conflict between Soviet and American forces, of agreeing to national technical means of verification as unavoidable and useful, of avoiding unnecessary crisis measures which would provoke undesired escalation by the other side, and so forth.

One can get carried away with the idea of regime, to the point at which some may envision regimes as progenitors of regional security communities that supplant the governments of states.[4] This outcome is highly improbable, and might in the end prove to be very dangerous. If states perceive that regimes are being constructed around and under them, they are apt to withdraw their cooperation, with adverse consequences for peace and stability in Europe. Instead, the regime-building process should draw from states their common interests in redefining the terms of an interstate security community in Europe, recognize certain non-state actors as critical supports for that process. The building blocks of new concepts of European security community are the affinities of states for policies and programmes which reduce the risk of war, lower the costs of arms races in peacetime, and diminish the expectation that states are arming because as a matter of course they distrust one another's intentions.

With regard to the relationship between state and non-state actors in post-Cold War Europe, the roles of CSCE, EC and WEU will obviously be important in general, although the specifics remain to be defined. CSCE is the most inclusive group, allowing the non-aligned, NATO and former Warsaw Pact states to grapple with security problems under a single umbrella. CSCE's post-Helsinki agenda in 1992 will certainly include further proposals for confidence and security building measures (CSBMs) in Europe, seeking to improve on the precedents set in Stockholm in 1986. In particular, the objective of transparency of states' intentions, ascertained by observation of force postures, troop movements, military doctrines and other indicators, will remain uppermost on the CSCE agenda. Measures to promote increased transparency are one kind of *operational* arms control, which aims to reduce misperceptions of states about the allegedly aggressive intentions of one another. Operational arms control was less visible and impressive than *structural* arms control during the Cold War years, but the importance of operational arms control in Europe after 1990 should enhance the role of CSCE as a forum for scheduling and monitoring the appropriate negotiations.

The European Community remains poised to expand from twelve to fourteen nations even before considering the possible accession of the newly democratic states of East and Central Europe. The accession of those states to Community protocols about trade, banking and investment, and social regulation would ultimately dissolve the economic wall that remains between Eastern and Western Europe, even after the military and political wall created by extended Leninism has been destroyed. The European Community is thought by some to be the nucleus of a new Europe which will develop true supranational powers, including supranational powers in defense and foreign

129

policy-making. The Commission of the EC undoubtedly has an important European agenda-setting function, and much that it does touches directly on foreign and defense policy. Nevertheless, the EC is not presently constituted to assume the role of superstate. Were it to so aspire, it might set off centrifugal tendencies which would destroy the web of obligations and commitments that it has already established.

The European Community has important roles apart from aspiring to transcend the nation state, a misguided mission for it or any other European organization for at least the next few decades. Among its more important roles from a security standpoint after the Cold War, the European Community encloses a reunited and resurgent Germany within a European policy-making framework. This benign enclosure of German policy within a European framework sensitizes Germans to the concerns of other states in Europe about latent German tendencies toward military recidivism and economic imperialism. As early as 1990, for example, it was clear that Polish defense planners regarded Germany as their major concern, not Russia.[5] Germany's Community orientation in turn reassures the French that they need not align with Russia or absent America from the continent of Europe, as they did before the First World War and tried unsuccessfully to do between the wars.

The reference to a possible American military withdrawal from Europe is more fully dealt with in the next section, but its relationship to the political issue of a redefined security community is significant here. The paradox of US relations with Europe after the Cold War is that the more successful Europeans can be in creating a security community without US defense guarantees, the less necessary is the permanent stationing of US forces on the European continent. The rationale for US forces deployed under NATO auspices was that those forces were necessary as a tripwire which would ensure a potentially full commitment of US military power to prevent a Soviet conquest of Western Europe. Repolarization of European politics now makes plural the source of potential threats to peace and stability. Since the source of threat is uncertain, the requirement for a prompt US engagement is not obvious. Under some conditions, a continuation of US military presence in Europe could serve as a lightning rod which attracted domestic political hostility, as American force commitments have done in Latin America and in the Middle East. This hostility is especially likely to develop if US forces were used in conditions of communally-based civil war, as in Yugoslavia in 1991 and 1992.

The role of NATO in post-Cold War Europe remains unclear. Even before the demise of the Soviet Union and its transformation into the Commonwealth of Independent States (CIS), NATO had already taken decisions which transformed its military strategy and its political character. German reunification challenged the relevancy of forward defense and its siamese twin in NATO strategy, flexible response. US strategy under Bush meanwhile underwent fundamental rethinking, basing future planning on regional contingency operations and allowing for an estimated warning time of months to years for the reconstitution of forces needed to fight a major war in Europe or a global war. Although NATO's past contributions to regional security cannot be denied, its future relationship to any new European security community remains to be defined. NATO can serve as a bridge to another organization whose origins and rationale are less Cold War dependent, but expert analysts and political leaders in the West are not of one mind about the future role of NATO in building European self-sufficiency.

Important steps in groping toward a definition of NATO's new relationship with post-Cold War Europe took place in 1990 and 1991. First, the London Declaration issued following the meeting of NATO heads of state and government in July 1990 called for an action program in five areas: establishment of a new relationship with the states of Eastern and Central Europe; development of a new military strategy; strengthening of the Conference on Security and Cooperation in Europe (CSCE) as a forum for resolving interstate disputes by empowering it with permanent institutions; commitment to continue the arms control process beyond the conclusion of the CFE (Conventional Forces in Europe) agreement reached by NATO and the Warsaw Pact before the dissolution of the latter; and encouragement of a European defense identity in the form of a European pillar' within the Atlantic alliance. Implicit in the fourth of these objectives, continuation of arms control beyond CFE, was further progress on military transparency and force reductions in order to reduce the probability of surprise attack and large-scale offensives.[6] This objective of structural and operational arms control for the purpose of improving defenses relative to offenses has special pertinence to the third section of this chapter, 'Non-Offensive Defenses and Security Dilemmas', where its theoretical implications receive explicit consideration.

NATO's review of its military strategy resulted in the publication of the alliance's new Strategic Concept at its Rome summit in November, 1991. The special Strategy Review Group set up by NATO to develop the new concept had had to optimize between two very different requirements. They had to provide a document which gave adequate guidance to military planners for future development of armed forces. In addition, they had also to write guidance which could be made public as an explanation of NATO's new strategy to the world at large. Among the more important features of the new strategic concept were these: reliance on smaller, more flexible and mobile forces instead of static and linear defenses; development of multinational forces to assume roles formerly assigned to allied forces under single state command; increased emphasis on reconstitution, mobilization and reinforcement compared to immediate force readiness; less dependency on nuclear escalation, including the reduction of NATO's sub-strategic nuclear weapons deployed in Europe. In addition to these 'guidelines for defense', the new NATO strategic concept also called for a 'broad approach to security' placing increased emphasis on crisis management and conflict prevention.[7]

As a conceptual basis for future NATO military planning, the new strategic concept had to address the future relationship between Atlantic and European concepts of security. The development of a new European security identity, as perceived by NATO, would amount to a stronger European pillar within the Atlantic alliance. The assumption of a stronger European defense identity which remained within the NATO defense umbrella, as opposed to a European defense identity which transcended NATO, was a source of continuing controversy among NATO allies and within the broader European defense and foreign policy community. A stronger 'Europillar' within a basically Atlantic version of security community amounted, according to some, to continued European dependency on American leadership on security and defense issues. Although the immediate danger of threat to the survival of democratic Europe was gone, an Atlanticist security community might drive European defense policies toward American 'out of the area' priorities instead of European ones.

The meeting of the Council of the European Community in Maastricht in December 1991 called for a version of European defense identity which was not necessarily dependent on a viable NATO. One result of this EC summit was a proposed treaty on European Political Union; another was its call for the military expression of a European security identity to take place through a strengthened Western European Union.[8] Plans to move the WEU Secretariat to Brussels, probable overlap of state representatives to NATO and WEU, and WEU dependency for some time on NATO logistics and other assets for military operations left open the possibility of a benign and collaborative relationship between NATO and WEU. NATO's proposed Rapid Reaction Force might also be dual-hatted and act on behalf of the WEU.[9] On the other hand, implicit in the Maastricht declaration was, according to some ministers, the assumption of an EC-subordinated WEU which might foster the growth of European defense identity not so compatible with Atlanticism. The Communiqué of the NATO Defence Planning Committee in December 1991 attempted to have the best of both worlds, contending that NATO's new security concept envisioned that 'the WEU will be developed as the defence

132

component of the European Union and as a means to strengthen the European pillar of the Atlantic Alliance'.[10] The role of NATO forces inside and outside of the alliance was further complicated by the Franco-German decision of 22 May, 1992 to establish a joint army corps, and by their invitation to other member states of the European Community to join.[11]

CSCE has been advanced by some as the all-European security organization to include participants from Vancouver to Vladivostok. Although it has the advantage of maximum inclusiveness, CSCE for that very reason is unlikely to acquire sharp deterrent or defensive teeth. Its usefulness as a forum for the consensual development of regime norms and procedures for operational arms control would be in contradiction with a new role in regional policeman-ship or supranational deterrence. Others have suggested that the reborn Western European Union could, either under the aegis of the EC or as a European pillar within NATO, establish itself as the interstate organization of record for the monitoring of threats to peace and for the organization of timely and appropriate responses. However, it is not clear that the EC is willing to accept military responsibilities, and it is also unclear whether the WEU would be able to extend its reach into East and Central Europe for the purpose of peacekeeping and security. Certainly the WEU would be limited in its eastward reach if it were seen as a cat's paw for NATO. NATO Secretary General Manfred Worner issued a statement on 21 May, 1992 to the effect that NATO had taken a landmark decision to assume a wider European peacekeeping role, including support for peacekeeping efforts of CSCE. US defense officials, although they declined to rule out this possibility, responded quickly to Worner's statements about an expanded NATO peacekeeping role, cautioning that any such undertaking would have to be approved by NATO foreign ministers.[12]

Some have envisioned a security and peacekeeping role for CSCE by subdividing its efforts regionally and functionally, allowing for the specialization of smaller groups of states to offset the cumbersome problem of carrying on negotiations in a thirty-five state forum. Charles A. Kupchan and Clifford A. Kupchan have proposed a new European security organization based on the Concert of Europe of the early nineteenth century.[13] They propose a two-level design for a future CSCE as the institutional expression of a modern concert. A security group would include the US Britain, France, Germany and Russia as permanent members and other CSCE states as rotating members.[14] Other CSCE states would have input into security group deliberations, but the other states would focus their efforts on confidence and security building measures (CSBMs), human rights, promotion of democracy, and other issues of less apparent controversiality among CSCE members. Fred

Chernoff notes that Europe might be broken into subregions, permitting negotiations among only those states immediately concerned with a local issue (for example, Greece, Turkey, Bulgaria and Romania discussing manpower in the Eastern Mediterranean).[15]

As noted by Professor Chernoff and other experts, there are several important reasons for doubting that CSCE can assume the role of a comprehensive European security organization. First, the authority of the CSCE parliament will remain limited until all of its members become representative democracies. Second, the complexity of arms control and transparency negotiations among thirty-five states is much greater than it was when essentially two blocs were attempting to attain some rough measure of bloc to bloc parity. A two-sided process has essentially been replaced by a thirty-five-sided one. Third, the consensus decision rules of CSCE allow a single dissenting state to prevent agreements and progress: 'CSCE's history is replete with examples of a single state blocking progress where the other 34 solidly agreed'.[16] Fourth, some of the strongest military powers in CSCE perceive security interests outside of Europe to be as important, or more so, than vital interests within Europe in the aftermath of the Cold War. This substantively complicates the already procedurally complicated CSCE forum for reaching agreement on sensitive issues such as force sizes and operational transparencies.[17]

The problem of sub-regional military balances within a larger European security framework looms larger as a result of the completion of the CFE treaty, signed in November, 1990. Focussed as it was on ensuring equitable balances between the then-constituted eastern and western blocs, CFE could not prevent the survival of sub-regional force imbalances into the next decade. Ivo Daalder notes, for example, that Germany will retain an almost two to one advantage in ground force equipment over residual Polish, Czech or Hungarian forces.[18] In addition, the CFE sufficiency guideline allows the Commonwealth of Independent States to deploy two-thirds of the former Warsaw Pact states' holdings of Treaty Limited Equipment. This means in practice that the military balance in conventional land and tactical air forces between Russia and her newly democratic former allies will be one very favorable to Moscow. Nevertheless, it is a fair verdict that CFE accomplishes what can realistically be done in pursuit of the 'preventative' aspect of arms control (reducing the likelihood of war) for the Atlantic-to-the-Urals (ATTU) region as a whole. Sub-regional preventative arms control efforts will remain important, as indicated. On the other hand, the political function of arms control contributes to improved relations, and some theorists suggest that the very process of conducting arms control negotiations has a dampening effect on hostility. As Daalder notes, arms control enhances the opportunities for potential adversaries to communicate, and it offers one platform for upgrading common interests should they choose to do so.[19]

My view is that, for the obvious political reasons, NATO authorities have attempted to paper over the divergence in regional security concepts, between the older world of a US dominant Atlanticist security community and the emerging world of European self-reliance. A WEU dependent on a continuation of NATO in its present form, albeit with a new strategic concept, does not immediately threaten the relevancy of continued US troop deployments and security guarantees to Europe. However, a WEU as the military arm of the EC could also be strengthened apart from NATO by means of movement toward political union, and therefore to common defense policy, among EC states. It is therefore conceivable that Europeans might direct their defense affinities more toward the WEU essentially subordinate to the EC, with NATO's role adjusted to a political instead of a military presence. In this NATO-reduced and EC-enhanced framework, cooperation between the trans-Atlantic and European organizations would not be precluded. But NATO would no longer serve as the single institutional locus for war planning and force development, and it might not continue as the dominant voice in Europe on those issue areas.

SPLIT-LEVEL DETERRENCE AND US STRATEGY

The traditional distinction between deterrence and defense is that deterrence relies upon the credible threat of retaliatory punishment, whereas defense is based on the physical capability to deny to an aggressor territory, economic assets, or other values which are threatened.[20] The distinction between deterrence and defense is not necessarily the same as that between the use of nuclear and conventional weapons. But in practice, many academics and US policy planners during the Cold War assigned deterrent missions primarily to nuclear forces, and defense missions exclusively to conventional forces. NATO strategy, for example, was thought to rest on a capability for immediate conventional resistance to aggression, supported by the credible threat of nuclear escalation. Once it became clear that NATO would never approach its Lisbon conventional force goals set in 1952, the threat of nuclear retaliation became the mainstay of US and allied NATO military strategy for dealing with a possible Soviet incursion into Western Europe.

The assumption on which NATO strategy was based during the Cold War was that the primary source of threat to US as well as West European security was the Soviet Union. The immediate threat was posed by Soviet military power potential weighed against that of Western Europe. Without a guarantee of American support, Europe's vulnerability to Soviet aggression was fore-ordained. The model of deterrence in a single package assumed that any Soviet or allied Warsaw Pact incursion against a NATO country would be a signal that global war was on. Since the member states of the Pact were judged to be entirely subordinated to Soviet dictation, partial wars in Europe between minor powers were not taken seriously as planning possibilities. The super-powers and their alliances, according to the assumptions of US and allied NATO Cold War planners, effectively ruled out anomic wars not connected to the larger aims of the Kremlin.

However valid these assumptions might have been for the Cold War years, they are clearly insufficient to support a coherent US or NATO policy for the next decades. The focus of much strategic debate across the Atlantic on these points has so far been very institutional. NATO has reformulated its declaratory strategy to take into account the reduced likelihood of any Russian invasion of NATO territory. Future NATO force planning will emphasize three kinds of forces: rapid reaction; main battle forces; and reconstitution forces. This schematic is not coincidental. It is an attempt by NATO to lock into the shifting sands of a reformulated US military strategy, set in motion in 1990 and given additional impetus by the apparent irreversibility of the Soviet collapse. The 'new military strategy' as explained by Secretary of Defense Richard Cheney and Chairman of the Joint Chiefs of Staff General Colin Powell called for reduced forward deployments and more emphasis on crisis response capability. If and when necessary, forces needed for the conduct of a major coalition war in Europe or for a global war will be reconstituted. (Fiscal constraints made it unlikely that the election of any Democrat to the White House in 1992 would change the essence of force plans and structures proposed by Bush for fiscal year 1997, although the emphasis in declaratory policy about perceived threats would be open for debate and discussion. Threat assessment would be especially controversial if Senator Sam Nunn or Congressman Les Aspin, respective chairs of their Armed Services Com-mittees, assumed the office of Secretary of Defense under President-elect Clinton.)

Although most of the policy debate surrounded the size of the Bush proposed crisis response forces, equally significant would be decisions taken about the 'presence' forces to be permanently forward deployed in post-Cold War Europe by the US. Bush planners estimated that a minimum effective force remaining in Europe by the end of Fiscal Year 1993 would be some 150,000 US service personnel. This would provide an effective corps equiva-lent for three general roles: supporting diplomacy and crisis management in

Europe; providing complements for NATO's newly designed multinational force structure; and, third, crisis reaction and deployment for combat missions within or outside of European territory. US experience in the Gulf War of 1991 and the preceding redeployment of the VII Corps from Europe to Saudi Arabia had suggested that some time would be saved by rapid deployment of forces from Europe to the Middle East/Southwest Asia theater of operations, compared to deployment from the continental United States, *if* very favorable assumptions about logistics and infrastructure were realized.[21]

Reconstitution as conceived by Bush defense planners is not quite the same thing as mobilization. Reconstitution involves the rebuilding of defense industrial and other economic capabilities during a prolonged buildup to war. Under the Bush planning guidance as explained in public sources, the US 'Atlantic force' would include residual forces remaining in Europe after US deployments have been drawn down to approximately 100,000–125,000 troops.[22] The forces remaining in Europe after the implementation of Bush defense guidance by 1997 will probably amount to two army divisions and three tactical fighter wings. These capabilities will be supported by US maritime forces, including European-assigned and forward-deployed Marine units capable of forcible-entry operations. The forward presence and deployed Atlantic forces will be backed up by large reserve forces capable of being deployed rapidly. According to General Powell, Atlantic force reinforcement and sustaining forces could include: four active, six reserve and two cadre reserve army divisions; two active and 11 reserve air force tactical fighter wings; five navy carrier battle groups; two marine expeditionary brigades; and the US Marine Corps reserve component.[23] US mobility programs have as their objective the capability to move four army divisions, 30 air force tactical fighter squadrons, a marine expeditionary brigade and pertinent support to Europe within ten days.[24] US force packages of the future, according to this design, might appear as indicated in Table 4.1.

However, the Atlantic force will not be tasked only for crisis response and possible reinforcement in Europe. It will also have primary responsibility for responding to outbreaks of crisis in the Middle East and Southwest Asia. This reflects the changed emphasis in the Bush strategy, compared with that of previous administrations, from a focal scenario of Soviet global aggression beginning in Europe to a more open-ended scenario base. The experience of Desert Storm is relevant to the composition of the Atlantic force and to the design for the Contingency force, the second component of the 'base force' concept developed under the direction of Cheney and Powell. The Contingency force will be a force specialized for rapid crisis response outside of Europe, primarily in Latin America, Africa and other Third World areas where the scope of conflict is likely to be confined to the tactical level.

TABLE 4.1

US FORCE PACKAGES (1992 BUSH PLAN)

	Army	Navy	Marines	Air Force
ATLANTIC FORCES				
Europe	2 divisions	1 CVBG	MARG in Mediterranean MPS	3 wings
CONUS	4 active 6 reserve (+ 2 cadre) divisions	5 CVBG and support ships	2 MEBs (+ 1 RC)	2 active 11 reserve wings
PACIFIC FORCES				
Korea	1 division			1–2 wings
Japan		1 CVBG	1 MAGTF (to be specified)	1–2 wings
Hawaii/Alaska	1 division (light)		1 MEB	1 wing
CONUS		5 CVBG and support ships	1 MEB	
CONTINGENCY FORCES	4 divisions	Forces from Atlantic and Pacific 8 SL-7s and rest of RRF		7 wings inter-theater airlift

Special Operations Forces (SOF) of all services assigned to Contingency Forces.

STRATEGIC NUCLEAR FORCES

Ballistic Missile Submarines (SSBNs): About 18 Tridents.

Land-Based Strategic Missiles (ICBMs): About 500 Minuteman III, 50 MX (silo-based), other undetermined.

Bombers: Mix of B-52-H, B-1 and B-2 (ATB or Stealth) bombers.

Abbreviations:
CVBG = Carrier Battle Group
MAGTF = Marine Air-Ground Task Force
MARG = Mediterranean Amphibious Ready Group
MEB = Marine Expeditionary Brigade
MEF = Marine Expeditionary Force
MPS = Maritime Pre-positioning Ships
RC = Reserve Component
RRF = Ready Reserve Fleet

Source: Testimony of Admiral David E. Jeremiah, Vice Chairman of the Joint Chiefs of Staff, House Armed Services Committee, 12 March 1991, as noted in Gordon Adams and Lawrence J. Korb, co-chairmen, *Responding to Changing Threats: A Report of the Defense Budget Project's Task Force on the FY 1992–FY 1997 Defense Plan* (Washington, DC: Defense Budget Project, June 1991), p.15. The Project Senior Analyst was Natalie J. Goldring.

138

Included in the Contingency force will be army light and airborne divisions; marine expeditionary brigades; special operations forces; and, selected air force components.[25] Carrier and amphibious forces would be used to support the operations of the Contingency force as required by circumstances.

There is some potential tension within both the political and the military aspects of the Bush security strategy. The political tension is marked by the ambivalence between the desire to maintain forces which support the predominant power position of the US relative to that of any other state, on the one hand, and the obvious US interest in obtaining multilateral political support in any regional crisis. The tension between unipolarity and collective security is conceptual, but may be skated over in practice by artful diplomacy. Thus, for example, the US was able to mobilize against Iraq a diverse coalition that included major Arab powers, normally unwilling to attach themselves to US foreign-policy objectives in the Middle East or Southwest Asia. US military power served as the actual bludgeon to expel Iraq from Kuwait in 1991, but multilateral sanction for the operation was provided by a United Nations resolution and by the size and heterogeneity of the anti-Iraqi coalition. These fortuitous political circumstances which paved the way for the use of overwhelming force against Iraq, and which allowed US leaders to minimize the risk of horizontal escalation, may never be repeated.

The military tension in the new strategy rests on the greater burden placed on conventional deterrence without nuclear escalation. This strategic design is taking hold although the Bush administration programmed an approximately 25 per cent reduction in US active duty and reserve force size between fiscal years 1992 and 1997. US active and reserve forces programmed for 1997 under the Bush 1991 plan are estimated as shown in Table 4.2.

The Bush administration 1991 plan also called for reductions in defense budget outlays of about 20 per cent by 1997. From estimated outlays of $322 billion in 1991, expenditures were projected to drop to $288 billion in 1997. This represents an approximate three per cent average annual reduction in projected defense outlays, according to the projections built into the 1991 Bush plan.[26] The 1991 Bush projections were dead on arrival in Congress. Sentiment for cutting even further into the defense budget was strong on Capitol Hill as a result of the Soviet collapse and the condition of the US economy. The Congressional Budget Office outlines an alternative scenario which is consistent with some proposals made in Congress for greater reductions than those proposed in the 1991 Bush plan. This alternative path assumes that reductions in defense outlays are approximately double the rate projected by the Bush administration, or about six per cent per year in real (inflation-adjusted) dollars.[27] According to this second and more pessimistic projection from the DOD standpoint, defense outlays in 1997 would be about $258 billion instead of the $288 billion projected by Bush, or a reduction of 29 per cent from the 1991 baseline figure compared to the Bush-projected reduction of 20 per cent (in 1992 dollars). The relevant figures by year are as shown in Table 4.3.

TABLE 4.2

US MILITARY FORCE REDUCTIONS, 1990–1997 (1991 BUSH PLAN)

	1990	1997	Percentage reduced
Active Forces			
Ground forces			
Army divisions	18	12	33
Marine brigades	9	7	22
Naval forces			
Aircraft carriers	13	12	8
Carrier air wings	13	11	15
Ships	545	448	18
Air forces			
Tactical fighter wings	24	15.5	35
Strategic forces			
ICBMs	1,000	550	45
SLBMs	608	432	29
Bombers	228	181	21
Reserve Forces			
National guard divisions	10	6	40
Marine brigades	3	3	0
Carrier air wings	2	2	0
Tactical fighter wings	12	11	8

Source: Statement of Gen. Colin Powell, Subcommittee on Defense, House Committee on Appropriations, 25 Sept. 1991, as revised by Congress of the United States, Congressional Budget Office, *The Economic Effects of Reduced Defense Spending* (Washington, DC: Congressional Budget Office, Feb. 1992), p. 4.

The importance of these lower-than-Bush-projected reductions is that they will take place within a strategic context that places even more reliance upon conventional forces for *deterrence* than did US Cold War military planning. Since Cold War scenarios were focussed on war in Europe involving eventual, if not immediate, clashes between US and Soviet forces, the makeweight of deterrence was thought to rest on nuclear forces, especially on US strategic nuclear weapons. With the replacement of US–Soviet rivalry by cooperation between Russia and the United States, the most plausible scenarios involving the potential commitment of US military power are those in which nuclear weapons would be irrelevant. The 'good news' from Desert Storm was that high-technology conventional forces could accomplish large operational or theater objectives for which the US and its allies might have relied on nuclear weapons during any earlier war in Europe. The 'bad news' for proponents of nuclear deterrence was that nuclear weapons, in the aftermath of the Gulf War of 1991, seemed irrelevant to the continuation of deterrence of regional contingencies.

TABLE 4.3

DEFENSE OUTLAY REDUCTION PROJECTIONS:
BUSH PLAN AND CBO ALTERNATE

	1991	*1992*	*1993*	*1994*	*1995*	*1996*	*1997*
Bush 1991 plan							
Authority	328	291	291	292	295	298	303
Outlays	322	313	296	292	289	289	288
Percentage change							
outlay	8	2	−5	−9	−13	−17	−20
CBO option							
Authority	328	281	275	270	266	261	256
Outlays	322	302	281	273	267	262	258
Percentage change							
outlay	8	−1	−10	−15	−20	−24	−29

Note: Authority data are given for comparison purposes. Budget authority includes commitments carrying over from previous years. Outlays are expenses vouchered within a given fiscal year. Percentage changes are computed with reference to a CBO calculated baseline case of no change in real defense budget authority.

Source: Congressional Budget Office, *The Economic Effects of Reduced Defense Spending* (Washington, DC: Congressional Budget Office, Feb. 1992), p.10.

Brookings Institution senior fellow and defense analyst Lawrence J. Korb contended that the conventional force reductions proposed by Bush and Cheney did not go far enough. Korb objected to the Bush plan on the grounds that it was too driven by domestic factors, including the need to maintain a healthy defense economic sector, and not sufficiently responsive to a coherent threat assessment.[28] Korb and House Armed Services Committee chair Les Aspin (D.-Wis.) argued for a budget based on specific threat assessments. As an alternative to the Bush base force projections for FY 1997, Korb proposed his Base Force II concept. Korb's Base Force II would reduce total military service personnel to two million instead of Bush's 'Base Force' of 2.6 million by fiscal year 1997. According to Korb, the Base Force II, while saving $100 billion over five years, would still permit the US to field forces capable 'in

141

principle' of handling 'two Desert Storms simultaneously'.[29] Comparison of Base Force II, Bush's Base Force and Desert Storm Deployments appears in Table 4.4.

TABLE 4.4

BUSH BASE FORCE, KORB BASE FORCE II AND
DESERT STORM DEPLOYMENTS

	Bush Base Force	*Korb Base II*	*Desert Storm*
Ground divisions	22 (46)	17 (59)	10 (31)
Tactical air wings	26 (39)	20 (50)	10 (28)
Aircraft carriers	12 (50)	9 (67)	6 (43)
Carrier air wings	13 (46)	10 (60)	6 (40)
Ships	450 (22)	350 (29)	100 (20)
Personnel	2.6 million (21)	2.0 million (28)	550,000 (18)

Note: Numbers in parentheses give the size of forces deployed to the Persian Gulf during the Gulf War of 1991 as percentages of the total current or proposed force. For example, the ground divisions deployed for Desert Storm constituted about 31 per cent of the 1991 total active and reserve forces available. The same divisions would constitute 46 per cent of the Bush Base Force and 59 per cent of Korb's Base Force II.

Source: Lawrence J. Korb, 'Real Defense Cuts – and the Real Defense Issues', *Arms Control Today*, May 1992, p. 7.

Nuclear weapons would remain relevant to the relationship between the US and Russia so long as both sides retained large forces, even greatly reduced post-START forces in the neighborhood of 3,000 warheads or so. And US nuclear weapons would remain pertinent to the deterrence of any Russian remobilization against the former Warsaw Pact states. However, the most credible role for nuclear weapons was always the deterrence of a deliberate attack on the US homeland or of a nuclear attack against a NATO ally. Neither seems probable unless politics in Russia change drastically within the next few years.[30] Even anarchy within the Commonwealth of Independent States and a possible problem with 'loose nukes' among non-Russian republics does not provide any plausible US 'enemy' with the ambition, let alone the purpose, of attacking American or allied NATO soil with nuclear charges. Therefore, although US strategic nuclear weapons remain relevant to Type I or basic deterrence against homeland attack, their continuing relevance for deterrence of Type II attacks, against the territory of allies, becomes more and more negligible as the Cold War recedes.

NATO's London Declaration of July 1990 straddled the fence between nuclear continuity and discontinuity in declaratory policy.[31] Alliance leaders did not want to give up the role of nuclear weapons in raising uncertainty for any prospective attacker. On the other hand, they acknowledged that changed political conditions in Europe now allowed for the use of nuclear weapons as 'weapons of last resort'.[32] The later use of nuclear weapons, compared to the early first use not ruled out by NATO's formerly authoritative 'flexible response' guidance dating from 1967, coincided with adjustments in NATO's overall defence concept also noted in the London Declaration and in subsequent NATO policy decisions. NATO's conventional deterrent strategy of the future will rest less on the principle of 'forward defense' at some dividing line between East and West, and more on a revised concept of flexible operations based on longer warning times prior to attack and extensive mobilization for any large and protracted conflict.[33] The relationship between tactical nuclear weapons in Europe and forward defense was further attenuated by President Bush's initiative of September 1991 announcing the removal of US short-range land and sea-based nuclear weapons from the American inventory.

However, the rub with conventional high-technology forces for deterrence is that they are very expensive per unit compared with nuclear forces or low-technology conventional forces. Challenges to regional security can be mounted by potential hegemons in Southwest Asia or in other regions by means of low-technology conventional forces or by indirect aggression against regimes friendly to the United States through terrorism and insurgency. In other terms, the costs per unit of manpower and equipment for challenges to deterrence will be low, and the costs per unit of responses to those challenges will be high. A foretaste of the kinds of constraints which future US planners may face was provided by the fiscal environment of Desert Storm, which required Secretary of State James Baker to collect contributions from allies to cover the incremental costs of US and coalition military action against Iraq.

Classified scenarios developed by the Pentagon as a basis for future defense planning were leaked to the press in early 1992 and criticized in Congress and by defense analysts. Particular controversy surrounded a February 1992 draft of US Defense Planning Guidance for 1994 through 1999 which called for explicit American efforts to prevent the emergence of any other regional or global power capable of matching US military potential. According to news accounts based on leaks of the draft document, the Defense Guidance stated that preventing the emergence of a rival superpower is 'a dominant consideration underlying the new regional defense strategy' and that the US should 'endeavor to prevent any hostile power from dominating a region whose resources would, under consolidated control, be sufficient to generate global power'.[34] The references to Germany and Japan were as obvious as they were sensitive. In addition, the draft Guidance envisioned among possible scenarios for the employment of US military power a Russian invasion of Lithuania through Poland. The scenario called for a US-led counterattack by 24 NATO divisions, 70 fighter squadrons and six aircraft carrier battle groups.

By May, a revised and less controversial version of the Defense Guidance for fiscal years 1994–99 had been signed by Defense Secretary Cheney. References to maintaining the US's unique superpower status against potential challengers were expunged from the revised version.[35] Also removed from the revised guidance were references to Germany, Japan and India as potential regional hegemons whose ambitions posed potential challenges to stability. The revised guidance deleted the original discussion of extending US security guarantees against Russian aggression into Eastern Europe. Instead, the document now made reference to the objective of expanding a stable and democratic 'zone of peace' in Eastern and Central Europe.[36] References to the possibility that 'US strategic assets may be employed', if US combat forces fighting in a conventional war were unable to win a rapid victory, also disappeared in the revised version of the Guidance. The original draft had been criticized on the grounds that this passage suggested a willingness to engage in nuclear first use or blackmail against non-nuclear powers, contrary to US declaratory policy.

Of course, Poles might be delighted with the language in the Defense Guidance, preferring to see it as an invitation for future US containment of Germany. And reunited and demilitarized Koreans might welcome an assertive US unipolarity against the possibility of Japanese military assertiveness in South Asia. Israelis would undoubtedly prefer to put Iraqis and Syrians on notice that the US would be willing to repeat Desert Storm (able is another question) even after the Bush-projected reductions or even greater reductions in US forces and supporting budgets.

International relations theorists in academia and many persons in the US arms control community, on the other hand, will not welcome the implication of unipolarism or hegemony which critics drew from the leaked defense guidance. Theorists have felled forests arguing about the transition from a bipolar to a multipolar system: a truly unipolar system makes the debate irrelevant.[37] Arms control advocates fear that an assertion of US unipolarity sends the wrong message about American willingness to act within the constraints of multilateral diplomacy. NATO allies of the United States will cautiously weigh the implications of any hint that American power is seen by

144

US leaders as sufficient to accomplish their objectives without reliance on coalition partners for more than window dressing.

Bush administration defense planning also called for the ability to deter, not just to defeat, insurgencies and revolutions which threatened to destabilize friendly governments and thereby place American interests in jeopardy. Presumably this meant keeping hostile forces from control over the Panama Canal, over Middle East oil fields, and over vital waterways and choke points through which the US Navy must pass. It also implied the deterrence of reborn Soviet or Russian use of fifth columns to destabilize East European democracies. The case for deterrence of revolutionary warfare and insurgency against governments friendly to the US becomes weaker, however, as the Cold War recedes from institutional and public memory. Without the linkage to Soviet global objectives, the rising of even avowedly Marxist revolutionary regimes, as well as others less devoted to ideologies which provoke American Presidents, represent no obvious threat to US security. Repugnant regimes in Haiti, the Philippines or in formerly Soviet Georgia may cause disgust among those favoring the spread of global democratic institutions, but it is doubtful that any US military intervention would be useful in order to obtain a preferred political outcome in these cases.

US conventional military power even at the height of Cold War defense spending had limited reach into improvement of the internal politics of allies outside of Europe. If the vulnerability of Third World regimes to coups or other non-democratic seizures of power is no longer an obvious US strategic interest, neither is the US capability for manipulating these situations likely to be enhanced by future defense budgets and planning guidance. Success in counterinsurgency requires that the political aspect of US efforts be as carefully developed as the military component. Security assistance alone cannot substitute for competent indigenous governments with broad popular support. The record of US covert action during the Cold War years was one in which accomplishments fell well below the level of expectations. In addition, various US covert actions were undertaken by components of the executive branch under quasi-legal or illegal authorizations. When the uncertain character of these dubious justifications and borderline authorizations came to light, the effectiveness of US intelligence was compromised in the minds of Congress and other players in the domestic policy-making process.[38]

The US military especially dislikes being thrust into ambiguous situations of civil conflict in foreign countries, which appear to professional officers as a no-win situation. And the growing high-technology character of the US and other Western armed forces makes them even less suitable for protracted counterinsurgent roles in other states. The diminished role of the CIA in covert action after the Cold War, relative to its robust involvement over four preceding decades, opens a window through which some military planners might wish to crawl. But this window is not a window of opportunity insofar as the dominant professional orientations and skill concepts of the US armed forces are concerned.[39] Rapidly concluded and decisive interventions, such as operation *Urgent Fury* in Grenada, will, if the Department of Defense has its way, be done with overwhelming force, primarily of the conventional, not unconventional, variety. Thus the deterrence of hostile revolutions outside of Europe and the important Gulf states rests on the same forces and mind-sets which are mostly designed for the conduct of theater air–land battle against heavily-armed and state-controlled forces. Conventional forces after the Cold War will, by all indications, be stretched in mission to cover contingencies formerly thought subject to deterrence only by the threat of nuclear escalation. Conventional forces will also be expected to provide whatever deterrence is available against various forces seeking to remove friendly regimes by internal as opposed to external aggression. This split-level deterrent requirement for future US conventional deterrence is as unavoidable as it is pregnant with potential credibility gaps.

NON-OFFENSIVE DEFENSES AND SECURITY DILEMMAS

Security Dilemmas and Ideal–Typical Strategies

European strategic thinkers and others dissatisfied with the military postures of the Cold War years studied various alternatives for individual or coalition defenses based on territorial self-defense or on other concepts excluding surprise attack and large-scale conventional offensives.[40] The 'solutions' to regional stability offered by superpower extended deterrence and offensively poised conventional forces did not commend themselves especially to the non-aligned states of northern Europe. Even NATO member states produced leading advocates of non-offensive defenses, and some US and European analysts were willing to endorse non-military, in addition to non-offensive, defenses as the basis of regional security. The development of interest in non-offensive defenses was interesting not only as an alternative to the superpower-oriented bloc politics of the Cold War. Non-offensive defense also offered an alternative to those states which sought to transcend Cold War military postures, but which distrusted supranational solutions in the form of politically powerful multilateral institutions. States such as Sweden and

Switzerland offered different forms of non-offensive defense while reserving to themselves the right to decide when and where their forces would be committed to battle.

Regardless of the pros and cons of non-offensive defense as seen from the Cold War perspective, the future European environment should be more conducive to the implementation of non-threatening defensive alignments and reduced security dilemmas.[41] The security dilemma is a construct that refers to the propensity for one state's search for greater security to cause another state to feel more insecure, on account of being threatened by the first state.[42] States' intentions in force building or in mobilizations may be benign and not, in their own minds, designed to destabilize the existing equilibrium in a particular region or in the system as a whole. However, the stability of any particular balance of power among states is determined by their perceptions of one another's intentions as much as by the 'reality' of state intentions that an objective observer might describe. The security dilemma suggests that there is a significant difference, for the inferences that leaders will draw about the probable intentions of potential adversaries, between those force deployments and modernizations that appear preparatory to attack, compared with those that appear to have been motivated by defensive, that is, self-protective goals.

As Charles A. Glaser has noted, states not only need to know the intentions of potential adversaries, but also the motivations underlying those intentions.[43] Two essential independent motivations are greed and insecurity. Aggressors motivated by greed or ambition might need to be deterred more than reassured: those motivated by insecurity might need more reassurance than deterrence. Classifying states' motivations and sense of security along two dimensions, Glaser develops a typology of potential adversaries based on their potential motives for aggression. This typology is constructed as depicted in Table 4.5.

Glaser's typology builds on the insights of Robert Jervis and others who have studied the relationship between states' perceptions of their adversaries' intentions or capabilities and the likelihood of avoiding war.[44] Jervis notes that decision-makers act in terms of vulnerability that they perceive, and this perceived vulnerability can differ from actual conditions.[45] These subjective security requirements of states exist along at least two different dimensions. First, states differ with regard to how much security they think that they require. Some states value security above all else, and others may value it very little compared with other values. This insight on the part of Jervis is uncommon and counter-intuitive. It is generally supposed by international relations theorists that security is the primary motivation of state actors, pre-empting other objectives. However, the primacy of state security concerns over other policy objectives is highly context dependent.

147

TABLE 4.5

TYPES OF ADVERSARIES
(BY MOTIVATION AND DEGREE OF PERCEIVED SECURITY)

	GREEDY	NOT GREEDY
SECURE	Deterrence model	Satisfied with status quo
INSECURE	Extremely unstable	Spiral Model

Source: Adapted from Charles P. Glaser, 'Political Consequences of Military Strategy', *World Politics*, No. 4 (July 1992), p. 503. I have changed some of the terminology in order to suit my own research objectives, I trust without distorting the author's originally intended meanings. For example, Glaser's descriptor for the top-right cell is 'ideal state', which may be appropriate for the conceptualizations he seeks to develop, but it would be quite misleading here. The contrast between deterrence and spiral models is drawn from Robert Jervis, 'Cooperation under the Security Dilemma', *World Politics*, No. 2 (Jan 1978), pp. 167–214.

Therefore, Jervis notes that the second aspect of subjective security is the degree of perceived threat felt by one state with regard to other states which might have the capability or the intention to attack it.[46] As he argues, 'a state that is predisposed to see either a specific other state as an adversary, or others in general as a menace, will react more strongly and more quickly than a state that sees its environment as benign'.[47] One aspect of this problem of threat perception is the degree to which the military technologies and military doctrines of prospective adversaries contribute to mistaken threat perceptions of intent to attack. States operate in an imperfect world in which the line between offensive and defensive force deployments or military doctrines is not always clear to others. Equally important and vexatious for policy-makers is the requirement to estimate whether the offense or the defense has the advantage if deterrence fails.[48] Jervis develops a taxonomy of four worlds and estimates their relative degrees of stability based on the two dimensions: whether an offensive posture can be clearly distinguished from a defensive one, and whether offense or defense has the advantage. The resulting matrix is depicted in Table 4.6.

The most dangerous among these alternative worlds is obviously the upper left condition: offensive and defensive military postures are relatively indistinguishable, and offense has the advantage. Two-sided nuclear forces with only MIRVed ICBMs deployed in silos provide one hypothetical illustration of such a world. An example of this unstable condition with conventional forces would be a situation in which two sides confronted one another with offensive and defensive deployments not clearly distinguishable, and each side preferred a strategy of annihilation to one of attrition as the key to victory. Annihilation and attrition are ideal types of offensive and defensive strategies,

148

respectively. The polarity between these two types of strategies helps to bring out some of the pertinent features of past and future military postures among great powers and their potential for stability or instability in Europe (as discussed in an earlier chapter).

An ideal condition for stability in Europe after the Cold War, according to the preceding schematic, occurs when conditions approximate those in the

TABLE 4.6

ALTERNATIVE WORLDS FOR STABILITY
(BASED ON EXPECTATIONS ABOUT OFFENSE AND DEFENSE)

	OFFENSE HAS THE ADVANTAGE	DEFENSE HAS THE ADVANTAGE
OFFENSIVE POSTURE INDISTINGUISHABLE FROM DEFENSIVE	Most dangerous combination, very unstable	Security dilemma exists, but states' security needs may be compatible
OFFENSIVE POSTURE DISTINGUISHABLE FROM DEFENSIVE	No security dilemma, but aggression is possible. Status quo states and aggressors can follow different policies	Very stable

Source: Robert Jervis, 'Cooperation under the Security Dilemma', in Art and Jervis (eds), *International Politics*, p. 203. Some text deleted.

lower right quadrant: offensive military postures can be distinguished clearly from defensive ones; and, defense has the advantage over offense in terms of available military technology and strategy. It would be a mistake for policy-makers or theorists to assume that the Europe of the future will reach this benign condition any time soon. However, it is an attainable goal for policy-makers to guarantee against a drift of events leftward and upward on Table 4.6, toward its most dangerous combination of indistinguishable offensive and defensive postures together with an assumed advantage for the offensive form of war. In other words, Europe after the Cold War need not create the instability of the July crisis of 1914, or that inherent in the multipolar power system of 1937–39.

The breakdown of peace in 1914 and in 1939 has led many scholars to conclude that multipolar systems of more than two major powers are neces-sarily more stable than bipolar systems, based on the stability of the Cold War. This prejudgment is mistaken. Multipolar systems are not all of one kind. The Napoleonic wars were not fought within the same kind of multipolar system that witnessed the outbreak of the First World War. And the system which was in place before Hitler's attack on Poland in 1939 was different from both the international systems of the Napoleonic and Wilhelmine eras. Obsession with the relationship between system structure and peace can obscure equally important relationships between system *texture* and the likelihood of war.

System texture includes the policy aspirations and diplomatic finesse of states as well as their military power and potential. States go to war for causes, at least putative ones, and they make war within a context defined by diplomats. Diplomats on behalf of heads of state help to determine, the duration, intensity and frequency of wars. Wars ill-prepared diplomatically are likely to fail regardless of the combat proficiency of armed forces, as Germany's experiences in two world wars of this century attest. Better diplomacy might have avoided either world war and yet obtained for Germany a greater respect for its power. And better diplomacy might have extricated Germany from overcommitment against so many foes that its enemies' sheer resources were able to outlast its strategic cleverness and military campaign proficiency. As another example, the diplomacy of Metternich in support of the Concert of Europe, even after it had been weakened by dealignment into two more or less opposed blocs, added a stabilizing factor to a system riven by civil war and interstate conflict about the basic ordering principles of political rule.[49] By incorporating the revolutionary nationalisms of Germans into the imperial system of that state, Prussian and German Chancellor Otto von Bismarck shifted the entire balance of power in Central Europe and immediately created for France and Russia a serious security dilemma.[50]

The most significant outcome of the end of the Cold War and the deconstruction of the former Soviet Union is that the center of gravity in European politics shifts eastward. Reunited Germany is now the policy pivot in East Central Europe, and on Germany's web of aspirations and commitments much of Europe's future depends. If Germany chooses autarchy and nationalism, then others have two basic policy options: they can 'bandwagon' with a rising German strength, or they can 'balance' against that strength unilaterally and by making coalitions in order to aggregate their individual capabilities into collective strength.[51] German pre-eminence in Central Europe could be balanced in a variety of ways, but several generic strategies suggest themselves. First, Germany could be incorporated into a larger political union of the kind envisioned in the Maastricht agreement among the members of the European Community in December 1991. Second, British, French and Italian power could operate as a coalition of 'majors' drawn from former NATO Europe to restrain Germany from hegemonic ambitions. Third, the US through NATO could reinsure united Germany against threats emanating from elsewhere in Europe. The third option assumes that NATO continues to provide a meaningful forum for European security discussions.

Fourth, Germany could essentially go its own way, making deals with a newly constituted Czechoslovakia, Poland and Russia.[52]

European security institutions such as WEU and CSCE have thus far had little success in putting out the fires of war in former Yugoslavia. The multilateral intervention that has occurred has taken place under United Nations auspices. Eastern European trilateralism in the form of a security pact linking Poland, Czechoslovakia and Hungary was proposed but abandoned in the aftermath of Soviet disintegration.[53] A case can be made for the continuing existence of NATO in some form, allowing for multinational military formations which would include German forces as are now being implemented. NATO's long-range future is undetermined, however; it offers merely an available and non-controversial option. Franco-German reinsurance of one another is an acceptable option for containment of German political or military aspirations westward, but it does not answer the problem of Germany's potential for expanding to the east. In fact, Franco-German cooperation may help to loosen restraints against German assertiveness in the directions of Poland and Czechoslovakia.

With regard to multinational European security institutions of the future, WEU seems the most probable candidate for the role of military arm of the new European Union. WEU will build on NATO infrastructure and experience in supporting peacetime military preparedness, but its role perception will have to be very different from that of NATO during the Cold War. WEU will be even less supranational than NATO was, which was not very much. And WEU will lack the military impressiveness of a bloc of 16 states headed by an American theater commander-in-chief (CINC). Therefore, WEU will have to be supplemented by other fora for the purposes of conflict mediation and confidence-building measures, including monitoring of military exercises and inspections to detect offensively intended force buildups. CSCE, now with more than 50 members, looms as the most inclusive forum for confidence building, but its size and heterogeneity preclude a very assertive role in strictly military measures.

Much of the future of European stability depends on how the former Soviet Union, especially the Ukraine and Russia, evolves. If Russia and the Ukraine can be stabilized politically and economically, then Eastern Europe should not boil over into regional anarchy, and the reach of West European security institutions can be extended to the Urals. If, however, Russian federation dissolves in to civil war or if Ukrainian nationalism leads to friction with Russia or Romania (over Moldova, for example), the stability of East Central Europe is put at risk and a go-it-alone philosophy among the region's formerly cooperative states becomes more likely. The psychological reach of US and

Russian nuclear deterrence into the center of Europe is now attenuated by the reunification of Germany and the demise of the Soviet Union. The situation is one that for all practical purposes is beyond military deterrence: there is no attack for which a nuclear threat is a plausible response. Nuclear weapons have been stranded on both sides of the Atlantic insofar as their future potential for contributing to European stability is concerned.[54]

CONCLUSION

Repolarization of European politics, split-level demands imposed on conventional forces for deterrence across the spectrum of conflict, and fundamental rethinking of US and European military strategies make the transition from the Cold War to the future a precarious but manageable one. Non-state actors and state actors whose military postures and plans are strategically defensive can push the system in the direction of greater stability through reduced fears of surprise attack and large-scale offensives. On the other hand, high-technology conventional forces in a partly or totally denuclearized world can be used to support offensive strategies of annihilation, as well as defensive or attrition strategies. In addition, the security dilemma almost guarantees that one state's defensive buildup will be perceived by another as potentially offensive. The versatility of modern weapons technology makes the clear distinction between benign and malign weapons all the more difficult, and it was never easy.[55]

NOTES

This chapter draws upon 'Security in Europe after the Cold War, Part I', *European Security*, Vol. 2, No. 2 (Summer, 1993), pp. 163–89.

1. On the relationship between polarity and war, see Bruce Bueno de Mesquita, 'Systemic Polarization and the Occurrence and Duration of War', *Journal of Conflict Resolution*, No. 2 (June 1978), pp. 241–67; Michael Brecher, Patrick James and Jonathan Wilkenfeld, 'Polarity and Stability: New Concepts, Indicators and Evidence', *International Interactions*, No. 1 (1990), pp. 49–80; Jack S. Levy, 'The Polarity of the System and International Stability: An Empirical Analysis', in Alan Ned Sabrosky (ed.), *Polarity and War* (Boulder, CO: Westview Press, 1985), pp. 41–66. Much of the literature on polarity and stability disputes whether bipolar or multipolar systems are more stable: deductive arguments can be made for either system as relatively more stable, and the results of empirical studies depend on operational definitions for variables such as stability. Levy, for example, disaggregates stability into seven different attributes. Brecher, James and Wilkenfeld argue that eruption of war is too narrow a criterion for determination of instability: they propose to include crisis as well as war as a valid indicator of instability. For a discussion of the problem of measuring polarity, see Frank Whelon Wayman and T. Clifton Morgan, 'Measuring Polarity in the International System', in J. David Singer and Paul F. Diehl (eds), *Measuring the Correlates of War* (Ann Arbor, MN: University of Michigan Press, 1990), pp. 139–56. The case for the greater stability of multipolar compared to bipolar systems is argued in Kenneth N. Waltz, *Theory of International*

Politics (Reading, MA: Addison-Wesley, 1979), pp. 161–93. For counterarguments in favor of multipolarity as more stable, see Karl W. Deutsch and J. David Singer, 'Multipolar Power Systems and International Stability', *World Politics*, Vol. 16 (1964), pp. 390–406. Bueno de Mesquita, 'Systemic Polarization and the Occurrence and Duration of War', contends that theories connecting the static aspects of polarity to the probability or duration of war are generally false, although he found strong relationships between directional change in system tightness (intra-bloc solidarity) and the occurrence and duration of war, especially twentieth-century war.

2. For a lucid account of the modern relationship between international politics and economics which keeps its focus on the political, see Susan Strange, *States and Markets* (New York: Basil Blackwell, 1988).

3. According to Robert O. Keohane, the concept of regime is defined in terms of four main components: principles, norms, rules and decision-making procedures. See Keohane, *After Hegemony: Cooperation and Discard in the World Political Economy* (Princeton, NJ: Princeton University Press, 1984), p. 59.

4. For a critique of regime concepts, see Susan Strange, '*Cave! hic dragones*: a critique of regime analysis', in Stephen D. Krasner (ed.), *International Regimes* (Ithaca, NY: Cornell University Press, 1983), pp. 337–54.

5. Army War College Delegation, Visit to Eastern Europe, Special Report, *Changing Security Perspectives in Eastern Europe* (Carlisle, PA: Strategic Studies Institute, US Army War College, 15 August 1990), pp. 3–6.

6. Manfred Worner, 'NATO transformed: the significance of the Rome Summit', *NATO Review*, No. 6 (Dec. 1991), pp. 3–8, provides an excellent summary of decisions taken in London which prepared the ground for subsequent policy decisions announced at the Rome summit in November 1991. The text of the London Declaration appears in *NATO Review*, No. 4 (Aug., 1990), pp. 32–3.

7. Michael Legge, 'The making of NATO's new strategy', *NATO Review*, No. 6 (Dec. 1991), pp. 9–14. See also Gen. John Galvin, 'From immediate defence towards long-term stability', *NATO Review*, No. 6 (Dec. 1991), pp. 14–18.

8. The Western European Union originally included the original six Common Market countries (France, Germany, Italy, Belgium, Netherlands, and Luxembourg) plus the United Kingdom. It was an outgrowth of the Brussels Defense Treaty of 1948, which failed to transform itself into a European Defense Community (EDC) as some had hoped in the early 1950s. Portugal and Spain joined WEU in 1990. For background and perspective, see Willem Van Eekelen, 'Building a new European security order: WEU's contribution', *NATO Review*, Aug. 1990, pp. 18–23.

9. Ambassador G. von Moltke, 'NATO takes up its new agenda', *NATO Review*, No. 1 (Feb. 1992), pp. 3–7, esp. p. 4.

10. Defense Planning Committee *Communiqué*, Brussels, 12–13 Dec. 1991, published in *NATO Review*, No. 1 (Feb. 1992), pp. 30–2.

11. *Philadelphia Inquirer*, 25 May, 1992, p. A5.

12. Ibid.

13. Charles A. Kupchan and Clifford A. Kupchan, 'A New Concert for Europe', Ch. 8C in Graham Allison and Gregory F. Treverton (eds), *Rethinking America's Security: Beyond Cold War to a New World Order* (New York: W.W. Norton, 1992), pp. 249–66.

14. The authors actually propose the Soviet Union for the security group, but I assume they would adopt Russia as its most logical politico-military successor and have so defined it.

15. Fred Chernoff, 'Arms Control, European Security and the Future of the Western Alliance', *Strategic Review*, No. 1 (Winter, 1992), pp. 19–31.

16. Ibid., p. 26.

17. Ibid.

18. Ivo H. Daalder, 'The Role of Arms Control in the New Europe', *Arms Control*, No. 1 (May 1991), pp. 20–34, esp. p. 26.

19. Ibid., p. 23.
20. Glenn H. Snyder, *Deterrence and Defense: Toward a Theory of National Security* (Princeton, NJ: Princeton University Press, 1961), pp. 14–15.
21. My understanding of this is very much in debt to Don Snider, Center for Strategic and International Studies, Washington, DC, who bears no responsibility for arguments or opinions here.
22. James J. Tritten, 'America Promises to Come Back: A New National Security Strategy', *Security Studies*, No. 2 (Winter, 1991), p. 182.
23. Ibid., p. 183.
24. Ibid., p. 187.
25. Ibid., p. 185.
26. Congress of the United States, Congressional Budget Office, *The Economic Effects of Reduced Defense Spending* (Washington, DC: Congressional Budget Office, Feb. 1992), p. 10.
27. Ibid., p. 12.
28. Lawrence J. Korb, 'Real Defense Cuts – and the Real Defense Issues', *Arms Control Today*, May 1992, pp. 5–9. Korb was assistant secretary of defense in the Reagan administration for manpower, reserve affairs, and logistics.
29. Ibid., p. 7.
30. Draft US Department of Defense Guidance of 18 Feb 1992 apparently referred to the need for continued aiming of US nuclear weapons at Russian targets which leaders in Moscow 'value most'. See Barton Gellman, *Washington Post News Service*, 'Pentagon revises key plan', in *Philadelphia Inquirer*, 25 May 1992, p. A3. It would be reasonable to assume, nevertheless, that the entire concept of the Single Integrated Operational Plan (SIOP) for nuclear war planning is being revisited by the Office of the Secretary of Defense. A deconstructed SIOP is a logical outgrowth of a post-Cold War world in which the Soviet Union no longer even exists, and the retargeting of missiles away from US and Russian homelands is a logical derivative of a progressively warmer political relationship. In the interim, the disconnection of theater nuclear from strategic nuclear warfare is a *fait accompli* in Europe, with the Bush-Gorbachev initiatives of autumn 1991 on the withdrawal and dismantling of short range nuclear forces having resolved the 'use or lose' problem for NATO.
31. Ambassador Henning Wegener, 'The transformed Alliance', *NATO Review*, Aug. 1990, pp. 1–9, esp. p. 5.
32. London Declaration, Para. 18, in *NATO Review*, Aug. 1990, p. 33.
33. Wegener, 'The transformed Alliance', p. 5.
34. Barton Gellman, 'The US Aims to Remain First Among Nonequals', *Washington Post*, National Weekly Edition, 16–22 March, 1992, p. 19.
35. Barton Gellman, 'Pentagon revises key plan', *Washington Post* news service, in *Philadelphia Inquirer*, 25 May, 1992, p. A3.
36. Ibid.
37. For an argument that the international system is now actually unipolar and that this development is favorable for international peace and security, see Charles Krauthammer, 'The Unipolar Moment', Ch. 8F in Allison and Treverton (eds), *Rethinking America's Security*, pp. 295–306.
38. For an asssessment of US covert action during the Cold War, see Gregory F. Treverton, *Covert Action: The Limits of Intervention in the Postwar World* (New York: Basic Books, 1987).
39. Sam C. Sarkesian, 'US Strategy and Unconventional Conflicts: The Elusive Goal', Ch. 10 in Sarkesian and John Allen Williams (eds), *The US Army in a New Security Era* (Boulder, CO: Lynne Rienner, 1990), pp. 195–16.
40. See, for example, Horst Afheldt, 'New Policies, New Fears', *Bulletin of the Atomic Scientists*, Sept. 1988, pp. 24–8, and John Grin and Lutz Unterseher, 'The Spiderweb Defense', *Bulletin of the Atomic Scientists*, Sept. 1988, pp. 28–30. According to Stephen J. Flanagan, there are four basic types of non-offensive defense concepts: area defense; wide-area covering defenses; the fire barrier; and integrated and interactive forward defense. See

Flanagan, *NATO's Conventional Defenses* (Cambridge, MA: Ballinger Publishing Co., 1988), Ch. 7, esp. pp. 110–20; Andreas von Bulow, 'Defensive Entanglement: An Alternative Strategy for NATO', in Andrew J. Pierre (ed.), *The Conventional Defense of Europe: New Technologies and New Strategies* (New York: Council on Foreign Relations, 1986), pp. 112–152; and Von Bulow, 'O nesposobnosti k napadeniyu' (On the Inability to Attack), *Kommunist*, No. 7 (May 1989), pp. 122–5.

41. For an informed assessment, see Richard H. Ullman, *Securing Europe* (Princeton: Princeton University Press, 1991)
42. Robert Jervis, 'Cooperation under the Security Dilemma', *World Politics*, No. 2 (Jan. 1978), pp. 167–86, in Robert J. Art and Robert Jervis (eds), *International Politics: Anarchy, Force, Political Economy and Decision Making* (New York: Harper Collins, 1985), pp. 86–101, esp. p. 88.
43. Charles L. Glaser, 'Political Consequences of Military Strategy: Expanding and Refining the Spiral and Deterrence Models', *World Politics*, No. 4 (July 1992), pp. 497–538.
44. Robert Jervis, *Perception and Misperception in International Politics* (Princeton: Princeton University Press, 1976), esp. Ch. 3.
45. Idem., 'Cooperation under the Security Dilemma', as reprinted in Robert J. Art and Robert Jervis (eds), *International Politics: Anarchy, Force, Political Economy and Decision Making* (New York: Harper Collins, 1985), p. 91.
46. Ibid.
47. Ibid.
48. This is treated at length in George H. Quester, *Offense and Defense in the International System* (New Brunswick, NJ: Transaction Books, 1988 edn).
49. A.J.P. Taylor, *The Struggle for Mastery in Europe, 1848–1918* (Oxford: Clarendon Press, 1954), Ch. 1.
50. Ibid., p. xxxiii.
51. These terms are explained in Stephen M. Walt, 'Alliance Formation in Southwest Asia: Balancing and Bandwagoning in Cold War Competition', Ch. 3 in Robert Jervis and Jack Snyder (eds), *Dominoes and Bandwagons: Strategic Beliefs and Great Power Competition in the Eurasian Rimland* (New York: Oxford University Press, 1991), pp. 51–84, esp. p. 52. See also Walt, *The Origin of Alliances* (Ithaca, NY: Cornell University Press, 1987).
52. For a discussion of security and stability problems in Eastern and Central Europe, see Otto Pick, 'Reassuring Eastern Europe', *NATO Review*, No. 2 (April 1992), pp. 27–31.
53. Ibid., p. 29.
54. On the role of nuclear weapons in future Europe, see Ullman, *Securing Europe*, pp. 83–106.
55. For documentation, see George H. Quester, *Offense and Defense in the International System*.

5

Nuclear Proliferation and Civil–Military Relations: Managing Old Risks in New Environments

According to American military strategists, the technique for making adversaries yield to threats without actually engaging in war is brinkmanship.[1] Nuclear weapons were ideal tools for Cold War brinksmen, or so it seemed. Their highly destructive and indiscriminate character created a terroristic aura about them, suitable for intimidation of foreign leaders and general publics. It followed that skillful persuasion by means of nuclear brinkmanship should have permitted the US and the Soviets, once they attained nuclear sufficiency, to 'win' crises that they would otherwise 'lose'. History turned out otherwise, according to the interpretation offered here: fewer than 20 years into the Cold War, US and Soviet leaders were forced to improvise around brinkmanship and other risky nuclear bargaining tactics.

The issue, whether nuclear coercion worked during the Cold War as it was supposed to, carries significant baggage into the new world order of the 1990s and thereafter. Nuclear coercive diplomacy is the lubricant of nuclear deterrence, the necessary dynamic which makes deterrence something more than a purely static construct. If nuclear coercion can be relied upon as a support for stability after the Cold War, then it follows that nuclear proliferation is not necessarily as dangerous as some pessimists claim. A well-managed process of proliferation might be more stable than a nuclear disarmed world. On the other hand, if nuclear coercive diplomacy was not actually successful during the Cold War, under ideal conditions of an 'overdetermined' international stability, then a stronger likelihood exists that nuclear proliferation and instability will be highly correlated.

The first part of this study looks at two of the most serious superpower crises of the Cold War and asks whether leaders relied on brinkmanship, as suggested in some historical accounts, or whether they dodged the brinkmanship bullet and worked around it. The second section uses the former Soviet Union and the aftermath of the abortive Soviet coup of August 1991 to show how unproductive nuclear coercion might have been had it been practiced under these unexpected, and unwelcome, circumstances of instant nuclear proliferation. The last part asks what could happen if aspiring brinksmen were to assume political power inside or outside of Eurasia, placing big bets on the potential for nuclear coercion but without the painful nuclear learning forced on leaders in Washington and Moscow by history.

BRINKMANSHIP, OPTIONS AND NUCLEAR CRISES

Brinkmanship strategies involve the manipulation of risk by leaders of one state in order to deter or to compel desired behavior from another state. The risk-taking propensities of leaders are dependent upon many variables, including the international balance of military power, the reputation of a state for its willingness to defend its commitments, and the behavioral and psychological attributes of particular leaders. The policy-maker who is *living* through a crisis views the situation differently from the scholar who is trying to understand that crisis after the fact. For the scholar, the manipulation of risk is a seemingly rational process by which adversaries press one another in bargaining games until one side yields. For the policy-maker, crisis bargaining, especially with nuclear weapons and a possible outbreak of nuclear war in the pot, is a dangerous activity full of uncontrollable elements.

Where scholars look for 'manipulation of risk', political leaders are apt to perceive victimization by risks. The sense of loss of control over events can lead policy-makers toward alternatives which they might never have contemplated under other conditions. In two significant crises of the Cold War, described in more detail below, this sense of potential loss of control caused US or Soviet political leaders to draw back deliberately from the brink. Each side settled for less than maximum advantage and less than maximum stress on the other side's decision-making process. Each found a partial community of interest in avoiding the more dangerous aspects of crisis management once it became clear that leaders were in danger of chasing events instead of controlling them.

The sense of loss of control over events is an existential, not an analytical, phenomenon, experienced by those who participated in crisis decision-making and not by others. If nuclear crises were more existential than they were analytical, as perceived by those who were forced to manage those crises,

157

then what was being bargained about was not 'outcomes' or 'options' for settlement, as in labor–management negotiations. What was being negotiated was the inherent view held by US and Soviet leaders of military danger and political catastrophe.

The Cuban Missile Crisis of 1962

The Cuban missile crisis had many lessons, judged differently by US hawks and doves and by their Soviet counterparts. US hawks concluded that Khrushchev backed down in the face of overwhelming US nuclear and conventional force superiority. Soviet hawks concluded that their missiles had been sent to defend Cuba against a possible US invasion, and that Khrushchev bungled the clandestine deployments which could have temporarily removed a Soviet window of vulnerability to US coercion. American doves reasoned that the two sides had had a narrow escape from mutual disaster, and that the Cuban missile crisis had largely resulted from misperception of one another's motivations and political priorities. Soviet new thinkers of the Gorbachev era, allowing that the United States' hostility to Cuba had poisoned the atmosphere of US–Soviet relations, none the less acknowledged that Khrushchev had blundered in attempting to place Soviet nuclear delivery vehicles so close to US shores.[2]

There is no end to academic controversy about the reasons for Khrushchev's decision to deploy the Soviet missiles to Cuba, and US scholarly debates over the correctness of Kennedy's decision have continued from 1962 to the present. Whether one judges favorably the conduct of the two leaders and their principal advisors, one cannot help but notice that Kennedy's and Khrushchev's behavior during the Cuban missile crisis marks a turning point in superpower Cold War brinkmanship. For the Soviet leadership, the forced retreat in the aftermath of the US discovery of the missiles led to a reappraisal of the value of nuclear coercion in US–Soviet relations. Soviet diplomacy for the remainder of Khrushchev's tenure in office emphasized adherence to the political status quo as the basis of peaceful coexistence. The Kremlin ceased its pressures on Berlin, and US–Soviet agreements on a nuclear test ban and on the creation of a crisis management 'hot line' were in part the products of a post-crisis recognition of mutual interest in reducing reliance on nuclear arms and nuclear threats.[3]

Several conferences in 1987 sponsored by Harvard University benefited from the availability of newly declassified US research materials on the Cuban missile crisis. The Hawk's Cay conference brought together US crisis participants and American scholars in order to compare policy-makers' and academics' understandings of that seminal event. The second conference in Cambridge, Massachusetts included former US policy-makers and US and Soviet academics.[4] The results of the two conferences included the unsurprising finding, but a very significant one in this context, that policy-makers and academics saw the crisis very differently. James G. Blight and David A. Welch describe the difference between academics and policy-makers as the view from 'somewhere' and the view from 'nowhere'. 'Somewhere' is the view of policy-makers who participated in the Cuban missile crisis deliberations and felt the responsibility for any decisions that were taken. 'Nowhere' is the more analytical and detached perspective of academics who seek antiseptic facts and explanations apart from the feelings participants might have had at the time of the crisis.[5]

The differences between the view from somewhere and the view from nowhere remain profound throughout the Hawk's Cay and Cambridge conferences. One manifestation of this is that some US policy-makers, including former Secretary of Defense Robert S. McNamara, recalled that the balance of nuclear strategic power meant little to them in advising the President about crisis management options. The important thing for policy-makers who lived through the Cuban missile crisis, in the view of McNamara and other key Kennedy advisors, was the sense of danger and stress that all shared. The members of the ExComm, the crisis management advisory group assembled by the President, recalled the tense atmosphere of uncertainty surrounding the crisis and waved off academic questions that asked about their formal logics for decision-making. As McNamara explained:

> I don't think we've quite succeeded in re-creating the atmosphere at the time ... There were deep differences of opinion among us, and very strong feelings about Cuba, and the fact is that we weren't going through an unemotional, orderly, and comprehensive analytical decision making process.[6]

Equally frustrating for scholars was the acknowledgment by members of the ExComm that, for the most part, they made little effort during the crisis to extrapolate from their immediate decisions to contingencies which might result in further escalation. Although Kennedy's advisors worried a great deal in general about the possibility of US-Soviet conventional or nuclear conflict growing out of the crisis, members of the ExComm did not explore in any systematic way the alternatives open to Khrushchev in response to the US 'quarantine' (blockade). There were few if any explicit discussions of how escalation might be controlled in the event that the Soviet Union chose to run the blockade or to escalate the crisis to another theater of operations, say in Europe.[7]

The experience of the Cuban missile crisis suggested to participants, if not to scholars, that brinkmanship tactics in nuclear crisis management created an unfavorable ratio of acceptable and unacceptable risks. Khrushchev and Kennedy extricated themselves from a process of escalation which might have resulted in world war by using extraordinary diplomatic approaches, including backchannels and improvised decision-making ploys. Robert Kennedy's final démarche to Soviet Ambassador Dobrynin on 27 October, at the climax of the crisis, contained both an insistence on the Soviet withdrawal of their missiles from Cuba and a tacit recognition of the symmetry between Soviet missiles in Cuba and US missiles in Turkey. Dean Rusk revealed many years after the Cuban missile crisis that President Kennedy authorized Rusk to open a channel through the United Nations for a public trade of the missiles in Cuba for the missiles in Turkey.[8] If this report is accurate, it means that President Kennedy was prepared to authorize a missile trade in preference to ordering an air strike or invasion of Cuba.

Kennedy was apparently more impressed with the possibility of uncontrolled escalation than he was enticed by the prospect of successful brinkmanship in forcing Khrushchev to back down.

The Berlin Crisis of 1961

Readers might concede that the relationship between crisis management experience and wariness of brinkmanship was established for US leaders who participated in the Cuban missile crisis. In some ways, the Berlin crisis of summer and autumn, 1961 was analogous to the Cuban missile crisis of 1962. In both cases, extended deterrence provided by a superpower to an ally was under challenge: Soviet extended deterrence against any US invasion of Cuba, and US extended deterrence of any Soviet or East German effort to force the US, Britain and France out of West Berlin.[9] On the other hand, the Berlin crisis of 1961 provided a more explicit test of the connection between nuclear brinkmanship and flexible response. A situation calling for a determined US resistance to Soviet pressure on a European ally, especially the Germans, was just what the doctor ordered for those who suspected massive retaliation of military inflexibility.

US planning for the Berlin crisis of 1961 was the first major test of flexible response and graduated deterrence. The Kennedy administration was caught at an early stage of its effort to transfer the idea of graduated and flexible response from the realm of theory into military institutional practice.[10] Berlin crisis planning guided by the concept of flexible response included options ranging from very small conventional actions to large-scale nuclear war. Paul H. Nitze, Assistant Secretary of Defense for International Security Affairs who directed much of the Berlin crisis contingency planning, gave a speech on 7 September in which he expressed optimism about US graduated response capabilities if needed:

> We have a tremendous variety of warheads which gives us the flexibility we require to conduct nuclear actions from the level of large-scale destruction down to mere demolition work ... the number of delivery vehicles of all types which the United States possesses provides the flexibility for virtually all modes and levels of warfare.[11]

Despite this apparent optimism about flexible options on the part of his advisors, President Kennedy emphasized the avoidance of military incidents between US and Soviet forces, while still holding to the political tenet that allied rights in West Berlin would not be compromised. A test of the President's confidence in crisis management based on flexible military options was provided by the tense confrontation between US and Soviet tanks at Checkpoint Charlie, a well-known crossing point in the Berlin Wall constructed by the Soviets in August 1961. US leaders saw the 1961 Berlin crisis, and the events from 22–28 October, in particular, as a Soviet effort to intimidate the US and its Western allies by testing their resolve. The 1961 Berlin crisis had originated in Khrushchev's *aide-mémoire* of 4 June 1961, threatening to sign a separate peace agreement with East Germany and thus turning over to the DDR control of allied access routes to West Berlin. This *aide-mémoire* restated the essential points of an earlier note to President Eisenhower in 1958, provoking an earlier crisis over Berlin. The essential points included a demand for the neutralization of Berlin and insisted on a deadline of six months for negotiating the appropriate peace agreement.[12]

Raymond Garthoff, a senior fellow at the Brookings Institution who served in the US State Department during the 1961 Berlin crisis, has revealed new information about the confrontation between US and Soviet tanks at Checkpoint Charlie from 25 to 28 October. According to Garthoff, this confrontation, which could have erupted into a US–Soviet war, including nuclear war, was the result of both sides having misperceived the objectives and intentions of the other.[13] On 22 October the senior American diplomat in Berlin and his wife attempted to enter East Berlin at the Checkpoint Charlie crossing point to attend a theater performance. When East German police demanded to see their passports, the Americans refused, departed, and returned with an escort of eight armed US soldiers, supported by four M-48 tanks and other US troops deployed near the checkpoint.[14] After several US probes and East German efforts to check documents, on 25 October General Lucius Clay, President Kennedy's special representative in Berlin, decided to concentrate ten M-48 tanks near the Wall. The next day a Soviet tank battalion (33 tanks) entered East Berlin, and on 27 October ten Soviet tanks moved forward to the East German side of the checkpoint. An eyeball-to-eyeball confrontation between US and Soviet tanks was now a reality.[15]

According to Garthoff, new documentation available in 1991 reveals that the Soviet leadership in late October of 1961 was not attempting to probe Western resolve by using East German inspections as a surrogate for Soviet coercive diplomacy. Instead, Khrushchev interpreted US actions as a challenge to the political and military status quo in Berlin. His interpretation was that the US actions of 22–27 October were efforts to intimidate the Soviet Union into reconsidering its decision to construct the Berlin wall. Khrushchev also apparently thought it was possible that the US was preparing a pretext for knocking down the wall with military force. In September, General Clay had authorized drills by US combat engineers in West Berlin in which a simulated portion of the wall was breached by bulldozers. Soviet intelligence certainly learned of these drills, and two retired Soviet military intelligence officers told interviewers that the GRU (main intelligence directorate of the Soviet General Staff) had actually photographed the exercises.[16] Thus it was not unreasonable, although incorrect, for Soviet leaders to infer that the US had established a definite plan to destroy the wall or breach it at selected points.

In addition, the general political and strategic context of US–Soviet relations at this time contributed to US and to Soviet pessimism about one another's objectives with regard to Berlin and Germany. The Kennedy administration had been determined to contravene the impression being given by Khrushchev since Sputnik that the Soviet Union had strategic nuclear forces superior to those of the US. The task of spiking Khrushchev's public diplomacy was given to Deputy Secretary of Defense Roswell Gilpatric.

Speaking for the administration in a policy statement on 21 October (one day before the confrontation between the senior US diplomat in Berlin and East German border guards), Gilpatric claimed US strategic nuclear superiority, indicated that there was no missile gap favorable to the Soviet Union, and contended that the US had 'a second strike capability which is at least as extensive as what the Soviets can deliver by striking first'.[17] For the Soviet leadership and for Khrushchev in particular, the Gilpatric speech must have been ominous. It meant that the United States had superior numbers of strategic nuclear delivery vehicles and warheads compared to the Soviet

Union, and that US officials were aware of their relative advantage. Further, US awareness of its advantage could only have come about through reconnaissance which was sufficiently competent to pinpoint the locations of the Soviet strategic rocket forces. Those forces based in the Soviet Union were vulnerable to first or second strikes in a way that their American counterparts were not. In addition, the political implications of Kennedy's willingness to go public with this announcement could reasonably have seemed rather ominous to Soviet audiences. After all, it was Kennedy who had used the missile gap as a major issue in his 1960 campaign for the Presidency. For Kennedy to now acknowledge that the missile gap was non-existent, or drastically in favor of the US, required major swallowing of domestic political swords in order to make a point with Moscow.[18]

Although aware of US advantages in the military balance, however, President Kennedy did not necessarily see them as useful bargaining chips in Berlin, any more than he did in Cuba. Instead of engaging in nuclear brinkmanship, the President opened a backchannel communication to the Soviet leadership through Soviet embassy press attaché Georgi Bol'shakov. On 27 October, Robert Kennedy passed a message from JFK to Khrushchev through Bol'shakov. President Kennedy asked Khrushchev to withdraw his tanks from their positions near Checkpoint Charlie and indicated in the same message that Khrushchev's cooperation would be followed by American reciprocity: US tanks would also be withdrawn.[19] Khrushchev agreed to this proposal by Kennedy and began withdrawal of the ten Soviet tanks on the morning of 28 October. Approximately half an hour later, the ten US tanks near the checkpoint also withdrew. Government officials and others on both the US and Soviet sides who were not privy to the backchannel communication between Kennedy and Khrushchev claimed victory in the crisis, alleging that the other side had backed down in the face of political resoluteness and military muscle. But the October 1961 confrontation over Berlin was not resolved by competitive brinkmanship, but by the avoidance of brinkmanship and by the decision on the part of both leaders to resolve the crisis on mutually acceptable terms.

Could Flexible Options Rescue Nuclear Brinkmanship?

The disinterest of Kennedy and Khrushchev in nuclear brinkmanship during the Berlin and Cuban missile crises was in part related to the discovery by both leaders of how inflexible war plans really were. In their Cuban missile crisis deliberations, as we have noted, both emphasized the possibility that events would carry military operations beyond the control of political leaders. At times US leaders actually doubted whether Khrushchev was still in control of his government, as when they received his second letter of 27 October contradicting a message of the previous day and stiffening terms for settlement of the crisis. What US officials did not know was that Khrushchev and his advisors also had doubts about the extent to which Kennedy could control his own advisors and forces. Soviet leaders wondered whether the US government was not under the control of a military–security clique, consistent with their ideologically biased understanding of American government, but also consistent with some indications presented to them before and during the crisis itself by unknowing US planners and decision-makers.

The connection between flexible options and nuclear brinkmanship on behalf of deterrence presupposes that signals are understood as intended by the recipients as well as by the senders. If unintended signals are sent, or if intended signals are nevertheless misunderstood by the recipients, leaders may be drawn into an escalatory conflict spiral instead of being helped to find a way out of an impasse. This psycho-social aspect of brinkmanship proved to be more significant for US and Soviet crisis managers than the numbers of weapons on either side or the assumed outcomes of any actual nuclear exchanges. The US and Soviets got into the 1961 Berlin and 1962 Cuban crises as a result of misperceptions about one another's motives and resolve. When the ability of each side to take into account the perspective of the other was enhanced by the sobering impact of crisis diplomacy, each adopted the image of an adversary more interested in compromise than in conflict over core values.

Three episodes which took place during the Cuban missile crisis raise serious doubts that leaders were fully aware of the activities of their military and intelligence organizations. If not aware, then the heads of state and supreme commanders were to some extent acting on false premises about the sources of their own behavior. It is even less likely that leaders on each side could fully and correctly interpret the behavior of their opposite numbers in Moscow or in Washington. The first of these episodes was the U-2 'stray' which accidentally overflew Soviet airspace on 27 October; the second was the U-2 shootdown which took place over Cuba on the same day; and the third was a miscommunication from an important US spy in the Soviet Union in the midst of the crisis.[20]

In the first incident, a US U-2 reconnaissance spy plane accidentally strayed into Soviet airspace over the Chukhotsk Peninsula (north-east Siberia). The Soviets scrambled air defense fighter interceptors to attack the US aircraft.[21] In response, the US sent fighter aircraft from Alaska to escort the U-2 safely home. Under orders effective 22 October, the US interceptors were armed with nuclear air-to-air missiles.[22] The US government explanation was that the U-2 had strayed accidentally into Soviet airspace. Aurora borealis had prevented the pilot from proper use of celestial navigation to determine that he was off course. The prescribed U-2 mission was to collect air samples of radioactivity from Soviet nuclear tests.[23] Raymond Garthoff has suggested that the location of the U-2 'argued against its being taken as a serious military reconnaissance mission of the type that might be made on the eve of hostilities'.[24] Scott Sagan notes, however, that President Kennedy apparently feared the Soviets might believe that the flight was a last-minute 'pre-SIOP' reconnaissance mission, immediately preceding a nuclear attack.[25] Garthoff and Sagan agree that the incident was a dangerous one, given its timing and the uncertain implications of any shooting between US and Soviet aircraft during some of the most anxious moments of the Cuban crisis.

The second incident, which raised questions about the leaders' ability to control the crisis-related behavior of their own organizations, involved the shooting down of a U-2 over Cuba on 27 October by a Soviet surface-to-air (SAM) missile. US officials wondered whether the Soviet leadership had authorized this attack, and the same officials offered explanations for it, none of which turned out to be correct after the fact. Officials at the time speculated that Khrushchev might have directed the shootdown as a warning against further escalation by the US Others theorized that Khrushchev might have been directed to do so by other, and more hard-line, leaders in Moscow who then held the balance of power. It was also suggested that the Cubans might have been responsible for the shootdown, by somehow getting control of Soviet air defense missile installations. Last, US leaders had to entertain the possibility that the Soviet air defense commanders were simply following standard operating procedures which instructed them to attack any suspicious overflights.[26]

In fact, the decision to shoot down the US reconnaissance plane was taken by local Soviet air defense commanders without authorization from Moscow and in violation of the spirit, if not the letter, of their standing orders. The Soviet commander of SAM units in the eastern part of Cuba made the decision to shoot down the U-2, and the decision was approved by his commanding officer located in Havana. Standing orders had called for Soviet air defenses to attack any US planes which were part of an American attack on Cuba. The Soviet high command apparently meant by these orders that US aircraft participating in an *air strike* or *invasion* of Cuba should be attacked automatically. Local commanders in Cuba interpreted their discretion broadly, to include attacks against snooping enemy reconnaissance aircraft.[27] Having been informed of the U-2 shootdown over Cuba, the Soviet Defense

Minister quickly issued a reprimand to Soviet commanders in Cuba and made very specific the demand that they not fire on US reconnaissance planes.[28]

The third incident or situation which could have led to unexpected and undesired escalation in Cuba was the apparent deployment of tactical nuclear warheads with Soviet ground forces units deployed prior to the onset of the missile crisis. The existence of tactical nuclear weapons for surface-to-surface, short-range missiles with Soviet troops based in Cuba was not known to US leaders during the crisis. Further, the Soviet army field commander had apparent, contingent authorization to use these weapons against any force attacking Cuba and the Soviet forces deployed there.[29] At the Havana conference on the Cuban missile crisis in January 1992, Soviet Army General Anatoly Gribkov, who helped to plan the Cuban missile deployments, acknowledged the deployment in 1962 of nine tactical nuclear warheads in the 2–25 kiloton range along with six short-range tactical rocket launchers. According to Gribkov, General of the Army Pilyev, the Soviet military commander in Cuba, had received discretionary authority to fire the tactical nuclear weapons at any US invaders without seeking further clarification and approval from Moscow.[30]

The fact that the Cuban missile crisis did *not* erupt in war is taken by some as an argument for the successful coercion of the Soviet leadership by US nuclear brinkmanship. But the preceding illustration, with regard to a Soviet nuclear presence already in Cuba and unknown to American leaders and analysts, shows that Kennedy and Khrushchev were prudent to improvise against brinkmanship by hedging their bets and bundling their threats into larger packages with promises and reassurances. A premature US invasion of Cuba could have resulted, if General Gribkov's memory is accurate, in a nuclear first use in *Cuba* by Soviet forces against invading Americans. The potential for escalation into a larger regional or world war is too obvious for comment, and the resulting collateral damage for Cuba would have provided little consolation for Castro.

The tactical nuclear deployments in Cuba might well have been the products of organizational inertia: the same kinds of weapons were usually deployed with Soviet ground forces and tactical rocket launchers. This is hardly reassuring to those who would argue for leaders in command of organizations that can guarantee flexible and supple response to authorized commands. Had the commanders of Soviet ground forces in Cuba understood correctly Khrushchev's diplomatic and strategic as well as military needs, they or their superiors might have cautioned against deploying tactical nuclear warheads in the Caribbean. One might argue, of course, that the tactical nuclears were nothing compared to those intended for medium-range

166

ballistic missiles, but the dismissal confuses the importance of missile range with the importance of inadvertent escalation. The tactical nuclear weapons were not capable of striking the continental US by surprise, but they were more capable than their longer range cousins of getting caught up in a process not fully under the control of either side.

DEMISE OF THE SOVIET UNION: RELEASING NUCLEAR UNCERTAINTY

During the Cold War years US and other Western experts had only partial glimpses into the Soviet nuclear command and control system, and these glimpses were not always consistent.[31] It was assumed that the Politburo, led by the General Secretary of the Communist Party of the Soviet Union, would take the important decisions for war and peace, including decisions for the use of nuclear weapons. Gorbachev's accession to leading state and party positions led to reforms in defense decision-making during the period from 1985 through 1990. These reforms affected the political structure for supervision of the armed forces on matters of high policy. As Gorbachev sought to break the party monopoly on political power and to devolve more power from the central government to the periphery, it followed that the question of relations between party and state officials and military bureaucrats would become more complicated. Professional officers in the armed forces could be found across the spectrum of enthusiasm, or lack thereof, for Gorbachev's political reforms, including the impact of *perestroika* on the Soviet armed forces. To some extent these groupings of modernizers and conservatives, to over-simplify, followed along the lines of support for or disagreement with Gorbachev and revised views of strategy of the Soviet 'new thinkers'. Thus, Gorbachev's willingness to accept the dissolution of the Warsaw Pact, the reunification of Germany and the attachment of the new Germany to NATO amounted to a geopolitical revolution which had to affect strategic planning and the future composition of the Soviet armed forces.[32]

The Soviets passed through one phase of debates on the implications of *perestroika* for the professional armed forces and for their strategic doctrines between 1985 and 1990. The abortive coup of 19–21 August 1991 constituted another and more uncertain window of opportunity on these questions. It seemed clear, in the aftermath of the failed coup, that the relationship between the Soviet armed forces and the state political leadership, itself under siege, would undergo fundamental change. The party–state nexus having been shattered by Gorbachev's earlier reforms, the centralized Soviet state imploded in 1991 under the pressure of post-coup democratization. The Baltic republics of Estonia, Latvia and Lithuania were officially recognized as independent states by the government of the former Soviet Union and by others, including the United States and the leading NATO and non-aligned countries of Europe. Gorbachev and Boris Yeltsin, President of the Russian Federation, then attempted to cobble together a new, albeit temporary, framework for union, among the remaining 12 republics. The Ukrainian declaration of independence, approved by popular referendum on 1 December 1991, left the aspiring Union of Sovereign States as conceived by Gorbachev without its breadbasket and without other major economic assets critical for the survival of a post-Soviet voluntary federation of sovereign republics.

During the coup itself and in later autumn 1991 efforts to assemble a new union, Soviet political and military leaders were confronted with the problem of establishing reliable arrangements for nuclear command and control. Although Western media expressed some anxiety during the coup about which Soviet fingers were actually on the nuclear trigger, it became clear shortly thereafter that there had existed no substantial risk of accidental or unauthorized nuclear use.[33] Bruce G. Blair of the Brookings Institution noted in Congressional testimony that 'the situation would have to become much more dire ... involving clashes with military units inside the Soviet Union, before we would have to worry about a breakdown in nuclear command and control'.[34] Whether the same confidence in the integrity of the nuclear chain of command could have been held through a succession crisis continuing for weeks or months is another question; fortunately for all concerned, the August days were of short duration. Nevertheless, the coup attempt sensitized Western audiences to the issue more than before, and the conclusion was widely drawn that the process of democratization in the former Soviet Union had not fully worked out emergency arrangements for devolution of nuclear command authority.

The issue of devolution of nuclear command authority in the former Soviet Union during the coup and subsequently could be divided into two major components: who had and has access to the authentication codes for nuclear release; and how cohesive were and are the professional armed forces in response to presumably authorized commands from acting or permanent constitutional authority? During the coup, the status of constitutional authority was temporarily usurped by the State Committee for the State of Emergency (the gang of eight) a loosely knit group of party bureaucrats, military officers and KGB officials. Membership of this group included the persons whose backgrounds are summarized in Table 5.1.

This group spirited Gorbachev into house arrest and mistakenly assumed that Gorbachev's legacy would fall apart in the absence of its personal spokesman. The coup plotters both overestimated Gorbachev's importance and underestimated the more lasting impact that his reforms had had on the

TABLE 5.1

COUP PLOTTERS* IN THE SOVIET UNION, 19–21 AUGUST 1991
(MEMBERS OF THE STATE COMMITTEE FOR THE STATE OF EMERGENCY)

Name	Major Position at Time of Coup Attempt	Career Background
Gennadi Yanayev	USSR Vice-President	Komsomol,† party apparatus, official trade union
Vladimir Kryuchkov	Head of KGB	Komsomol, party apparatus, diplomatic work, KGB
Valentin Pavlov	Prime Minister	Official in state bureaucracy
Dmitriy Yazov	Defense Minister	General of the army, career military
Boris Pugo	Interior Minister	Komsomol, party apparatus, formerly headed Latvian KGB and Latvian Party
Oleg Baklanov	First Deputy Chairman, Defense Council	Factory manager, armaments specialist, state bureaucracy, CPSU Secretariat
Vasiliy Starodubtsev	Chairman, USSR Peasants Union and Russian Federation Agrarian Union	Kolkhoz chair, Novomoskovskoye Agro-Industrial Association
Aleksandr Tizyakov	President, USSR State Association of State-Owned Industrial, Construction, Transportation, and Communications Enterprises	Director, Kalinin Machine-Building Plant (artillery factory in Sverdlovsk)

* Also indicted for high treason were: Sergei Akhromeev, military advisor to President Gorbachev; Valeriy Boldin, Gorbachev's chief of staff; Anatoliy Lukyanov, Chairman, USSR Supreme Soviet; and Valentin Varrenikov, Commander in chief of the ground forces, among others.

† Komsomol refers to the Communist Party youth league, an almost obligatory stop in the career track for those aspiring to important CPSU positions in the former Soviet Union.

Sources: Joan DeBardeleben, 'Political Institutions', Ch. 29 in Mark Kesselman and Joel Krieger (eds), *European Politics in Transition*, 2nd edn (Lexington, MA: D.C. Heath & Co., 1992), p. 625; and Richard F. Staar, *The New Russian Armed Forces: Preparing for War or Peace?* (Stanford, CA: Hoover Institution, 1992), p. 2.

Soviet body politic. The armed forces were now divided into factions along professional and ideological lines. They could not be moved as a single entity in response to commands from the self-appointed coup makers. In effect, the leaders of the main arms of service for the most part defeated the coup by a bureaucratic sit-down strike. Without the support of the main elements of the ground forces, air force and other principal arms of service, the coup makers could not enforce their directives.

It was thought by US expert analysts that, under Gorbachev, at least three persons had to concur for nuclear release to be granted to the armed forces: Gorbachev, as President; the Minister of Defense; and the Chief of the General Staff of the Soviet Armed Forces.[35] Acting together, the three would presumably have provided the Soviet equivalent of the US National Command Authority.[36] The post-coup system may have increased the effective veto power of republic presidents or their representatives over the use of Russian strategic nuclear weapons. The 'Commonwealth' armed forces (fictitious with regard to the status of fully nationalized conventional forces throughout the former Soviet Union by the end of 1992) served as a useful stovepipe through which to maintain centralized command over nuclear weapons. The vast majority of nuclear-capable delivery systems which could reach the United States are located in the Russian Federation (about 80 per cent taking into account ground-launched, sea-launched and air-delivered munitions).[37] Other republics in which some strategic nuclear weapons were still deployed included the Ukraine, Belorussia and Kazakhstan. Boris Yeltsin and other Russian leaders expressed the opinion shortly after the failed coup that all nuclear weapons in the former Soviet Union should eventually be returned to the Russian republic. As of September 1991 strategic nuclear weapons were still deployed outside Russia in three republics of the former Soviet Union: the Ukraine; Belorussia; and Kazakhstan. The forces deployed in the Ukraine and in Kazakhstan amounted to several thousand strategic warheads (ICBMs and bomber bases in each case). In numerical totals, the strategic nuclear weapons of either the Ukraine or Kazakhstan as of September 1991 qualified either republic as a nuclear superpower, having more total nuclear force loadings than Britain, France or China.[38]

Leaders in the Ukrainian parliament and in other non-Russian legislative bodies appeared more interested in becoming 'nuclear-free zones' and in being rid of their nuclear weapons, both strategic and tactical, than they did in acquiring putative superpower status. On the other hand, republican politicians were not slow to recognize that their nuclear holdings created temporary bargaining chips for future dealings with the Russian republic. In late October 1991 Ukrainian leaders restated their preference for making the Ukraine a nuclear-free zone. They also called for talks among the various republican leaderships to establish a joint command for the use of nuclear weapons. One Ukrainian representative in Moscow noted that 'The Ukraine wants to be a nuclear free zone, but the Ukraine understands that this is a long process and it can take a long time'.[39] Earlier in the same month the Ukraine had asserted its authority over some 1.2 million Soviet soldiers deployed on its territory, and its political leadership also asserted a claim to part of the Soviet Navy's Black Sea Fleet. Most ominous for what remained of the central government in Moscow, Ukrainian politicians also announced plans to form a separate national army of almost 500,000 persons.[40]

Ukrainian assertions of the right to form a separate national army drew criticism from Gorbachev, but they pointed to the distrust in the minds of the non-Russian republics over the potential for Russian hegemony, including nuclear intimidation, in the post-coup world. Vladimir Lobov, Chief of the Soviet General Staff, stated on 23 October 1991 that all Soviet nuclear weapons should be based in Russia. Lobov was endorsing the earlier suggestion by Yeltsin to this effect. Lobov gave as one rationale for this recommendation the prevention of nuclear proliferation. Another reason for concentrating all nuclear weapons in Russia, in Lobov's view, was the need to guard against 'unsanctioned use' of nuclear weapons. But Vladimir Grinev, chairman of the Ukrainian parliament, suggested in a newspaper interview in October that the Ukraine could not shrug off responsibility for its 'weapons of mass destruction' by giving them to someone else. Grinev suggested that the four republics with strategic nuclear weapons establish a joint command.[41]

It would make little sense for any of the non-Russian republics of the former Soviet Union to use their nuclear weapons against a foreign nuclear power, even if they were able to gain access to the authentication and unlocking codes necessary to launch strategic nuclear weapons based on their soil. Nor would nuclear weapons be the weapons of choice for fighting a civil war. One can only imagine one potential 'use' for nuclear weapons of strategic range deployed outside of Russia. Republics which feared that they could not deter a future Russian invasion, due to their inferiority in conventional forces, might attempt to nationalize their nuclear weapons and to retain those weapons for use in the role of deterrence by punishment. Here, too, it would be a case of threatening suicide for fear of death, given the lopsided superiority of the Russian republic in long-range nuclear weapons.

A more plausible threat posed by nationalized nuclear forces located in republics outside Russia would have been a threat based on their use of tactical nuclear weapons, before the weapons were 'repatriated' to Russia. These weapons were more widely dispersed throughout the Soviet Union than were strategic nuclear weapons at the time that the Soviet flag was hauled down in favor of Russian sovereignty over the territory and forces of the Russian Federation in late December 1991. Under Cold War Soviet control, armed forces' tactical nuclear weapons were stored separately from their delivery vehicles, such as short-range missiles or artillery, and the storage sites were thought to be guarded by special troops under the jurisdiction of the Ministry of Defense. Sea-based Soviet tactical nuclear weapons, on the other hand, were assumed by expert Western analysts to be deployed already mated with their delivery systems, including torpedoes and cruise missiles. Testimony provided to the House Armed Services Committee suggested that only some of these land- and sea-based tactical nuclear weapons prior to the coup attempt were protected against unauthorized use by Soviet versions of US Permissive Action Links, or PALs.[42]

Several different problems are involved in estimation of the likelihood that unauthorized use of tactical or strategic nuclear weapons could take place in any of the former Soviet republics. These problems include the issues of *authentication*, *enablement* and *physical possession* of nuclear weapons.[43] Although the distinctions are not always carefully made in discussions of US or other developed Western arrangements for nuclear command and control, the distinctions are important to those commanders and operators who are entrusted with the responsibility for preventing accidental or unauthorized use. Authentication refers to procedures and codes which validate the identities of those decision-makers who are authorized to order the use of nuclear weapons on behalf of state policy. Authentication establishes, for example, that it is President Clinton or President Yeltsin who has actually given the political order for nuclear release, and not some pretender. The obvious reason for authentication is to prevent usurpers from ordering into action military forces for other than duly authorized state purposes.

Enablement of nuclear weapons results when the unlocking codes which bypass the electronic or mechanical locks on weapons are provided by higher authorities to field commanders. In theory, no US or Soviet nuclear weapons which were protected by coded locks could be fired by field commanders, terrorists or others who obtained possession of the weapons without knowledge of the unlocking codes. Collusion between field commanders and higher authorities in the armed forces would therefore seem prerequisite for the firing of weapons protected in this way. On the other hand, not all US and Soviet nuclear weapons prior to the coup attempt of August 1991 were so protected by US PALs or by their Soviet equivalents, code interlock devices. It was widely known that US naval nuclear weapons did not carry PALs, although President Bush's tactical denuclearization initiative of 27 September

1991 removed many of these from service. As noted earlier, it was thought that some, but not all, Soviet strategic and shorter range nuclear weapons are protected by electronic or mechanical locks.

There is considerable controversy within the relevant technical communities about how reliable PALs are and under what conditions they might be fallible.[44] In theory, a modern US PAL should disable the weapon after several unsuccessful tries by unauthorized users. In practice, some experts believe that unauthorized persons acquiring a nuclear weapon could sooner or later bypass almost any PAL. This might mean that PALs were tamper proof against renegade officers who would be apprehended well within the time frame of PAL protection by loyal officers. It is less clear that PALs would resist repeated efforts to enable nuclear weapons which were permanently acquired by hostile forces, either terrorists or dissident nationalists.

Therefore, the problem of nuclear enablement relates to the third issue, of possession of one or more weapons by unauthorized potential users. These might be dissidents within the armed forces, or terrorists who seize launchers or storage sites. It takes little imagination to write a scenario for either terrorist or dissident troop seizure of weapons stores or launch vehicles in parts of the former Soviet Union. Possession of weapons does not thereby equip dissidents or terrorists to launch them; the usurpers must still overcome the problems of authentication and enablement. For formerly Soviet strategic nuclear weapons which might fall into unauthorized hands, there is the additional problem that proper targeting information or retargeting capability might not be available to the illegals. A Soviet SS-19 made launch ready illegally by Ukrainians, for example, would not necessarily be usable unless it could be retargeted away from its previously programmed US aimpoints toward Moscow or some other destination in the Russian republic. For this purpose, access to relevant satellite technology, including imagery of the target site, weather and geodesy, would be imperative. Ballistic missiles of strategic (transcontinental) range are designed to fly exoatmospherically on trajectories very different from medium- and short-range missiles. Even if armed by surreptitious collusion between persons who could provide authenticating and enabling codes, ex-Soviet strategic nuclear weapons might still be useless to anyone who wished to employ them for internal war or for deterrence of inter-republican aggression. It would make more sense for Russia's nervous neighbors who sought a strategic deterrent to convert launchers for the delivery of advanced technology conventional weapons.

The agreement by other republics to return former Soviet tactical nuclear weapons to Russia by June 1992 was fortuitous for the preservation of post-Soviet nuclear command and control against nuclear terrorism or against

173

terrorist entrepreneurship. Possession of nuclear weapons by dissidents or terrorists was a serious danger both in terms of immediate and longer term risks. Even if unauthorized users could not promptly enable or launch nuclear weapons, they might learn a great deal about the assembly and security of nuclear weapons by disassembling an illegally acquired version of the technology. Tactical nuclear weapons could, by means of illegal transfer from Russian or other forces, find their way across the borders of the former Soviet Union into rogue state or terrorist hands. As RAND Corporation expert Edward L. Warner III (presently Assistant Secretary of Defense) testified to the House Armed Services Committee in 1991:

> Another chilling prospect that could emerge in the midst of widespread chaos and disorder in the Soviet Union would be the illegal sale of nuclear weapons by disaffected Soviet troops to international terrorist groups or the representatives of foreign nations. A severe breakdown of military discipline at a nuclear weapons storage site might put nuclear weapons on the market much as conventional weapons, including armored fighting vehicles, have already been given or sold to armed national groups over the past year or so.[45]

A report from Les Aspin, Chairman of the US House of Representatives Committee on Armed Services in September 1991 and later Secretary of Defense under Clinton, suggested that 'if civil war were to break out today, the security of the 12,000-plus tactical nuclear weapons in the Soviet Union – kept at hundreds of storage sites, many outside the Russian republic – could be impossible to guarantee'.[46]

The disintegration of the Soviet Union changed the context for negotiating the START (Strategic Arms Reductions) treaties. The START I Treaty was signed by the US and the Soviet Union on the last day of July 1991, and was awaiting ratification when the Soviet Union collapsed five months later. The Lisbon Protocol to START I was signed in May 1992 by the US and the four former Soviet republics, now independent states, with strategic nuclear weapons deployed on their soil: Russia, Belarus, Kazakhstan and the Ukraine. The four former Soviet republics are designated by the protocol as successor states to the Soviet Union for purposes of START. The Protocol also commits Belarus, Kazakhstan and the Ukraine to accede to the Nuclear Non-Proliferation Treaty (NPT) as soon as possible as non-nuclear weapons states. Russian foreign minister Kozyrev noted that, at the end of the seven-year START I implementation period, Russia would expect Belarus, Kazakhstan and the Ukraine to have eliminated all the strategic nuclear delivery vehicles *and* nuclear warheads on their soil.[47] The START II agreement signed by

Presidents Bush and Yeltsin in January 1993 assumes that the strategic nuclear arsenals of the US and Russia will be reduced to the levels of 3,500–3,000 by the year 2003. START allows the contracting parties freedom to choose the order in which their forces are reduced to meet permissible levels: traditionally, older systems have been retired first to preserve newer and more capable systems. Following that criterion strictly in this case might not be as advisable as moving to the head of the list for reductions the strategic nuclear forces outside of Russia.[48] The totals of these forces, as of January 1993, are given in Table 5.2.

TABLE 5.2

FORMER SOVIET UNION STRATEGIC NUCLEAR WEAPONS OUTSIDE OF RUSSIA, JANUARY 1993

Republic	Delivery System	Number of Missile Launchers or Bombers	Warheads
Belarus	SS-25 missile	81	81
			Total = 81
Kazakhstan	SS-18 missile	104	1,040
	Bear-H bomber	40	370
			Total = 1,410
Ukraine	22-24 missile	46	460
	SS-19 missile	130	780
	Bear-H bomber	14	224
	Blackjack bomber	16	192
			Total = 1,656
Totals		431	3,147

Source: Thomas Bernauer, Michele Flournoy, Steven E. Miller and Lee Minichiello, 'Strategic Arms Control and the NPT: Status and Implementation', Ch. 1 in Graham Allison, Ashton B. Carter, Steven E. Miller and Philip Zelikow, *Cooperative Denuclearization: From Pledges to Deeds* (Cambridge, MA: Center for Science and International Affairs, Jan. 1993), p. 31.

To complicate matters further, the initial phase of START II overlaps with the seven-year implementation period for START I. For example, START I requires that the US and CIS eliminate 4,563 and 4,301 warheads respectively during the seven-year treaty implementation period. However, START II requires US reductions of at least 8,492 warheads and CIS reductions of at least 6,792 warheads. START II force limits are to be attained by the year 2003, or by 2000 if the US allocates sufficient funds to expedite Russian force reductions and eliminations. The implementation of START II would lead to the timetable of reductions indicated in Table 5.3.

According to a report of the 21 January 1993 CIS Defense Ministers' meeting, some issues of nuclear ownership between Russia and the Ukraine might remain unresolved even as arms control proceeded. Ukrainian political and military leaders continued to insist that the former Soviet strategic nuclear forces located on Ukrainian territory now belonged to the Ukraine, and not to Russia. Russian President Yeltsin and Ukrainian President Kravchuk agreed in 1992 that Russian specialists would be granted access to nuclear systems located on Ukrainian territory for operational checking, servicing and part replacement. Russia would, according to the same agreements, assume responsibility for Ukrainian nuclear security (presumably this meant security against unauthorized tampering with or seizure of weapons or launchers).[49] Also unresolved was the status of military space forces, including satellite communications systems as part of both CIS and Russian national forces. Regardless of ownership claims, control of strategic forces outside of Russia was said to be shared by the Russian and CIS heads of state and high commands.[50]

TABLE 5.3

TIMETABLE FOR START II FORCE LIMITS

	7 years(START I)	2000–2003
Total Warheads	3,800–4,250	3,000–3,500
MIRV ICBM Warheads	1,200	0
Heavy ICBM Warheads	650	0
SLBM Warheads	2,160	1,750

Source: Thomas Bernauer, et al., 'Strategic Arms Control and the NPT', p.33.

Presidents Yeltsin and Kravchuk met on 24 June 1992, and again on 4 August 1992 in order to resolve issues related to the disposition of the Black Sea Fleet. Pursuant to the 30 December 1991 Minsk meeting of the Commonwealth heads of state, the Ukraine had begun in January 1992 to nationalize and administer Ukrainian armed forces' oaths to military person- nel stationed in the Kiev, Carpathian and Odessa military districts of the former USSR, and to the Black Sea Fleet.[51] Boris Yeltsin moved to create a Russian Ministry of Defense in April 1992, and in doing so declared that the Black Sea Fleet belonged to Russia. The Black Sea Fleet commander was obviously sympathetic to Russia, and he was charged with waging a campaign of fear against officers who sought to take the Ukrainian oath of allegiance.[52] Yeltsin and Kravchuk agreed to dampen this controversy which had become 'heated to the maximum and fraught with "explosive" social potential' by withdrawing the Black Sea Fleet from the command of Russia and Ukraine for three years.[53] A subsequent 1993 agreement yielded the entire fleet to Russia in return for economic concessions to Kiev by Moscow.

The political value of nuclear weapons outside of Russia among the states of the former Soviet Union was that of bargaining chips, and not tantamount to the value of components of a viable nuclear strategic force.[54] Continuation of US–Russian amity and a responsible definition of self-interest by all sides within the CIS would almost certainly lead to denuclearization outside of Russia. The Soviet political disintegration had fortunately not led to a military disintegration of the nuclear command and control system, for a variety of reasons.[55] Among those reasons were the experiences and expectations of mature Soviet and Russian military establishments, who had learned that stable and secure nuclear command and control was a necessary component of international and internal political stability regardless of the shifting sands of internal politics.

The breakup of the Soviet Union was a dramatic lesson about the political disutility of nuclear weapons. Touted as the exemplary instruments for accomplishing strategic coercion without actually engaging in a war, nuclear weapons became, in the hands of a disintegrating empire, potential fuses for an outbreak of accidental or inadvertent war. The presumption that the nuclear sword would always be held by a politically accountable government and a militarily sophisticated brain could no longer be taken for granted in the post-Cold War Eurasian world. A sleeping expert and lay community on arms control was rudely awakened from nuclear complacency in August 1991. Although everyone knew that nuclear weapons were highly destructive, no one anticipated a situation of complete political dissolution in an imperial state which was still capable of historically unprecedented, and globally unacceptable, damage.

Not all experts are as pessimistic about nuclear proliferation, even within the former Soviet Union. John J. Mearsheimer contends that the United States should have encouraged the Ukraine to remain a strategic nuclear power, based on the force it inherited in the breakup of the former Soviet Union.[56] Mearsheimer relies on the logic of deterrence as it appeared to most US officials and analysts during the Cold War years: nuclear weapons are a more secure deterrent than conventional weapons. A race between Russia and the Ukraine in conventional military power is much more likely to result in war than is a Ukrainian nuclear deterrent. Mearsheimer's suggestion is that a secure Ukrainian deterrent which could inflict a hundred warheads or so against Russia after a surprise first strike would be sufficient to deter Russian military adventurism. This logic is consistent within the Cold War deterrence paradigm, but stability was *over-determined* during the Cold War by a bipolar international system, by offsetting asymmetries in US and Soviet conventional land and sea power, and by the nuclear learning about crisis management

177

which took place during the first decades of the atomic age, especially between 1949 and 1963.[57] The last point is crucial: the nuclear learning could take place because both the US and the Soviet Union had time to develop the nuclear command and control systems which could, each in its own way, balance the 'always' and 'never' requirements for authorized nuclear use.

Had a serious crisis been in progress between the Soviet Union and one of its political adversaries in August 1991, the coup and its aftermath might have turned out differently. In addition, the Russian perspective on national defense remains one of siege, created by new friends and old enemies as well as former Soviet republics whose own concerns about Russian imperialism have some historical justification. The Yeltsin regime in Russia, after it assumed most of the former Soviet military mission for state defense, declared for a course of continued political rapprochement and military détente. Denuclearization was part of this perspective, with some understandable reluctance from military quarters. Nevertheless, the August 1991 failed coup and subsequent Russian power struggles attest to the good fortune that habits of nuclear command and control held over from the Cold War years trans-ferred from the older world to the newer. It was also fortunate that no political confrontation between the Soviet Union or Russia and NATO, China or Japan was taking place during the transition from empire to aspiring demo-cracy.

The preceding point is important because some have argued that it was nuclear weapons which prevented Soviet military adventurism at the time of the failed coup and Russian adventurism thereafter. Without nuclear weapons to complicate matters, it might be thought, the former Soviet armed forces could have afforded to bring about an East–West crisis in order to defuse internal opposition and to justify the continuing rule of the emergency committee of August 1991. Perhaps in a world in which nuclear technology was unknown, and nuclear weapons had never been invented, the point has some logic. On the other hand, leaders cannot return to this kind of nuclear innocence, and large arsenals, once assembled, become themselves important political symbols of international status. If US and Russian arms reductions now seem like potlatch in reverse, it is only because their Cold War experience permitted survival through learning that aggressive nuclear exploitation of crisis bargaining was better in theory than in practice.

PRAETORIANS AND THE FUTURE OF BRINKMANSHIP

If the preceding section offers a reasonable prognosis, the unsettled political situation in the former Soviet Union will probably resolve itself against any serious risk of accidental or unauthorized nuclear use. The controllability of nuclear forces and the propensity for nuclear brinkmanship, in aspiring or existing polities outside of Europe and North America, offers a scene of somewhat greater indeterminacy. States with regional ambitions, undemocratic regimes and delivery vehicles for weapons of mass destruction also aspire to join the nuclear club. Some of these states have already attempted coercive diplomacy through brinkmanship against regional rivals, and one refused to blink in the face of US and allied compulsion in 1990, forcing a war.

During the Iran–Iraq war of the 1980s, the two sides used ballistic missiles for terror attacks against one another's urban areas in their 'war of the cities'. Current third world ballistic missiles armed with conventional warheads are not as efficient for destroying military targets with high accuracy as are aircraft. Aircraft can carry larger payloads over longer distances. But ballistic and cruise missiles have other attributes which may make those missiles attractive to future third world users. Ballistic missiles have a short time from launch to detonation and would not be detected by most air defenses. Ballistic missile defenses are not indigenous to the third world and the technology would have to be imported from the US, Russia or other countries with research and development programs for theater missile defense. Conventionally armed cruise missiles would lack speed comparable to that of ballistic missiles, but cruise missiles could be given sufficiently small radar cross sections to evade most air defenses now available to countries outside of Europe and North America.[58]

Regional antagonisms provide opportunities for the use of third world ballistic missile forces as part of crisis or wartime coercive bargaining strategies, including brinkmanship strategies. Five states which are candidate belligerents in a future war against Israel, for example, now have ballistic missiles of various ranges: Iran; Syria; Saudi Arabia; Libya; and Iraq.[59] As a result of the Gulf War of 1991, Iraq is under UN supervision with regard to its weapons of mass destruction and delivery vehicles for those weapons. Saudi Arabia fought in the conflict on the side of the UN coalition. Israel stayed out of the war. In any future Arab–Israeli conflict, these alignments would be very different. Thus Israel must focus its contingency planning on the capabilities of potential opponents, including their capabilities for delivery of chemical weapons by ballistic missiles. Chemical attacks on Israel's largest cities could change the political character of a war even if those attacks did not materially affect the fighting power of the IDF. The Chinese CSS-2 missiles sold to Saudi Arabia have a range of 1,600 to 1,860 miles delivering a payload of 4,500 pounds. Syria as of 1991 had Soviet-supplied Frog-7, Scud-B and SS-21 short-range ballistic missiles capable of delivering a thousand pound payload over distances of 40, 190 and 75 miles respectively.[60] Israel has domestically produced the Jericho I and Jericho II ballistic missiles with approximate ranges of 400 and 900 miles, and the potential exists for Israel to convert its Shavit three-stage rocket for satellite launch to a ballistic missile with ranges from 1,500 to 2,200 miles.[61]

The spread of ballistic missiles in the Middle East is combined with unstable political factors, including military praetorianism and regional hostilities. Iraq and Syria remain as 'republican' governments in which military support for Ba'athist party leadership is absolutely decisive. Israel's small territory means that even short-range ballistic missiles launched from Syria or Iraq can reach vital centers of population and industry. A pre-emptive Syrian missile attack on Israel's major cities could undermine Tel Aviv's doctrine of limiting damage by moving any conflict promptly into the opponent's territory by means of Israeli counteroffensive or pre-emptive strikes. Israeli military planners might also worry that Syrian missile attacks could disable airfields and destroy Israel's air defense envelope during the initial period of war. Israel has in past wars depended on its air superiority, especially in the first hours of war, to prepare the way for its ground forces counteroffensives leading to decisive victory over Arab adversaries.[62]

The potential for a relationship between praetorianism and pre-emption is mediated by variables other than military capabilities and regional political hostilities. Among these variables, the quality of the politico-military command and control systems of the various regional powers and aspiring hegemons is highly significant. Potential third world disputants with ballistic missiles and potential access to weapons of mass destruction, including nuclear weapons, include Israel, Iraq, Syria, Iran, Pakistan, India, and North and South Korea. Among these states, only India and Israel are representative democracies or civic polities. India is the only acknowledged nuclear power among these states, but analysts generally credit Israel with the possession of 100 or more nuclear weapons.[63] The short distances between the capital cities or major military installations of third world states that may acquire nuclear weapons allows little time in many scenarios for a delayed and considered reaction to plausible threats. Table 5.4 summarizes the distribution of third world ballistic missiles and weapons of mass destruction.

Experts now admit, in the aftermath of the Gulf War of 1991 and other revelations, that the problem of detecting unacknowledged nuclear weapons production is more challenging than ever before. Approaches to the detection of secret nuclear activities take two paths. The first path is the International Atomic Energy Agency (IAEA) safeguards system, using on-site inspections of suspect facilities and other techniques. The second path is the evidence collected by US and other intelligence agencies through a variety of technical and other means, including communications intercepts, satellite photography and human intelligence. When the Nuclear Non-proliferation Treaty entered into force in 1970, these two approaches were judged to be sufficient. In addition, so little civilian plutonium or highly enriched uranium was in circulation that inspectors assumed a country would have to conduct a full scale nuclear test in order to be a nuclear power.[64] The almost completed Iraqi nuclear weapons capability of the 1980s showed that the IAEA and Western intelligence agencies could not always detect incipient nuclear activities. And the nuclear programs of Pakistan and South Africa showed that it was not necessary to conduct full-scale tests in order to become a nuclear armed state.[65] Table 5.5 summarizes international inspection agency knowledge of formerly secret nuclear production plants.

TABLE 5.4

THIRD WORLD BALLISTIC MISSILES AND WEAPONS OF MASS DESTRUCTION:
COUNTRIES EQUIPPED OR ATTEMPTING TO ACQUIRE

Country	Ballistic Missiles	Nuclear Weapons	Chemical Weapons	Biological Weapons
Afghanistan	yes			
Algeria	yes			
Argentina	yes	possible	possible	
Brazil	yes	possible		
Burma			likely	
Cuba	yes		possible	
Egypt	yes		likely	
Ethiopia			likely	
India	yes	yes	likely	
Indonesia	planned		possible	
Iran	yes	possible	likely	
Iraq	yes	possible*	yes	likely
Israel	yes	yes	likely	
Korea (North)	yes	possible	likely	likely
Korea (South)	yes		likely	
Kuwait	yes			
Libya	yes	possible	likely	
Pakistan	yes	likely	likely	
Saudi Arabia	yes		possible	
South Africa	yes	unlikely**	possible	
Syria	yes		likely	likely
Taiwan	yes		likely	likely
Thailand	possible		possible	
Vietnam	possible		likely	
Yemen	yes			

* Iraq's nuclear capability was largely if not entirely demolished by the Gulf war of 1991.
** This judgment disagrees with the source for this table, which judged South Africa likely in this category.

Source: Steve Fetter, 'Ballistic Missiles and Weapons of Mass Destruction', *International Security*, No. 1 (Summer 1991), p. 14.

181

Table 5.5 lists nuclear production plants as 'secret' in the sense that they were not officially acknowledged as such until some time after they had been established by their respective governments. As indicated in the table, there are two approaches available to a state which chooses to make its own nuclear weapons: uranium enrichment or plutonium separation. One might suppose that the large investments, personnel and infrastructure necessary for a state to go either route to nuclear status could not go undetected. But several cases remind us that the ability to detect cheating (on the part of non-nuclear signatories to the Nuclear Non-proliferation Treaty) or unacknowledged

TABLE 5.5

SECRET NUCLEAR PRODUCTION PLANTS

	Technology	Plant	When Revealed	How Revealed
Argentina	Gaseous diffusion	Pilcaniyeu	1983	Announced
	Plutonium separation	Ezeiza	1978	Announced
Brazil	Centrifuge	IPEN	early 1980	Intelligence
	Centrifuge	Aramar	mid-1980s	Announced
Iraq	Calutrons	Tuwaitha	1991	Defector/Inspection
	Calutrons	Tarmiya	1991	Defector/Inspection
	Centrifuge	Tuwaitha	mid-1980s	Iraqi declaration
	Centrifuge	Rashidiya	1992	Defector/Inspection
	Centrifuge	Al Furat	1991	Iraqi declaration
	Plutonium separation	Tuwaitha	1991	Inspection/Declaration
India	Plutonium separation	Trombay	1950s	Announced
	Centrifuge	Trombay	1980s	Announced
	Centrifuge	Mysore	mid-1980s	Intelligence
Israel	Reactor	Dimona	late 1950s	US intelligence
	Plutonium separation	Dimona	1960s	US intelligence
North Korea	Reactor	Yongbyon	1984	Intelligence
	Plutonium separation	Pyongyang	1992	IAEA Inspection
	Plutonium separation	Yongbyon	late 1980s	Intelligence
Pakistan	Centrifuge	Kahuta	late 1970s	Intelligence
South Africa	Aerodynamic separation	Valindaba	1970	Announced

Source: Condensed from David Albright, 'A Proliferation Primer', *Bulletin of the Atomic Scientists*, June 1993, p.17.

nuclear production is very contingent. Investigators may find only what they have been looking for. Much about the Iraqi programs to develop weapons of mass destruction during the 1980s escaped international intelligence agencies and export controls, among other reasons, because 'Western governments did not aggressively pursue leads about Iraqi nuclear efforts or seriously impede Iraq's nuclear program during the 1980s'.[66]

It is now clear, as a result of the Gulf War of 1991, that Iraq was working toward the eventual deployment of nuclear weapons, and Iraq's attacks on Israeli cities during that war with conventionally armed Scud ballistic missiles showed the potential danger of short flight times combined with high destructive potential. Although the US Patriot theater missile defenses system provided some capability for deflecting Iraq's Scud attacks, against a nuclear-armed ballistic missile Patriots or similar technologies would be unable to limit destruction to acceptable levels. The US interest in the Bush version of SDI, or GPALS (Global Protection Against Limited Strikes), is motivated in part by the desire to have near term deployment options for the protection of allied territory in the Middle East or in Europe against nuclear attacks from rogue states. In terms of the problem of brinkmanship as discussed here, highly competent theater defenses might prevent coercion of US allies by aspiring hegemons or other aggressors who possessed small nuclear forces.

The problem of command and control for third world nuclear forces is twofold. First, it is not clear that the forces or the command systems of nuclear-armed states outside of Europe will be survivable against even small first strikes. Thus, the forces and command systems may invite attacks on themselves in a crisis. Second, the 'ownership' of the nuclear forces may not be clear, or, if clear, may not be accountable to duly constituted civilian authority. The nuclear command and control system for North Korea or Pakistan has not yet emerged. But it is not inconceivable that the safeguards against accidental launch or mistaken pre-emption would be less competent than those which the US and the Soviet Union have developed through decades of experience. Command and control systems of third world states may be designed to emphasize 'fail deadly' procedures more than they are built on 'fail safe' assumptions, and this decision might be reasonable from a military-technical standpoint. The short flight times of ballistic missiles to intended targets and the uncertain state of warning and assessment capabilities could lead to threat assessment which was highly susceptible to crisis inflation.

Pessimistic threat assessment would be all the more likely in cases where the military institutions themselves would be threatened with public humiliation and disgrace, or prompt destruction, for a mistaken 'don't launch' decision. Military rulers who identified their military corporate status with the fate of the state itself could be prompted by ambiguous indicators to launch 'on warning' or 'under attack', given a reasonable expectation that failure in prompt retaliatory launch would prevent any coherent retaliation. Even for the US and other powers experienced in the operation of nuclear forces, the problem of launch 'under attack' poses strains for the command system. US officials have repeatedly stated in public testimony that the deterrent does not *depend* on a launch under attack or on warning option. But they have also refused to rule out this option as a possible response. Testifying in 1979 on the requirements for US nuclear warning and attack assessment systems, US Air Force General Thomas Stafford, then Deputy Chief of Staff for Research, Development and Acquisition, explained that additional minutes of warning might be crucial for the execution of certain retaliatory missions. According to Stafford, 'the difference is if you know specifically [deleted] is under attack, there is no doubt that they are attacking high value really non-military targets [deleted] and the response of our forces would be different than if they were attacking only military targets.'[67] Stafford's reference to high value, other than military targets was to command and control targets, especially to the national command authority. The implication is that procedures for devolution of authority would be activated as rapidly as possible in the event that prompt threats to the US national command authority were detected.

Small nuclear forces might be vulnerable not only to nuclear pre-emption but to pre-emptive attack without nuclear weapons. The US and its allies demonstrated in the Gulf War that a potential nuclear capability could be subjected to devastating attacks by means of conventional, high-precision weapons. The long range delivery of precision-guided munitions has been demonstrated in the technology of the cruise missile. Ballistic missile re-entry systems could be made accurate enough to destroy some targets previously reserved for nuclear destruction, thereby avoiding the collateral damage attendant to nuclear strikes.[68] Some Bush Pentagon planners touted small, low-yield miniature nuclear weapons as substitutes for the larger and more destructive weapons of this type. But even smaller nuclear weapons cannot get away from the negative symbolism attached to nuclear first use, and improvements in reconnaissance, communications and precision aiming already available to US planners, or those soon foreseeable, should make the use of any nuclear weapons irrelevant for any missions other than deterrence of nuclear attack.[69] However, not all states can afford the advanced technologies required for high technology conventional munitions, delivery systems and the command and control which is associated with those technologies and systems. Nuclear weapons might be more appealing to some of those states as a means of rapid transition into a favorable position from which to coerce regional allies.

Pre-emption-prone praetorians could appear not only in the developing societies of Asia, Africa and the Middle East, but also within the 'common European home' stretching from the Atlantic to the Urals.[70] Praetorianism in post-Cold War Europe would not necessarily take the form of coups by juntas against civilian governments accused of political corruption, inept performance or ideological incorrectness.[71] Amos Perlmutter has identified three general types of military organization produced by modern nation states. Each of these three types represents a different kind of reaction to the quality of civilian political institutions. In stable political systems, the classical 'professional soldier' predominates. In an environment of political instability, the praetorian soldier assumes increased importance. Revolutions produce a soldier whose expertise is oriented to socio-political values and whose client is a revolutionary party-movement (out of power) or party-state (once in power).[72] According to Perlmutter, each of these three types of military perspective is a form of military corporate professionalism, although the revolutionary soldier is essentially non-corporate and frequently anti-corporate in his professional orientation. The corporate or organizational perspective of professional soldiers is the strongest predictor of their political behavior, in his view.[73]

There is considerable consensus among students of praetorianism that civil institutions which have undergone loss of political legitimacy are ripe for military overthrow. Samuel P. Huntington has discussed praetorianism as a product of the relationship between the rate of social mobilization (including political participation) and the development of political institutionalization. In his *Political Order in Changing Societies*, Huntington described a praetorian political system as any system lacking cohesive and authoritative institutions for interest articulation and aggregation, and also deficient in legitimacy based on shared political values and expectations between leaders and followers.[74] A condition of political normlessness results from a gap between political institutionalization, or the capacity of political institutions to process inputs into acceptable outputs, and political participation. As this gap becomes larger, civil institutions are unable to make authoritative decisions and to resolve the diverse and conflicting claims of interest groups. Civilians strike and riot to get what they want; military officers who fear for their corporate or organizational interest engage in coups.

Following the demise of the Soviet contiguous empire in Eastern and Central Europe, it cannot be taken for granted that civil institutions in those states will acquire democratically based support and a sense of legitimacy

185

necessary to withstand praetorianism. In one sense, the former Warsaw Pact states underwent 'imposed praetorianism' when they were occupied by Soviet forces after the Second World War and required to follow Moscow's political line for decades thereafter. The Polish self-invasion against Solidarity in the early 1980s may represent a nationalist-conservative form of praetorianism, deliberately undertaken by President Jaruzelski and his colleagues in order to forestall direct Soviet intervention. Having gone through its own period of praetorianism Poland may be better able than other former Warsaw Pact states to develop strong political parties and a sense of democratic constitutional legitimacy.[75] Jack Snyder has suggested that within a neo-liberal institutional framework, three patterns of pluralistic politics – civic democracy, praetorianism and corporatism – offer useful categories for analysis of the possible futures for former Soviet bloc states. Civic polities are marked by mature electoral competition among parties which contest for the allegiance of the largest numbers of voters in the middle of the political spectrum. In democratic corporatism, most of the important interests in a society are included in an umbrella coalition within which key political trade-offs are arranged. Either democratic corporatism or civic polities allow for interest articulation and aggregation without the destructive pattern of praetorianism, in which naked competition among groups and classes is not mediated by any authoritative and legitimate civil institutions.[76]

The connection between praetorianism and proliferation in Europe after the Cold War requires more than the collapse or incapacity of civic institutions. It also requires incompatible political objectives among states in east, central or southern Europe for which states are willing to fight, or threat perceptions which appear to justify states' decisions to arm themselves with weapons of mass destruction.[77] The initiatives by French and German leaders in 1991 to create a Franco-German military force which might serve as the nucleus of a future European army, exclusive of NATO, represented one form of response to uncertainty about future stability in Europe. A Euroforce would provide for the contingency of US virtual or total withdrawal from post-Cold War Europe. It would also offer to contain the aspirations Germans might otherwise have for military autonomy outside of NATO, including a national nuclear force. There is the obvious parallel in the minds of leaders in Paris and Bonn with Jean Monnet's approach to European economic union after the Second World War. By linking the economies of France and Germany within the framework of the European Coal and Steel Community, and later within the European Economic Community or Common Market, postwar Europeanists used transnational economic ties to create political expectations of a security community.

The division of Germany and the inclusion of West Germany in NATO served to constrain German military autonomy during the Cold War years. The reunification of Germany and the possible eclipse of NATO in Europe open the door to new security arrangements that include existing NATO, former Warsaw Pact and non-aligned states. The Conference on Security and Cooperation in Europe (CSCE) is the obvious candidate as a broader forum for creating confidence-building measures to forestall military buildups and to expose interest in offensive military doctrines. The Western European Union might provide an alternative forum for joint European military planning, either for a European pillar within NATO or for a European force constituted without NATO. US officials shudder at the thought that NATO could follow the Warsaw Pact into historical obsolescence, but the more important issue is what follows NATO. If a power vacuum in Europe which invites exploitation by aggressive nationalism, irredentism or other anti-stability forces results from the deconstruction of NATO, peace between the Atlantic and the Urals will be at risk.

On the other hand, many scholars think that peace in Europe after the Cold War is threatened less by aggression from sources external to Europe than it is by sources within the common European home. The transformation of NATO into a looser security guaranty from North America to Western Europe is not incompatible with this widely held vision that internal, not external, threats to Europe are most likely to jeopardize peace. The US could maintain an over-the-horizon presence outside of Europe by means of America's uncontested maritime power and nuclear weapons, even at greatly reduced levels of nuclear arms. Of course, this solution does not provide an answer to the questions: 'What do we do about Yugoslavia in 1993, or about the possible disintegration of the Russian Federation in 1994?' NATO, however, might not be the body best constituted to answer this question, or to do anything about it if preventive diplomacy or military intervention are called for.

The connection between praetorianism and proliferation, of nuclear or other weapons of mass destruction, is not automatic in Europe or anywhere else. Options available to the US and other countries seeking to restrain proliferation include deterrence and arms control, preventive diplomacy or military intervention, and the providing of forums for the resolution of unrequited territorial or other claims between hostile and heavily armed neighbors.[78] With or without NATO, Europeans fearful of threats to stability generated within or outside of Europe have options to impose constraints on praetorian proliferators. Equally important, however, is the acknowledgment that stability is not all of one piece. Stability at any price is not what Europeans

187

really want; the stability of the Cold War years was purchased for costs that the citizens of Poland, Hungary, East Germany, Czechoslovakia, Romania and Bulgaria did not choose to pay.

Whether proliferation is highly correlated with praetorianism or not, substantial Cold War evidence and the initial phases of the post-Cold War world do not offer much support for neorealist arguments sympathetic to 'well managed' nuclear proliferation.[79] Even if we assume that those non-nuclear states that acquire nuclear forces in the next two decades or so have politically accountable militaries, reliable command and control systems and survivable weapons, it does not follow that nuclear weapons spread dissuades putative attackers and strengthens the resolve of defenders. Nuclear weapons of the Cold War were not born into military strategies supportive of the geopolitical status quo. The symbiosis between weapons of mass destruction and the political stabilization of US–Soviet relations was gradually worked out through peacetime diplomacy, including arms negotiations, and crisis driven learning experiences. Will time and circumstances permit this luxury of learning curve again?

CONCLUSIONS

The combination of praetorian political systems and mature weapons tech-nologies poses potential risks to international political stability. One of the most important is the likelihood that unstable or illegitimate military govern-ments will engage in risky bargaining tactics based on new arsenals of unprecedented lethality. Although Cold War history may suggest to some that the strategy of brinkmanship worked to US or to Soviet advantage at various stages of their political and military competition, the image is misleading for future imitators of US and Soviet good fortune. In fact, US–Soviet confronta-tions during the Cold War years were notable for the lack of confidence leaders had in nuclear brinkmanship and risky bargaining tactics. Leaders in Washington and Moscow embraced brinkmanship warily while improvising ways around it in the most important crises of the Cold War years, including the Berlin crisis of 1961 and the Cuban missile crisis of 1962.

The finding that, in two of the most important crises of the Cold War, leaders sought to pull back from the brink instead of toward it has implications for neorealist and other arguments on behalf of a permissive proliferationism after Cold War. Since nuclear weapons are thought to favor the defense and to discourage putative attackers from adventurism, the spread of nuclear weapons to defensively minded states might support stability more than denuclearization would. This argument is clever, but wrongheaded. It ignores

188

the reality that new nuclear states of the next century will not experience the crisis-taught lessons about the risks of nuclear coercion, nor will their governments necessarily be in the hands of accountable civilians and obedient militaries. Granted that there has been some overselling of non-proliferation as an end in itself by its most boisterous partisans. But it remains the case that neither the 'internals' nor the 'externals' of nuclear accountability, as the case of the former Soviet Union shows, provide reassurance in favor of nuclear multiplicity.

NOTES

The author gratefully acknowledges Peter D. Feaver, Raymond Garthoff and Andrew J. Goodpaster for comments on earlier drafts or pertinent references and suggestions on this topic. They bear no responsibility for arguments or opinions.

1. For a discussion of brinkmanship in historical context, see Richard Ned Lebow, *Between Peace and War: The Nature of International Crisis* (Baltimore, MD: Johns Hopkins University Press, 1981), pp.57–100. See also Thomas C. Schelling, *Arms and Influence* (New Haven: Yale University Press, 1966), pp.99–105. Lebow denotes brinkmanship crises as those crises in which a state knowingly challenges an important commitment of another state with the expectation that the second state will yield to pressure (Lebow, *Between Peace and War*, p.57), and he studies 13 of these between Fashoda (1898) and the Arab–Israeli crisis of 1967. On US experience with nuclear brinkmanship during the Cold War, see Richard K. Betts, *Nuclear Blackmail and Nuclear Balance* (Washington, DC: Brookings Institution, 1987).
2. On the various contemporary and subsequent Soviet judgments about the Cuban missile crisis (Caribbean crisis), see Raymond L. Garthoff, *Reflections on the Cuban Missile Crisis*, 2nd edn (Washington, DC: Brookings Institution, 1989), pp.154–92. For the views of diverse US participants in Cuban missile crisis decision-making, see James G. Blight and David A. Welch, *On the Brink: Americans and Soviets Reexamine the Cuban Missile Crisis* (New York: Hill and Wang, 1989).
3. Michel Tatu, *Power in the Kremlin: From Khrushchev to Kosygin* (New York: Viking Press, 1968), pp.229–33.
4. Described in Blight and Welch, *On the Brink, passim.*
5. Ibid., p.116.
6. Ibid., p.123.
7. Ibid., p.124–5.
8. Ibid., p.114.
9. On the concept of extended deterrence, see Paul K. Huth, *Extended Deterrence and the Prevention of War* (New Haven, CT: Yale University Press, 1988), pp.15–18.
10. For development of this point, see Richard K. Betts, *Nuclear Blackmail and Nuclear Balance* (Washington, DC: Brookings Institution, 1987), pp.92–108.
11. Nitze quoted in ibid., p.104.
12. Ibid., p.92. For additional background and analysis on the Berlin crisis, see Trachtenberg, *History and Strategy*, pp.169–234.
13. Raymond L. Garthoff, 'Berlin 1961: The Record Corrected', *Foreign Policy*, Fall 1991, pp.142–56.
14. Ibid., p.144.

15. Ibid., pp.144–5.
16. Ibid., p.148.
17. Ibid., p.151.
18. Kennedy's sensitivity to the implications of public diplomacy for inferences about military power was evident in his handling of the Cuban missile crisis. The relevant episodes are noted in Graham T. Allison, *Essence of Decision: Explaining the Cuban Missile Crisis* (Boston: Little, Brown, 1971).
19. Garthoff, 'Berlin 1961', p.152.
20. Sources for this discussion are Scott D. Sagan, *Moving Targets: Nuclear Strategy and National Security* (Princeton, NJ: Princeton University Press, 1989), pp.145–8, and Garthoff, *Reflections on the Cuban Missile Crisis*, pp.63–5, 82–9.
21. Sagan, *Moving Targets*, p.147.
22. Garthoff, *Reflections on the Cuban Missile Crisis*, p.89, n. 154.
23. Sagan, *Moving Targets*, p.147; Garthoff, *Reflections on the Cuban Missile Crisis*, p.89.
24. Garthoff, *Reflections on the Cuban Missile Crisis*, pp.89–90.
25. Sagan, *Moving Targets*, pp.147–8.
26. For a resume of the US speculations, see Garthoff, *Reflections on the Cuban Missile Crisis*, p.82.
27. Ibid., pp.84–5.
28. Ibid., p.84.
29. Raymond L. Garthoff, 'The Havana Conference on the Cuban Missile Crisis', *Cold War International History Project Bulletin*, No.1 (Spring, 1992), pp.2–4.
30. Ibid., pp.2–3.
31. On Soviet nuclear command and control see Bruce G. Blair, *The Logic of Accidental Nuclear War* (Washington, DC: Brookings Institution, 1993); Stephen M. Meyer, 'Soviet Perspectives on the Paths to Nuclear War', Ch.7 in Graham T. Allison, Albert Carnesale and Joseph S. Nye, Jr. (eds), *Hawks, Doves and Owls; An Agenda for Avoiding Nuclear War* (New York: W.W. Norton, 1985), pp.197–205; and Meyer, 'Soviet Nuclear Operations', Ch.15 in Carter, Steinbruner and Zraket (eds), *Managing Nuclear Operations*, pp.470–534. Additional and more recent information pertinent to Soviet nuclear strategy and expectations about limiting or controlling major war appears in Garthoff, *Deterrence and the Revolution in Soviet Military Doctrine* (Washington, DC: Brookings Institution, 1990), Ch.5.
32. For informative views on these points, see William C. Green and Theodore Karasik (eds), *Gorbachev and His Generals: The Reform of Soviet Military Doctrine* (Boulder, CO: Westview Press, 1990).
33. This subject is well covered in Les Aspin, Chairman, House Armed Services Committee, *A New Kind of Threat: Nuclear Weapons in an Uncertain Soviet Union*, White Paper (Washington, DC: House Armed Services Committee, 12 September 1991). The committee study drew from expert testimony, including statements by Bruce G. Blair, Brookings Institution, and Edward L. Warner III, RAND Corporation.
34. Blair, cited in 'Nuclear Arsenal as Safe as Ever, Experts Say', *Washington Post*, 20 August 1991.
35. Aspin, *A New Kind of Threat*, p.5.
36. According to some reports, Gen. Mikhail Moiseiev, Chief of the Soviet Armed Forces General Staff during the attempted coup period, for several hours had in his possession all necessary codes for launching a nuclear attack. One set of codes was seized from Gorbachev at his vacation home in the Crimea on the first day of the coup. This set of codes was then taken to the Defense Ministry in Moscow. Since the other two sets of codes were presumably authorized for Defense Minister Dmitri Yazov and Moiseiev, the defense minister and the chief of staff acting together possessed all necessary codes for nuclear release. Yazov was among the coup plotters; Moiseiev's role is less clear. When Yazov on 2 August went to the Crimea with other coup plotters to meet with Gorbachev, Moiseiev would apparently have held all three sets of codes. *Philadelphia Inquirer*, 10 Nov. 1991, p.16-A. Possession of the

codes would not have sufficed to authorize nuclear release if authentication procedures included biophysical authentication of leaders, such as Gorbachev's palm print or a retinal scan, as some accounts have suggested.

37. Aspin, *A New Kind of Threat*, p. 4.
38. Ibid.
39. *Philadelphia Inquirer*, 21 Oct. 1991, p. 12–A.
40. Ibid.
41. Ibid.
42. Aspin, *A New Kind of Threat*, p. 6. I am grateful to Bruce Blair and Peter Feaver for clarifying pertinent issues here.
43. See Peter Douglas Feaver, *Guarding the Guardians: Civilian Control of Nuclear Weapons in the United States* (Ithaca, NY: Cornell University Press, 1992), p. 38, on the distinction between authenticating and enabling codes.
44. See Peter Stein and Peter Feaver, *Assuring Control of Nuclear Weapons: The Evolution of Permissive Action Links* (Lanham, MD: University Press of America, 1987), and Feaver, *Guarding the Guardians*, p. 17.
45. Edward L. Warner III, testimony to the House Armed Services Committee, cited in Aspin, *A New Kind of Threat*, p. 6.
46. Aspin, *A New Kind of Threat*, p. 6. Stephen M. Meyer, professor and director of the Soviet studies research center at MIT and an expert on Soviet nuclear command and control, testified to Aspin's committee that in the event that some military units obtained access to tactical nuclear weapons and decided to oppose the regime, 'that could be interesting'. *Washington Post*, 20 August, 1991.
47. 'Written statement by the Russian Side at the Signing of the Protocol to the START Treaty on 23 May 1992 in Lisbon', cited in Thomas Bernauer, Michele Flournoy, Steven E. Miller and Lee Minichiello, 'Strategic Arms Control and the NPT: Status and Implementation', Ch. 1 in Graham Allison, Ashton B. Carter, Steven E. Miller and Philip Zelikow (eds), *Cooperative Denuclearization: From Pledges to Deeds* (Cambridge, MA: Center for Science and International Affairs, Harvard University, Jan. 1993), p. 54.
48. Ibid., pp. 31–2.
49. See comments by Russian Defense Minister Pavel Grachev on 21 Jan. 1993 Defense Ministers' Council Session, *Krasnaya zvezda*, 23 Jan. 1993, p. 1, JPRS-UMA-93-004, 3 Feb. 1993, p. 10.
50. Philip Zelikow, 'Ownership and Control over CIS Nuclear Forces', Appendix 1-E in Bernauer, *et al.*, 'Strategic Arms Control and the NPT', pp. 72–8.
51. Lt. Col. (Ret.) Vladimir Lartsev, 'For the Sake of Our Ukrainian Homeland's Security', *Narodna armiya* (Kiev), 17 Oct. 1992, pp. 2–3, JPRS-UMA-93-006, 24 Feb. 1993, pp. 53–7.
52. Ibid., p. 56.
53. Text of agreement between Russia and Ukraine on the Black Sea Fleet, *Morskoi sbornik*, No. 10 (Oct. 1992), pp. 17–18, JPRS-UMA-93–006, 24 Feb. 1993, pp. 32–3. See especially Articles 2 and 3. The Presidents of Russia and the Ukraine were designated as joint commanders of the fleet during a transitional period. Manpower acquisition during this period divided conscripts from Russia and the Ukraine in equal proportion (50 per cent for each state), with each conscript taking the oath of his respective state. In autumn 1993 Ukraine conceded the entire Black Sea Fleet to Russia.
54. This is clearly not the view of some Ukrainian military commanders and political leaders. Col. Vladimir Ivanovich Tereshchenko, chief of the Missile and Artillery Troops Directorate of the Main Staff, Ukrainian Armed Forces, noted in an interview in Nov. 1992 that 'the Missile and Artillery Troops are an independent combat arm waging combat and are not supplementing someone. That means we need the appropriate command and control of this combat arm from bottom to top.' Interview with Col. Tereshchenko in *Narodna armiya* (Kiev), 5 Nov. 1992, p. 1, JPRS-UMA-93–006, 24 Feb. 1993, p. 51.
55. Not all anomalies in the command and control of CIS nuclear forces have been resolved. For

example, the Ukrainian government announced in Nov. 1992 that 'Ukraine has neither direct nor indirect control over the nuclear charges of the Strategic Forces and has no intention to control them'. On the other hand, Ukrainian President Kravchuk is alleged to have publicly declared: 'I am able, from a juridical and administrative point of view, to prevent the Ukrainian missiles from being launched, even if Yeltsin and General [sic] Shaposhnikov, commander of the CIS strategic forces, wanted to push their button in Moscow.' Cited in Zelikow, 'Ownership and Control over CIS Nuclear Forces', p. 74.

56. John J. Mearsheimer, 'The Case for a Ukrainian Nuclear Deterrent', *Foreign Affairs*, No. 3 (Summer 1993), pp. 50–66.

57. See especially, on this point, Michael R. Beschloss, *The Crisis Years: Kennedy and Khrushchev, 1960–1963* (New York: Harper Collins, 1991). For other arguments against proliferation within the former Soviet Union, see Steven E. Miller, 'The Case Against a Ukrainian Nuclear Deterrent', *Foreign Affairs*, No. 3 (Summer 1993), pp. 67–80.

58. Third world ballistic missile forces are discussed in Janne E. Nolan, *Trappings of Power: Ballistic Missiles in the Third World* (Washington, DC: Brookings Institution, 1991). See also Steve Fetter, 'Ballistic Missiles and Weapons of Mass Destruction: What Is the Threat? What Should be Done?', *International Security*, No. 1 (Summer 1991), pp. 5–42; W. Seth Carus, 'Iran's growing missile forces', *Jane's Defence Weekly*, 23 July 1988, pp. 126–31, and Joseph S. Bermudez and W. Seth Carus, 'The North Korean "Scud-B" Program', *Jane's Soviet Intelligence Review*, April 1989, pp. 177–81. I am grateful to W. Seth Carus for pertinent background on the issue of third world ballistic missiles; he bears no responsibility for arguments here.

59. Nolan, *Trappings of Power*, p. 75.

60. Ibid., pp. 68–9.

61. Ibid., p. 76.

62. Ibid., p. 77.

63. See Alan Dowty, 'Going Public with the Bomb: The Israeli Calculus', in Louis Rene Beres, *Security or Armageddon: Israel's Nuclear Strategy* (Lexington, MA: Lexington Books, 1986), pp. 15–28.

64. David Albright, 'A Proliferation Primer', *Bulletin of the Atomic Scientists*, June 1993, pp. 14–23.

65. Ibid., p. 15.

66. Ibid.

67. Department of Defense Appropriations for 1980, Hearings before a Subcommittee of the Committee on Appropriations, US House of Representatives, 96th Congress, 1st Session, Part 3, p. 878, cited in Sagan, *Moving Targets*, p. 218.

68. For informed discussion of possibilities, see Carl H. Builder, *Strategic Conflict without Nuclear Weapons* (Santa Monica, CA: RAND Corporation, April 1983).

69. A thoughtful discussion of this issue appears in Andrew J. Goodpaster, *Tighter Limits on Nuclear Arms: Issues and Opportunities for a New Era* (Washington, DC: Atlantic Council of the US, May 1992). I am grateful to Michael N. Pocalyko for calling this study to my attention.

70. Samuel P. Huntington suggests that the fault lines between civilizations will be the principal axes of conflict in the future. If so, cultural conflicts rather than statist conflicts should encourage rather than discourage praetorian proliferation. See Huntington, 'The Clash of Civilizations?', *Foreign Affairs*, No. 3 (Summer 1993), pp. 22–49.

71. For a discussion of praetorian governments and military coup making, see Eric A. Nordlinger, *Soldiers in Politics: Military Coups and Governments* (Englewood Cliffs, NJ: Prentice Hall, 1977), and Amos Perlmutter, *The Military and Politics in Modern Times* (New Haven: Yale University Press, 1977), pp. 1–20, 89–114.

72. Perlmutter, *The Military and Politics in Modern Times*, p. 16.

73. Ibid., p. xvi.

74. Samuel P. Huntington, *Political Order in Changing Societies* (New Haven: Yale University Press, 1968).

75. For a suggestion to this effect in the context of a discussion of the prospects for praetorianism or other politics in post-Cold War Europe, see Jack Snyder, 'Averting Anarchy in the New Europe', *International Security*, No. 3 (Winter 1990/91), in Sean M. Lynn-Jones (ed.), *The Cold War and After: Prospects for Peace* (Cambridge, MA: MIT Press, 1991), pp. 104–40, esp. pp. 121–2.

76. Ibid., pp. 117–19.

77. Some possible sources of future instability in Europe, including nuclear proliferation, are noted in John J. Mearsheimer, 'Back to the Future: Instability in Europe after the Cold War', *International Security*, No. 1 (Summer 1990), pp. 5–56, and in Lynn-Jones (ed.), *The Cold War and After*, pp. 141–92. Mearsheimer emphasizes the importance of polarity in the determination of systemic stability, anticipating as a result that the post-Cold War period will be characterized by multipolarity and less stability compared to the Cold War. See also Stephen Van Evera, 'Primed for Peace: Europe after the Cold War', *International Security*, No. 3 (Winter 1990/91), in Lynn-Jones (ed.), *The Cold War and After*, pp. 193–243.

78. For a discussion of options for restraining proliferation of weapons of mass destruction, see Steve Fetter, 'Ballistic Missiles and Weapons of Mass Destruction: What is the Threat? What Should be Done?', pp. 5–42.

79. John J. Mearsheimer, 'Disorder Restored', Ch. 8A in Graham Allison and Gregory F. Treverton (eds), *Rethinking America's Security: Beyond Cold War to New World Order* (New York: W.W. Norton, 1992), pp. 213–37. See also Mearsheimer, 'The Case for a Ukrainian Nuclear Deterrent', *Foreign Affairs*, No. 3 (Summer 1993), pp. 50–66. Counterarguments to the preceding citation appear in Steven E. Miller, 'The Case Against a Ukrainian Nuclear Deterrent', *Foreign Affairs*, No. 3 (Summer 1993), pp. 67–81. Given the stresses already placed on the Russian and other former Soviet armed forces, the preservation of secure nuclear command and control is remarkably fortuitous, but not to be taken for granted. See Stephen M. Meyer, 'The Military', Ch. 4 in Timothy J. Colton and Robert Legvold (eds), *After the Soviet Union: From Empire to Nations* (New York: W.W. Norton, 1992), pp. 113–46.

6

Deterrence Stability with Smaller Forces: Prospects and Problems

The end of the Cold War and the improved relations between the United States and Russia/Commonwealth of Independent States have opened the door to strategic nuclear force reductions even more drastic than those agreed to under the START (Strategic Arms Reduction) Treaty. Presidents Bush and Yeltsin have agreed in principle to consider proposed reductions at or below the level of 3,500–3,000 strategic nuclear warheads. Expert testimony and various studies have suggested that future US and Russian forces might be reduced in the near term to 3,000 warheads and ultimately to 1,000, assuming favorable political conditions continue between Moscow and Washington and provided that other major nuclear powers follow suit with proportional reductions.[1]

The kinds of forces deployed, their operational environments, and the alerting and warning expectations of political and military organizations are all pertinent to the issue whether nuclear weapons will contribute to an outbreak of war. Unless and until US and Russian weapons are no longer targeted against one another's home territories, the transitional problem of nuclear deterrence stability cannot be wished away. It may turn out that deterrence becomes a more interesting and more problematical construct during the transition from Cold War to a new world order of uncertain polarity than it was during the Cold War years. Future Russians may need more reassuring than deterring about the prospects for deterrence stability. Ironically, few US planners or academic analysts anticipated the potential self-destruction of former Soviet military capability, including the capability for preserving stable strategic nuclear deterrence, that now looms in Russia and its associated republics in the Commonwealth of Independent States (CIS).

Getting from the Cold War condition of mandated deterrence to a security community in which deterrence is no longer necessary involves a way station through phased nuclear force reductions and minimum deterrence. Can this

194

way station be managed successfully? This chapter compares the nuclear deterrence stability of START-compatible US and Russian/CIS forces of the early 1990s with possible alternatives: a 6,000 RV 'true START' deployment for each side; 3,000 RV; 2,000 RV; and 1,000 RV in two variations. It then discusses the viability of these deterrents for different missions, and it offers conclusions about the implications of these findings for future nuclear forces planning.

APPROACH

This chapter uses notional forces for the United States and Russia/CIS (assumed to have inherited provisionally the strategic nuclear forces of the former USSR, although we make no further assumption about permanent political durability) at five different levels in order to develop indicators of strategic force viability under various scenarios. The five force levels discussed here are: (1) the US and Russian/CIS strategic nuclear forces adjusted for compatibility with the START guidelines and according to the Bush modernization plan for the US; (2) both sides limited to 6,000 actual RVs; (3) both sides limited to 3,000; (4) both sides limited to 2,000; (5) both sides limited to 1,000. The force structures used for the 6,000, the 3,000 and the 1,000 thresholds were adapted from those developed by the Congressional Budget Office for its analysis of future US strategic and arms control options.[2] In addition, a second 1,000 level notional force described by Ted Corbin, Arsen Hajian and Kosta Tsipis was used for comparison with the 1,000 CBO case, since that case represents the smallest force sizes examined here.[3] These forces have the attractive properties for this analysis that they were designed to provide roughly symmetrical, survivable and flexible force deployments for each side, maintaining land-, sea- and air-based components of their strategic nuclear forces as multiple hedges against nuclear strategic surprise. In addition, the author generates a 2,000 RV case of his own also emphasizing survivable and roughly symmetrical deployments.

To determine whether these or other forces would provide for stable deterrence, it is necessary to subject the forces to dynamic exchange modelling. Dynamic exchange models allow the user to approximate the kinds of targeting decisions and war strategies that military planners could be tasked to develop by their political leaderships. Leaders would lack confidence in their deterrents if, for example, their general staffs reported that their forces were first strike vulnerable. However, vulnerability is a matter of degree, and assessments of vulnerability, such as the debate over the US ICBM 'window of vulnerability' during the latter 1970s and early 1980s, do not always take

195

into account the diverse operational environments of US or Russian forces. In addition, missions for which forces are tasked help to determine the extent to which force survivability is important and the kinds of forces which need to survive.

Broadly speaking, theorists have distinguished two categories of missions for strategic nuclear forces: counterforce strikes directed against the opponent's weapons and command systems, and countervalue attacks against population, economic values and other non-military targets. This distinction is commonly used despite the recognition by most analysts that the destructiveness of nuclear weapons makes inevitable significant collateral damage to countervalue targets from counterforce attacks. In addition, policy planners and some theorists have judged counterforce/countervalue distinction to be one which is more misleading than helpful. In terms of target categories as they have been defined in publicly available US war plans, a more faithful distinction might be:

(1) hard nuclear threat targets, such as ICBM silos and some fortified command and control centers;
(2) other nuclear threat targets;
(3) other military targets, sometimes referred to as OMT, general purpose force or force projection targets;
(4) economic targets, including industrial facilities and transportation infrastructure.[4]

Targeting strategies based on these categories of targets could be described in endless ways. The literature and experience of US strategic planners suggests that at least the following possible strategies could be described in terms of their inclusiveness of various target categories:

TABLE 6.1
POSSIBLE TARGETING STRATEGIES

Types of Strategy	Target Classes			
	1	2	3	4
hard-target counterforce	x			
general counterforce (including HTCF)	x	x		
countermilitary	x	x	x	
general	x	x	x	x
assured destruction				x
limited countermilitary			x	
limited general counterforce		x		
limited hard target counterforce	x			

Note   1 = targets in class 1, as described above, and so on for classes 2, 3 and 4. I am grateful to Paul K. Davis, RAND Corporation, for his insights and suggestions in developing this schematic. He is not responsible for its incarnation here.

196

Some of these targeting strategies commend themselves to aficionados of game scenarios more than they do to real military planners. The first strategy represents the oft-posited missile duel which was a notional absurdity as well as irrelevant with regard to policy. The second or counterforce strategy is the damage limitation strategy first described by former US Secretary of Defense Robert S. McNamara and later de-emphasized in his declaratory policies in favor of assured destruction.[5] Department of Defense references to assured retaliation often implied the third kind of targeting strategy: general nuclear response. Once US weapons became abundant this developed as the *de facto* targeting strategy regardless of emphases in declaratory policy. Assured destruction has many variations, as Robert Jervis has explained; its simplest and most basic variant is used here.[6] The constrained countermilitary and limited counterforce-limited HTCF options are variations on those themes imposed by policy-makers who desire more limited options intended to destroy smaller target sets within the category.

Analysts have generally supposed that the side striking first in a nuclear war would launch primarily counterforce attacks in order to destroy the other side's strategic retaliatory forces. It is less consensual or obvious what the retaliator, however war has begun, is supposed to do in response. Some have argued that proportional nuclear response (limited HTCF, CF or CM) to the scale and character of the attack is the preferred course of action. Others have said that only massive nuclear response against a wide variety of target sets is appropriate. Students of US nuclear strategic planning have noted that until the 1970s the US Single Integrated Operations Plan (SIOP) provided few if any options short of massive retaliatory response. Beginning with the 'Schlesinger doctrine' promulgated in 1974, US declaratory policy acknowledged a need for more selective nuclear strategic options well below the level of massive response, including limited counterforce options. Although academic communities and arms control advocates expressed considerable skepticism about limited strategic options, US Department of Defense planning guidance from Nixon through Reagan called for an expanded menu of selective nuclear options using US and allied NATO strategic and theater nuclear forces.[7]

Despite considerable interest during those years in selective nuclear options, no US administration departed from the bedrock of assured retaliation or assured destruction as the most important mission for retaliatory forces. The arguments subsequent to McNamara were for the most part about what else forces and their associated command and control systems might be expected to do.[8] But every administration since Eisenhower's maintained that second strike capability based on the ability to inflict unacceptable retaliatory

197

damage against Soviet society was the bedrock of stable deterrence. This policy consensus on the bottom line of mutual deterrence at the declaratory level did not resolve disputes about the operational definitions for assured destruction or unacceptable damage. Subsequent analysis will provide measurements for those criteria to assist in the estimation of viability for various force levels and configurations.

ASSURED DESTRUCTION AND ASSURED RETALIATION

Assured destruction as defined by McNamara equated to 200 equivalent megatons (EMT) inflicted on Soviet value targets even after US forces had absorbed a surprise attack. McNamara's estimates were that 200 EMT delivered by 400 warheads would result in either prompt fatalities among 25 to 33 per cent of the Soviet population and two-thirds of its industrial capacity, or 20 to 25 per cent of the Soviet population and 50 to 75 per cent of industrial capacity.[9] Assured destruction was not necessarily the same as unacceptable retaliation. What was acceptable to the first striker might not be known by the retaliator, and vice versa. US analysts admitted that US knowledge of Soviet leaders' definitions for unacceptable damage was subject to uncertainty. Although models of US abilities to destroy various classes of targets could be developed, Cold War Politburo leaders' scale of values for those target classes were not available except by guesswork.[10] During the Carter administration a major policy review concluded that Soviet leaders valued most their military forces and leadership survival. Both Carter and Reagan defense policy-makers therefore argued that these target sets should receive high priority, although not necessarily greatest time urgency, in US nuclear strategic target planning. These assumptions about Soviet valuation of objectives would not necessarily carry over into a democratic Russia or CIS, and the profound transformation in the former Soviet military, subsequent to the demise of the USSR, makes the relationship between leaders and followers in Moscow very different from Cold War contexts.

The difference between assured destruction as defined by McNamara and assured retaliation are at least two sided. First, assured destruction attempted to establish a metric for defining the optimal delivery of weapons on urban and industrial target classes. Weapons and destruction above the threshold suggested by this metric were superfluous. Assured retaliation prescribes no particular metric.[11] The assured retaliation criterion has been used by Pentagon planners, independent analysts and by critics of US nuclear deterrence strategy. A second difference between assured destruction and assured retaliation is that the latter concept begs the question how much retaliatory damage is unacceptable to a first striker. Theorists have attempted to get at this by defining 'unacceptable damage' at various thresholds. One definition, widely cited in the literature and used in the present study, was provided by McGeorge Bundy. Bundy's guideline was that ten one-megaton equivalent warheads directed at ten cities would constitute a 'disaster beyond history'.[12] Bundy's definition for unacceptable damage and McNamara's for assured destruction are used in this study, as explained below.

It might seem that assured destruction and unacceptable damage would be irrelevant to a minimum deterrent world. But either assured destruction or unacceptable damage could be defined as a sliding scale instead of a metric. The two metrics offer convenient upper and lower bounds for measuring the survivable retaliatory capability of different kinds of forces. On the other hand, neither assured destruction nor unacceptable damage provides a criterion for targeting and using nuclear forces. In order to determine whether leaders could be confident that forces could survive to inflict unacceptable damage or assured destruction, military and political leaders would first estimate force performances in the counterforce and countermilitary exchanges that would almost certainly precede countervalue attacks.

Lower levels of US and Russian forces denuded of most of their START-accountable prompt, hard-target counterforce could still be tasked for countermilitary missions by military planners in the early stages of any conflict. Forces remaining after countermilitary and counterforce exchanges it had been concluded, would be the available assured destruction or unacceptable retaliation forces. In Kosta Tsipis' terminology, planners would want forces which are stratolytic, capable of carrying out missions against opposed forces and other military targets, in addition to forces which are econolytic, or capable of destroying social and economic value.[13] One should not be deluded that counterforce attacks can be 'surgical' and somehow avoid creating unprecedented, and unacceptable to all except for lunatic leaders, levels of destruction. Thus there is some merit to the admonition by Von Hippel, Levi, Postol and Daugherty that 'it is the very reliance on counterforce strategies that blocks stabilizing nuclear-force reductions beyond those currently being considered in START negotiations'.[14] It is equally valid to recognize, on the other hand, the purposeful distinction between preserving flexible counterforce capabilities for deterrence and engaging in a counterforce potlatch, of the kind supported in some Cold War US policy pronouncements, in order to establish 'escalation dominance' or military victory if deterrence fails.[15]

The problem of preserving forces capable of assured retaliation defined as assured destruction, unacceptable damage or in some other fashion, seemed trivial in the days of US and Soviet Cold War forces which exceeded 12,000 and 10,000 strategic nuclear warheads respectively. Although specialists were understandably concerned about targeting decisions, at such force levels great redundancy almost guaranteed a wide variety of targeting options for responsive forces under any conditions.[16] As force levels are reduced from their Cold War levels and even well below START-accountable peaks, the problem of maintaining an assured retaliatory capability after absorbing a nuclear first strike cannot be taken as automatically solved. Smaller but equal forces do reduce the level of destruction attendant on any war actually fought by those forces, compared to larger forces. This is a welcome by-product of nuclear force reductions, but with nuclear weapons the result only matters if the smaller forces serve as viable deterrents. Smaller forces which are less survivable than the forces deployed by the other side, even under benign political conditions, are less reliable guarantors of stable deterrence than forces which are symmetrically survivable.

The ability of the US and Russia to guarantee survivable forces and assured retaliation at lower US and Russian levels of warheads and equivalent megatonnage is also relate to the two countries' efforts to prevent nuclear proliferation. On the one hand, each side's Cold War forces dwarfed by comparison those of any competitors, and the Soviet and American forces established a nuclear condominium between Washington and Moscow in favor of a bipolar strategic nuclear world. On the other hand, those larger arsenals were cited by potential proliferators as evidence that the Cold War nuclear superpowers were not willing to abstain from nuclear use in the same sense that Moscow and Washington were demanding of current non-nuclear states. This issue of US and Russian examples for others to follow has already been cited as an agenda item when the Non-proliferation Treaty comes up for renewal in 1995. It is thought by some experts on the problem of nuclear proliferation that further reductions in US and Russian arsenals would encourage both nuclear suppliers and potential proliferators to pay greater attention to the non-proliferation regime established by the treaty.[17]

Arms control and disarmament perspectives on the best ways to reduce US and Russian strategic nuclear forces may follow different prescribed paths. Disarmament advocates assume that the smaller the number of weapons, the more stable the relationship between the two states. An ideal condition for proponents of disarmament would be the elimination of nuclear weapons entirely from the arsenals of the US, Russia and other states. Arms control advocates focus more on the short-term management of deterrence stability than on the long-run objective of general and complete disarmament. Arms control proposals emphasize stable deterrence as a worthwhile end in itself, and one which is highly dependent on the circumstances of force attributes

200

and military strategy. Disarmers have little or no faith in deterrence even at drastically reduced levels of nuclear weapons, and some can draw on the arms control literature to support the argument that deterrence failure is more likely with smaller forces than between states with larger forces. Arms control emphasizes the elimination of weapons which are militarily superfluous for deterrence and supports the argument that the ability of forces to carry out their essential missions is essential for deterrence stability. Disarmers consider almost all nuclear weapons politically and militarily superfluous, and a disarmament-oriented perspective on minimum or finite deterrence would not be satisfied with freezing forces at low, but still significant, numbers of warheads and delivery vehicles.

This study clearly favors the arms controller's perspective to the disarmer's. Nevertheless, it concedes to the disarmer the recognition that arms control is a partial approach to stability which relies on the management of nuclear deterrent relationships, not on the abolition of nuclear weapons or nuclear crisis management. The dependency of stable nuclear deterrence on weapons which have survivable retaliatory capabilities is not the only dependency on which the avoidance of war in the nuclear age has rested. Equally important have been the abilities of the US and Soviet Cold War leaderships to avoid or to manage nuclear crises. The dynamics of Cold War nuclear crisis management have suggested to some that it was a very fragile enterprise which might easily have spilled over into war.[18] Arms control literature can draw on Cold War experience of the nuclear superpowers to argue that nuclear crisis management was successful, avoiding any actual outbreak of war between Moscow and Washington or between their respective allies in NATO and in the Warsaw Pact. Skeptics can point to the gory details of nuclear crisis management, including episodes from the Cuban missile crisis, to illustrate that even great force redundancy and assured survivabilty for US forces did not alleviate policy-makers' concerns about inadvertent escalation and nuclear war.[19]

The disarmer's pessimism and the arms controller's optimism about nuclear crisis management are pertinent here in order to remind us that prominent military strategists as well as lay people will never accept nuclear deterrence as anything but a way station to a nuclear disarmed world. Arguments against continued dependency on nuclear deterrence for the avoidance of war, implying the irrelevancy of criteria for measuring the adequacy of nuclear retaliatory forces, have been forcefully presented in a number of academic and policy studies.[20] Getting to 'nuclear zero' will have to be accomplished by means of a gradual rather than an immediate and drastic elimination of US, and Russian forces, barring political developments even more turbulent than those of the past few years. On that assumption that gradualism is the preferred approach to nuclear arms reductions, even leaders who favor stable deterrence as an interim condition only must grapple with force structure and targeting decisions during that interim.

PROCEDURES AND CAVEATS

Each of the notional forces was used as the basis for dynamic exchange models in which counterforce and countermilitary attacks were simulated and the remaining assured destruction or unacceptable retaliation capabilities were ascertained.[21] The model used here allows analysts to choose among eight scenarios for counterforce exchanges, including a range of missile and bomber attacks. The user must make basic strategic decisions about how to attack and what to attack. Analysts can vary assumptions about command and control survivability, good or bad targeting information, and pre-launch survivability of force components (among other assumptions) to suit their research objectives and their own estimates of operational performance.

To simplify matters, this study follows consistently the same attack and response scenario through each simulated exchange. In each case, either the US or Russia strikes first with missiles. The other side rides out the attack and then retaliates with missiles. The first side then conducts one bomber follow-up attack, and the sequence of counterforce attacks is concluded. Other scenarios can be developed, but they involve more extensive counterforce attacks which consume progressively larger proportions of the remaining forces of both sides. As force levels descend from 6,000 to 1,000 warheads, the point of diminishing returns for more than three waves of counterforce strikes sets in (see Tables 6.3–6.5). As apparent in the results reported below, even this very simplified model of counterforce exchanges presses some forces against the margin of survivability.

The simulations were divided into three principal subsets:

1. The first group modelled both US and Russian first strikes for the six force structure cases (START-accountable; 6,000 RV; 3,000 RV; 2,000 RV; and two 1,000 RV cases) when the forces of both sides were on *generated* alert. Generated alert means that forces are prepared for prompt response and retaliation under authorized command.

2. The second group of exchange models used the same force structures but placed forces of the both sides on *day-to-day* alert. Day-to-day alert is the normal peacetime condition for military forces, including nuclear forces.

202

3. The third group of models placed the forces of one side (the first striker) on generated alert and the forces of the retaliator on day-to-day alert. According to many strategic thinkers, the most likely scenario for an actual nuclear attack is one in which a political crisis has preceded the outbreak of war. Therefore, both sides will have had time to prepare their forces by raising their levels of readiness or alert.[22]

Although it might seem plausible to assume that the forces of both sides would be alerted by means of crisis warning prior to war, it cannot be assumed by military planners that this 'best case' for force readiness will obtain under all circumstances. For example, it is not known reliably whether Soviet nuclear forces were alerted during the Cuban missile crisis; US analysts suggest not, although Soviet Premier Khrushchev indicated otherwise.[23] Therefore, our third group of simulations posits that one side strikes with forces already alerted against a second side with forces at day-to-day readiness.[24] It would make little sense for a state with forces at day-to-day alert levels to attack a state with forces already generated. In addition, leaders who expected to conduct a surprise attack would want exactly the conditions depicted in this set of exchanges: a defender whose forces are not yet fully poised for retaliation subjected to an unanticipated strategic strike. This 'worse case' for defenders can be misused to drive all analysis to the extreme, however, without comparison between it and other cases assuming more favorable conditions for retaliators.

One advantage of using asymmetrical exchanges between ready and unready forces is that the US and Russian force structures of the near future will carry over operational habits and constraints, related to survivability, from the Cold War past. For example, the US during the Cold War routinely maintained a much larger proportion of its ballistic missile submarine (SSBN) force out of port (on station or on patrol) compared to the Soviet Union. Higher proportions of US strategic bombers, compared to Soviet bombers, were also kept on quick reaction strip alert (US airborne alerts were abandoned several decades ago).[25] As START and subsequent agreements shift force structures toward single warhead land-based missiles, submarines and bombers as preferred launchers, and away from MIRVed land-based (especially silo-based) missiles, the pre-launch survivability of bombers and submarines becomes even more important in the calculus of deterrence. This plays to US Cold War strengths and Soviet weaknesses, which the 1990s version of any Russian deterrent inherits.

For example, a Congressional Budget Office study published in 1983 showed the significance of assumptions about warning time for bomber pre-launch survivability, applied to the Reagan administration bomber force and projected forward beyond his term of office.[26] Under conditions of peacetime or day to day alert, the US strategic bomber force of the 1980s would have operated with approximately one-third of its primary alert aircraft (PAA) on alert: some 30 per cent of the B-52s and about 40 per cent of B-1s and ATB (Stealth, or B-2) aircraft.[27] On peacetime alert, bombers would require 6.5 minutes between breakwater caused by initial SLBM launches until the first alert bomber took off. On generated alert, 95 per cent of all primary authorized aircraft (PAA) would be on alert, and the required reaction time would be 2.2 minutes.[28] Thus, assuming notional SLBM attacks without depressed trajectories, the proportions of the 1983 and projected 1990 and 1996 US bomber forces, on generated and day-to-day alert, surviving a surprise first strike are indicated in Table 6.2.[29]

TABLE 6.2

DAY-TO-DAY AND GENERATED US BOMBER PRE-LAUNCH SURVIVABILITY
(1983 AND PROJECTED 1990 AND 1996 FORCES)

Per Cent of ALERT force survivable	Day-to-Day Alert	Generated Alert
1983	94	85
1990	95	89
1996	92	85
Per Cent of TOTAL force survivable		
1983	28	81
1990	29	85
1996	28	81

Source: Congressional Budget Office, *Modernizing US Strategic Offensive Forces* (Washington, DC: CBO, May 1983), pp. 104–5, and author's estimates. Attacking forces are presumably already generated.

There is reason to believe that Russian bomber operations under day-to-day or generated alert conditions would be far less effective unless and until a rethinking of bomber doctrine and a restructuring of bomber command and control operations took place. According to a US study published in 1991:

> The Soviet Union has never demonstrated much concern for the survivability of its bomber fleet: no indications are evident that Moscow keeps any of its bombers on runway alert, making the entire fleet vulnerable to surprise attack. This situation could reflect the small portion of the Soviet arsenal that is based on bombers, or could indicate little Soviet concern about surprise attack, or could indicate a belief that

204

warheads surviving on ICBMs and submarines would be enough to deter the United States.[30]

In 1991 US analyses assumed that about two-thirds of Trident submarines and 55 per cent of Poseidons were out of port at any given time. The Soviet Navy was estimated to deploy 15–25 per cent of its SSBNs at sea on day-to-day alert, and a surge capacity to get about 67 per cent out of port on generated alert.[31] However, construction has already been halted on some classes of Russian attack submarines, and the modernization of Russian SSBN forces in the near term faces an obstacle course that includes constrained funding and a diminished military–industrial complex. Another unknowable factor is the impact of military *glasnost* on the recruitment and training of naval personnel, including those authorized to serve on nuclear armed ballistic missile submarines. To some extent these personnel, resource and administrative concerns relative to force modernization also apply to post-Soviet Russian bomber and Strategic Rocket Forces (RVSN).[32]

The third set of simulations places both sides' forces on day-to-day alert at the START-compatible, 6,000, 3,000, 2,000 and 1,000 warhead levels. It might seem unlikely that war could ever break out with forces on both sides at alert levels below actual war readiness. However, nuclear forces are not alerted in the same ways or with the same consequences as are conventional forces, at least in mature command and control systems such as the US and Soviet Cold War systems. In the US case, for example, the consequences of raising nuclear alert levels have been judged sufficiently serious to require the approval of the highest level of civilian policy-makers, including the President. An outbreak of war owing to accidental or inadvertent nuclear use or escalation by one side might find the forces of both sides mostly at day-to-day alert levels, or at least far from the highest alert levels to which they might have been raised during an extended crisis.[33] On the evidence of US Cold War crisis management experience, the alerting and command–control of US nuclear and general purpose forces were marked by uneven implementation of policy-makers' decisions throughout the chain of command, and by diverse military service understandings of the implications of orders for subsequent operational and tactical decisions.[34]

Thus, it might turn out that some parts of the military command system were being raised to higher alert levels while others, operating at far remove from the immediate operational–tactical environment of land, sea or air combat, were percolating at lower levels of readiness. It might not be obvious to shore-based commanders during a crisis, for example, that nuclear attack or ballistic missile submarines were being subjected to a concerted attack as

205

part of a pre-emptive nuclear strike. Or, such a plan for anti-submarine warfare nuclear pre-emption might be mistakenly attributed to one side in a crisis after the other side had lost a submarine during a tactical engagement developing from trailing and shadowing maneuvers. Awareness that top US Navy commanders and policy-makers might not know the consequences of harassing Soviet submarines and surface vessels during the Cuban missile crisis led Secretary of Defense McNamara to insist upon micromanagement of procedures for intercepting and boarding Soviet ships. As Alexander L. George has explained:

> Coercive diplomatic strategy focuses upon the task of affecting the opponent's will and his utility calculations rather than negating his military capabilities. Thus, coercive diplomacy has an essentially *signalling, bargaining, negotiating* character – a feature that is absent or much diminished in traditional military strategy – which the policy-maker attempts to build into the conceptualization and conduct of military operations.[35]

Thus, for signalling purposes one side might deliberately not alert its forces, especially its nuclear forces, and the other side might respond with partial restraint on nuclear or other force alerting. Some think that the Soviet Union during the Cuban missile crisis chose not to alert its nuclear forces for precisely this reason. Soviet leaders may have reasoned that the US, holding nuclear and conventional military trump cards, could be pushed into inadvertent or deliberate escalation by dramatic movements of groups of Soviet forces contiguous to NATO borders, or by nuclear readiness measures which seemed preparatory to general war. Similar US restraint was exercised during the Soviet invasion of Czechoslovakia in 1968; certain NATO reconnaissance flights over Czech territory were temporarily discontinued in order to signal the understanding held by NATO leaders that the crisis was not perceived by them as a preparation for attack on Western Europe.

It can be expected that, as the normalization of political relations between the US and Russia and the absorption of Russia into a pan-European security community take place, the operation of US and Russian nuclear forces will be based less on the worst case of nuclear strategic surprise. Future US nuclear forces will, like general purpose forces if present political trends continue, be planned around contingency operations of uncertain locale and duration. Some of the implications of this emerging political environment for US nuclear strategic planning are discussed in a later section. The point here is that the already apparent changes in the European political landscape allow us to foresee the time when rapid and massive response to nuclear strategic surprise will no longer drive US force structure or war plans. The more benign political environment makes it less imperative to operate large numbers of forces in a peacetime condition of quick reaction. Warning and assessment can be more fault tolerant. And response patterns need not be frozen into a simple menu of preselected options, but can be varied for specific, if unforeseeable, scenarios of crisis management and deterrence stability.

In the simulations that are summarized below, certain levels of alert are assigned to US and Russian forces based on 1991 published estimates of system reliability and vulnerability. These estimates from public sources are obviously subject to great uncertainty. Nevertheless, the essence of the difference between generated and day-to-day alert can be modeled with acceptable accuracy. The issue is whether survivability to inflict unacceptable damage or, assured retaliation, or survivability for the other missions to which nuclear forces might be assigned, is affected by the alert statuses of otherwise symmetrical and basically survivable forces.

DATA

For each of the 36 simulated exchanges that follow, a table summarizes the numbers of warheads and equivalent megatonnage, the percentage of assured destruction capable of being inflicted by each side after counterforce exchanges, and the percentage requirements for causing 'disasters beyond history' with those same remaining forces. The simulations are grouped by size of force and by whether forces are: both on generated alert; both on day-to-day alert; or, the first striker has generated forces and the retaliator has day-to-day forces. The measure for assured destruction is the percentage of 200 EMT, and the measure for disasters beyond history is the percentage of 10 EMT or 10 RV capable of being used against urban industrial targets. The exchanges are numbered sequentially.

Simulation 1

Both Sides on Generated Alert
START Forces

Russian First Strike

	wh/emt	McNamara (pct. of 200 EMT) (Macs)	Disasters beyond history (DBH)
US totals	4017/2279	1140	40170 wh 22795 emt
Rus. totals	682/313	157	6824 wh 3138 emt

Simulation 2

Both Sides on Generated Alert
START Forces

US First Strike

	wh/emt	Macs	DBH
US total	1831/1082	541	18312 wh 10882 emt
Rus. total	1100/616	308	11006 wh 6168 emt

Simulation 3

Both Sides on Generated Alert
6,000 RV

Russian First Strike

	wh/emt	*Macs*	*DBH*
US total	1879/1006	503	18799 wh 10006 emt
Rus. total	661/287	144	6610 wh 2877 emt

Simulation 4

Both Sides on Generated Alert
6,000 RV

US First Strike

	wh/emt	*Macs*	*DBH*
US total	1270/662	331	12704 wh 6622 emt
Rus. total	1191/643	322	11911 wh 6436 emt

Simulation 5

Both Sides on Generated Alert
3,000 RV

Russian First Strike

	wh/emt	*Macs*	*DBH*
US total	328/153	77	3285 wh 1538 emt
Rus. total	400/221	111	4008 wh 2220 emt

Simulation 6

Both Sides on Generated Alert
3,000 RV

US First Strike

	wh/emt	*Macs*	*DBH*
US total	340/149	75	3408 wh 1474 emt
Rus. total	487/293	147	4871 wh 2935 emt

Simulation 7

Both Sides on Generated Alert
2,000 RV

Russian First Strike

	wh/emt	*Macs*	*DBH*
US total	593/326	163	5934 wh 3262 emt
Rus. total	188/134	67	1887 wh 1345 emt

Simulation 8

Both Sides on Generated Alert
2,000 RV

US First Strike

	wh/emt	*Macs*	*DBH*
US total	122/59	30	1224 wh 598 emt
Rus. total	582/388	194	5823 wh 3889 emt

211

Simulation 9

Both Sides on Generated Alert
1,000 RV (CBO Force)

Russian First Strike

	wh/emt	*Macs*	*DBH*
US total	123/63	32	1233 wh 637 emt
Rus. total	129/106	53	1294 wh 1061 emt

Simulation 10

Both Sides on Generated Alert
1,000 RV (CBO Force)

US First Strike

	wh/emt	*Macs*	*DBH*
US total	86/35	18	864 wh 355 emt
Rus. total	248/213	107	2489 wh 2134 emt

Simulation 11

Both Sides on Generated Alert
1,000 RV (Tsipis Force)

Russian First Strike

	wh/emt	*Macs*	*DBH*
US total	176/81	41	1760 wh 817 emt
Rus. total	113/81	41	1131 wh 813 emt

Simulation 12

Both Sides on Generated Alert
1,000 RV (Tsipis Force)

US First Strike

	wh/emt	*Macs*	*DBH*
US total	75/45	23	752 wh 458 emt
Rus. total	169/109	55	1699 wh 1097 emt

213

Preliminary Analysis

In all cases of generated alert, both sides retain survivable capabilities for a variety of counterforce and countermilitary as well as countervalue missions. Neither can disarm the other, and both retain over-abundant capacity to inflict numerous disasters beyond history. At 3,000 or 2,000 RV and more consistently at 1,000 RV, the sides have some difficulty maintaining survivable assured destruction capability (exclusive of reserve forces, which were approximately 200 RV for the START and 6,000 RV cases and 100 RV for the 3,000 and 1,000 cases). However, it is not obvious that 3,000 or smaller forces need to meet the criteria of assured destruction, defined as 200 EMT, if they are otherwise survivable and capable of accomplishing a variety of stratolytic and econolytic missions.

A consistent pattern emerges in that the retaliator usually does as well or better than the first striker. Such a condition reflects the fact that striking against the forces of a side whose strategic nuclear weapons and command and control systems are already on generated alert is as foolhardy a gamble with smaller but stable forces as it would be with larger forces. Although the survivable 3,000, 2000, and 1,000 RV forces cannot inflict as much damage on urban and industrial society as larger forces can, they can inflict enough to make war unprofitable and horrible beyond precedent. Thus, they are of adequate size and character to guarantee stable deterrence, provided they receive adequate warning.

The asymmetrical character of US and Russian forces shows up a little in these runs between two hypothetically generated forces, but even more so in the results that follow. Operational asymmetries are not too costly for the Russians once their forces have been generated, but small Russian forces on day-to-day alert pose survivability problems for them. There are deterrent and arms race stable solutions to this apparent asymmetry, however.

214

Simulation 13

Both Sides on Day-to-Day Alert
START Forces

Russian First Strike

	wh/emt	*Macs*	*DBH*
US total	2074/1197	599	20746 wh 11971 emt
Rus. total	113/39	20	1130 wh 398 emt

Simulation 14

Both Sides on Day-to-Day Alert
START Forces

US First Strike

	wh/emt	*Macs*	*DBH*
US total	1446/859	430	14464 wh 8594 emt
Rus. total	58/18	9	588 wh 188 emt

215

Simulation 15

Both Sides on Day-to-Day Alert
6,000 RV

Russian First Strike

	wh/emt	Macs	DBH
US total	1134/587	294	11341 wh 5872 emt
Rus. total	69/33	17	690 wh 335 emt

Simulation 16

Both Sides on Day-to-Day Alert
6,000 RV

US First Strike

	wh/emt	Macs	DBH
US total	1097/578	289	10976 wh 5788 emt
Rus. total	78/30	15	780 wh 303 emt

216

Simulation 17

Both Sides on Day-to-Day Alert
3,000 RV

Russian First Strike

	wh/emt	*Macs*	*DBH*
US total	259/123	62	2590 wh 1232 emt
Rus. total	33/11	6	336 wh 110 emt

Simulation 18

Both Sides on Day-to-Day Alert
3,000 RV

US First Strike

	wh/emt	*Macs*	*DBH*
US total	288/100	50	2880 wh 1002 emt
Rus. total	57/22	11	572 wh 221 emt

217

Simulation 19

Both Sides on Day-to-Day Alert
2,000 RV

Russian First Strike

	wh/emt	*Macs*	*DBH*
US total	280/146	73	2808 wh 1469 emt
Rus. total	25/10	5	252 wh 100 emt

Simulation 20

Both Sides on Day-to-Day Alert
2,000 RV

US First Strike

	wh/emt	*Macs*	*DBH*
US total	270/118 emt	59	2704 wh 1185 emt
Rus. total	12/5	3	126 wh 50 emt

Simulation 21

Both Sides on Day-to-Day Alert
1,000 RV (CBO)

Russian First Strike

	wh/emt	*Macs*	*DBH*
US total	94/42	21	942 wh
			422 emt
Rus. total	0/0*	0*	0 wh*
			0 emt*

* Forces reserved prior to the start of war not included in remaining totals.

Simulation 22

Both Sides on Day-to-Day Alert
1,000 RV (CBO Force)

US First Strike

	wh/emt	*Macs*	*DBH*
US total	100/43	22	1008
Rus. total	4/2	1	42 wh
			17 emt

219

Simulation 23

Both Sides on Day-to-Day Alert
1,000 RV (Tsipis Force)

Russian First Strike

	wh/emt	*Macs*	*DBH*
US total	128/68	34	1284 wh 685 emt
Rus. total	9/3	2	98 wh 39 emt

Simulation 24

Both Sides on Day-to-Day Alert
1,000 RV (Tsipis Force)

US First Strike

	wh/emt	*Macs*	*DBH*
US total	120/73	37	1200 wh 731 emt
Rus. total	14/5	3	140 wh 56 emt

Preliminary Analysis

In the case of war beginning with the forces of both sides on day-to-day alert, the asymmetries between the operational and deployment habits of Russian (based on Cold War Soviet traditions, and therefore subject to uncertainty) and American bomber and submarine forces become more significant. However, under all conditions, both sides retain survivable forces adequate to inflict historically unprecedented societal damage. Only in the case of 1,000 RV forces on day-to-day alert do the Russians fall short of warhead or EMT requirements equal to one disaster beyond history. Even then the surviving numbers of warheads could still inflict unacceptable damage for any sane US President. The exceptional case is the 1,000 CBO warhead case in which Russia strikes first. In this case Russia emerges with effectively no survivable retaliatory capability other than reserves withheld before the war.

Does this virtual elimination of Russia's retaliatory capability for assured destruction or disaster beyond history effectively negate the viability of a 1,000 RV deterrent on day-to-day alert? Hardly, since the calculations of survivable warheads are based on estimates of those 'reliable and deliverable' as a subset of total surviving warheads. US officials could not assume that such calculations, made conservatively by the program (and by the Russians, in the event) would work in their favor. No President would bet the farm on the total negation of Russia's deterrent even allowing for the presence of strategic reserves (assumed to be withheld by both sides for post-conflict bargaining).

Moreover, the 'Tsipis' 1,000 RV force leads to results that are more symmetrical than the 1,000 CBO force, although this does not mean that one force is better than another. The differences between CBO and Tsipis force (1,000 RV) outcomes are neither statistically nor substantively significant. In each case both sides retain enough capability to cause historically unprecedented retaliatory damage to countervalue targets after two waves of counterforce attacks. If the Russians worried about lack of survivable countervalue capability under these conditions, they could target fewer weapons on US counterforce or countermilitary targets and attack value targets sooner. Our model deliberately forces both sides into a three-strike counterforce sequence of missile and bomber attacks before tabulating survivable countervalue capabilities.

Although both sides on day-to-day alert retain some capacity for counter-value retaliation after their forces are subjected to counterforce attacks, asymmetries are apparent as a result of the lower survivability of Russian bomber and submarine forces. The latter issue may be of concern to Russian planners of the future if modernization lags and US anti-submarine warfare makes possible conventional ASW pre-emption of major parts of the Soviet SSBN force.

221

Simulation 25

Attacker on Generated Alert
Retaliator on Day-to-Day Alert
START Forces

Russian First Strike

	wh/emt	*Macs*	*DBH*
US total	1913/1100	550	19138 wh 11000 emt
Rus. total	680/324	162	6800 wh 3244 emt

Simulation 26

Attacker on Generated Alert
Retaliator on Day-to-Day Alert
START Forces

US First Strike

	wh/emt	*Macs*	*DBH*
US total	1726/1012	506	17264 wh 10129 emt
Rus. total	25/5	3	252 wh 54 emt

222

Simulation 27

Attacker on Generated Alert
Retaliator on Day-to-Day Alert
6,000 RV

Russian First Strike

	wh/emt	*Macs*	*DBH*
US total	1014/516	258	10149 wh 5164 emt
Rus. total	573/260	130	5736 wh 2601 emt

Simulation 28

Attacker on Generated Alert
Retaliator on Day-to-Day Alert
6,000 RV

US First Strike

	wh/emt	*Macs*	*DBH*
US total	1404/749	375	14048 wh 7493 emt
Rus. total	573/260	130	5736 wh 2601 emt

Simulation 29

Attacker on Generated Alert
Retaliator on Day-to-Day Alert
3,000 RV

Russian First Strike

	wh/emt	*Macs*	*DBH*
US total	187/80	40	1870 wh 808 emt
Rus. total	357/201	101	3578 wh 2020 emt

Simulation 30

Attacker on Generated Alert
Retaliator on Day-to-Day Alert
3,000 RV

US First Strike

	wh/emt	*Macs*	*DBH*
US total	276/124	62	2760 wh 1240 emt
Rus. total	41/14	7	412 wh 149 emt

Simulation 31

Attacker on Generated Alert
Retaliator on Day-to-Day Alert
2,000 RV

Russian First Strike

	wh/emt	Macs	DBH
US total	277/146	73	2776 wh 1469 emt
Rus. total	196/138 emt	69	1966 wh 1385 emt

Simulation 32

Attacker on Generated Alert
Retaliator on Day-to-Day Alert
2,000 RV

US First Strike

	wh/emt	Macs	DBH
US total	207/89	45	2072 wh 898 emt
Rus. total	12/5	3	126 wh 50 emt

225

Simulation 33

Attacker on Generated Alert
Retaliator on Day-to-Day Alert
1,000 RV (CBO Force)

Russian First Strike

	wh/emt	*Macs*	*DBH*
US total	71/35	18	718 wh 352 emt
Rus. total	128/107	54	1285 wh 1078 emt

Simulation 34

Attacker on Generated Alert
Retaliator on Day-to-Day Alert
1,000 RV (CBO Force)

US First Strike

	wh/emt	*Macs*	*DBH*
US total	76/27	14	768 wh 280 emt
Rus. total	4/2	1	42 wh 17 emt

226

Simulation 35

Attacker on Generated Alert
Retaliator on Day-to-Day Alert
1,000 RVs (Tsipis Force)

Russian First Strike

	wh/emt	*Macs*	*DBH*
US total	118/62	31	1180 wh 621 emt
Rus. total	105/83	42	1052 wh 832 emt

Simulation 36

Attacker on Generated Alert
Retaliator on Day-to-Day Alert
1,000 RV (Tsipis Force)

US First Strike

	wh/emt	*Macs*	*DBH*
US total	92/56	28	920 wh 560 emt
Rus. total	14/5	3	147 wh 58 emt

Preliminary Analysis

At START and 6,000 RV levels, the two sides generally retain sufficient countervalue retaliatory capability following a sequence of counterforce attacks to inflict assured destruction and many times the level of unacceptable damage, the latter defined as ten warheads on ten cities or 10 EMT. The only exceptions are US first strikes with generated forces against Russian forces on day-to-day alert, which drive down surviving Russian assured destruction totals but leave intact the capacity for disaster beyond historical precedent. A US first strike in the START force case also reduces survivable Russian EMT below the level of unacceptable damage (10 EMT), but some 250 warheads remain exclusive of those reserved prior to war.

At the 3,000, 2,000 and 1,000 RV levels, there are major differences in the survivability of US and Russian forces following a short sequence of missile and bomber attacks. Russian forces caught on day-to-day alert by generated US forces are less survivable than their US counterparts when the tables are turned. The outcomes reflect the greater survivability and reliability of US bombers and submarines, especially at levels of 1,000 RV and even with evenly balanced force structures. (Offsetting asymmetries allow the US more sea-based and airborne power and Russia greater capability in mobile land-based missiles in the CBO 1,000 RV force. The Tsipis 1,000 RV force is symmetrical for each leg of the strategic triad.) Russia and the US retain under all conditions the capability to inflict historically unprecedented, and in all likelihood politically unacceptable, damage. Even 1,000 RV forces tested here allow for some survivable warheads, exclusive of prewar reserve forces of about 100 RV and after counterforce attacks.

In order to obtain a clearer fix on the extent to which meaningful differences in survivable systems exist, we calculated a measure of Relative Force Advantage (RFA) for those cases in which the forces of *both sides* or those of the *attacker only* were on generated alert. In other words, the cases of two-sided day-to-day alerts were excluded. This left 24 cases: 12 with the forces of both sides poised for first strike or prompt retaliation, and 12 with the attacker at high readiness and the defender on day-to-day alert. For each case the RFA is calculated as a ratio of the US surviving forces to the Russian surviving forces. A ratio of unity means that the US and Russia have equal remaining forces; a ratio greater than unity favors the US by the stated number, and a ratio less than unity favors the Russians.

Each RFA is calculated by adding the square root of the surviving EMT to the number of remaining warheads for each side. Then the Russian EMT-warhead figure is divided into the US EMT-warhead figure to produce the measure of Relative Force Advantage, stated as the US per cent of Russian forces. For example, an RFA of 5.0 means that the relative force advantage of surviving US forces compared to Russian forces is 500 per cent, or five times as large. The square root of the EMT was chosen because EMT numbers get large very quickly even at relatively small force levels. The results of this calculation for all cases involving one- or two-sided generated alerts are summarized in Tables 6.3 and 6.4.

TABLE 6.3

BOTH SIDES ON GENERATED ALERT: RELATIVE FORCE ADVANTAGE AS A
RATIO OF US TO RUSSIAN SURVIVING FORCES

Forces	First Striker	RFA	Advantage
START	Russia	6.06	US
START	US	1.66	US
6,000	Russia	2.82	US
6,000	US	1.07	US
3,000	Russia	0.81	Russia
3,000	US	0.70	Russia
2,000	Russia	3.12	US
2,000	US	0.22	Russia
1,000 (CBO)	Russia	0.94	Russia
1,000 (CBO)	US	0.35	Russia
1,000 (Tsipis)	Russia	1.52	US
1,000 (Tsipis)	US	0.46	Russia

TABLE 6.4

ATTACKER ON GENERATED ALERT: RELATIVE FORCE ADVANTAGE AS A
RATIO OF US TO RUSSIAN SURVIVING FORCES

Forces	First Striker	RFA	Advantage
START	Russia	2.79	US
START	US	65.11	US
6,000	Russia	1.76	US
6,000	US	24.30	US
3,000	Russia	0.53	Russia
3,000	US	6.38	US
2,000	Russia	1.40	US
2,000	US	15.43	US
1,000 (CBO)	Russia	0.55	Russia
1,000 (CBO)	US	16.20	US
1,000 (Tsipis)	Russia	1.11	US*
1,000 (Tsipis)	US	6.19	US

* Tsipis 1000 force with Russian first strike results in survivable warheads favoring US and survivable EMT favoring Russians as a result of the kinds of forces deployed. My composite measure gives more credit for warheads than for EMT, perhaps overstating the US advantage when the difference is so close as to appear non-existent.

Congressional Budget Office force projections of 1991 assumed reasonably that Bush administration modernization plans would be made compatible with the limitations agreed to in START. The START 90 forces in our analysis reflect that projection: US forces included 500 small, silo-based ICBMs, 18 Trident SSBNs with 24 D-5 SLBMs per boat, and 75 B-2 bombers. This projection was at least in temporary danger of being overtaken by new developments. In his January 1992 State of the Union message, President Bush announced changes in US strategic modernization plans, including the cancellation of the small ICBM program, cessation of production of D-5 warheads, and the halting of B-2 procurement at 20 aircraft. Bush also announced new US arms control proposals to be presented to the Russian government. These included a US offer to entice the Russians to eliminate all of their MIRVed ICBMs: if Boris Yeltsin would agree to do so, the US, according to Bush, would eliminate the MX ICBM with ten warheads, download existing Minuteman ICBMs to a single warhead per missile, reduce the number of warheads on US SSBNs by about one-third, and convert a significant portion of the US strategic bomber fleet to primarily conventional missions.[36] Whether Russian leaders will sign onto these proposals is unknown. There is some apparent resistance among Russian civilian and military leaders to wholesale divestiture of the Russian MIRVed ICBM capability and some rethinking of Gorbachev's assumptions about the benefits of denuclearization.

Consistent with the possibility that Bush's declared force modernization changes will take hold, we also project their implications for the previously analyzed START 90 and 6,000 warhead cases by adjusting those US forces accordingly (B-2 numbers were reduced to 20, more Poseidon C-4 missiles were deployed on submarines instead of Trident D-5s, and small ICBMs were eliminated in favor of additional warheads on submarines or bombers. The adjusted forces were engaged in simulation with Russian forces in order to compare the post-Bush 1992 relative force advantages (RFAs) for two kinds of cases: both sides are on generated alert, or only the attacker is. The following results, quite consistent with the findings for earlier simulations with forces of similar size, are tabulated in Table 6.5.

Tables 6.3 to 6.5 suggest that the forces of the two sides produce highly symmetrical outcomes when both sides are on generated alert, regardless of force size. When alerted forces attack those at day-to-day readiness and independently of force size, US forces significantly outperform Russian forces. For example, in Table 6.4 a Russian first strike with START-accountable forces leads to a US Relative Force Advantage of 2.79. A Russian first strike with 'true START' forces still leaves the US with a small RFA of

TABLE 6.5
START AND 6,000 RV FORCES (ADJUSTED FOR US DECLARATORY CHANGES IN FORCE STRUCTURE, 1992; SMALLER FORCES NOT AFFECTED)

Size	Alert Status (Attacker to Defender)	Side Striking First	Relative Force Advantage		
			Warheads Attacker/Defender	EMT Attacker/Defender	RFA (Ratio of US to Russian Surviving Forces)
START	Gen.–Gen.	Russia	1,033/3,954	625/2,010	3.78
START	Gen.–Gen.	US	1,226/1,134	657/649	1.08
START	Gen.–Day	Russia	945/1,478	598/717	1.55
START	Gen.–Day	US	1,305/35	718/16	34.15
6,000	Gen.–Gen.	Russia	637/1,626	280/871	2.53
6,000	Gen.–Gen.	US	1,190/1,178	566/659	1.01
6,000	Gen.–Day	Russia	600/890	295/480	1.48
6,000	Gen.–Day	US	1,262/75	574/16	16.27

1.76, and a Russian first strike with 2,000 RV forces leaves the US with an RFA of 1.40. Only in the 3,000 and 1,000 RV (CBO) cases does a Russian first strike leave them 'better off', and even in these cases the margins are small.

On the other hand, US relative force advantages, when striking with alerted forces against Russian forces not on alert, are much greater than Russian forces when the situation is reversed. In Table 6.4, US generated forces at START levels achieve an RFA of more than 65; at 6,000 RV levels, an RFA greater than 24; at 3,000 RV, an RFA greater than six; at 2,000 RV, a relative advantage greater than 15; and for the two 1,000 RV forces, RFAs of more than 16 and six, respectively. Table 6.5 adjusts the findings in Table 6.4 for the 1992 US expected reductions in D-5 production and in B-2 procurement, and for the expected elimination of Midgetman from the US arsenal. Results of these initiatives do not improve significantly the picture for Russia.

The only 'good news' for Russia is that reducing force size per se does not make the situation worse. It is not force size but operating characteristics and alert levels of the Russian forces compared to American forces which make them comparatively more vulnerable. While these comparative vulnerabilities may not be significant now, the uncertainties surrounding the future Russian military–industrial complex and weapons procurement bureaucracies make the issue more meaningful. One should remember that the present calculations assume that future Russian forces will perform about as well as past forces, in terms of alert levels and operational deployments. Actual Russian forces of the future may fall below these standards if military self-destruct continues, or may exceed these standards if the transition to military–industrial modernization can be made.

ASSESSMENT AND CONCLUSIONS

During the Cold War years the US and Soviet strategic nuclear arsenals were of such size and diversity that more than enough weapons existed to fulfill the requirements for any mission assigned by policy-makers. The early years of the nuclear age challenged theorists to rethink important problems of strategy and defense, including the very concept of deterrence itself.[37] By the mid-sixties original thinking on the subject of nuclear deterrence strategy had been largely played out in the academy and in the policy arena.[38] Successor generations nibbled at the edges of seminal works by Brodie, Schelling, Wohlstetter and other giants of the first half of the Cold War.[39] After the arrival of acknowledged US–Soviet strategic nuclear parity in the 1970s, declaratory refinements in nuclear strategic doctrine occurred more for the exercise and for the satisfaction of new administrations in Washington than as indicators of any meaningful change in strategic targeting plans or basic deterrence concepts.

The present study makes plausible but modestly favorable assumptions about the future performance attributes of US and Russian strategic nuclear forces based on present force attributes. It then asks whether smaller forces remain survivable, after a minimum number of counterforce attacks, in order to guarantee either assured destruction or unacceptable retaliation. The results suggest that even if US and Russian strategic nuclear forces undergo major, symmetrical reductions in size, the impact on the true survivability of their deterrents will be asymmetrical. At very low force sizes Russia will be quite vulnerable to strategic attack without warning, absent future force modernization and operational rethinking of the kind that Russia may be unwilling or unable to undertake. In some political environments, US–Russian nuclear deterrence may no longer matter, but in other environments the sensitivity of strategic stability to Russian military stasis could threaten progress toward a stable world of no, or few, nuclear weapons.

As the Russian armed forces work to develop their post-Cold War identity, evidence thus far suggests a continued concern on the part of General Staff and other military planners about strategic nuclear deterrence, stability and the avoidance of vulnerability to nuclear surprise attack. Several presentations given at the General Staff Military Academy's Military-Science Conference held from 27–30 May 1992 support this assumption. For example, in his discussion of the system of strategic leadership for the future Russian armed forces, Major-General S.K. Lopukhov enumerated functions which the future Russian armed forces command and control system 'must' provide.[40] Among these 'must' functions are included 'timely receipt of reliable information from strategic and tactical warning systems' about enemy aerospace or nuclear missile attack either in preparation or already in progress, and efficient command and control of strategic nuclear forces including 'guaranteed communication of centralized battle management orders (signals) to fixed and mobile ground launchers, strategic missile submarines, and Long-Range Aviation aircraft platforms' about the onset of enemy nuclear missile or aerospace attack.[41]

At the same conference, other experts noted that the disintegration of the Warsaw Pact and the elimination of many tactical nuclear weapons strengthened Western superiority in conventional military forces compared to Russia. Therefore, according to Lieutenant General L.I. Volkov, chief of a scientific research institute, the Russian strategic nuclear forces and especially their 'basis', the Strategic Missile Troops 'remain the last military–political force preserving constant combat readiness, supporting the strategic balance in the world and Russia's security, and *preventing its transition into the category of secondary states*.[42]

The evidence presented here shows that projected nuclear forces, even those reduced in size drastically, have the survivable countervalue and flexible countermilitary power to maintain stable deterrence *provided* that reduced force components perform about as well as their 1990 predecessors would have. In the US case the assumption seems safe; for Russia, it is less certain, given domestic political and economic uncertainties. Alert rates and operational procedures of the various force components become progressively more important as force levels are reduced from 6,000 down to 1,000. As a study for Lawrence Livermore Laboratory and the Brookings Institution noted, at levels below 6,000 RV 'the survivability and alert rates of the forces become more and more important if a disarming first strike is to remain an impossibility and if there are to be enough residual forces to carry out the specified military missions and maintain reserves'.[43] An appreciation of deterrence stability offered at a Russian General Staff conference in May 1992 argued that reductions to 6,000 START-accountable warheads and 1,600 delivery vehicles over a seven-year period was 'most advisable': however, according to the same analyst, additional reductions to 4,500 or 4,700 warheads 'should not be accepted', until the START treaty was fully implemented over a seven-year period.[44]

It is apparent from these simulations that Russia faces a significant challenge if it wishes to retain a survivable strategic nuclear deterrent force over the next several decades. START and post-START reductions will tilt the balance of nuclear strategic deterrent capability toward weapons systems operated with far greater survivability and lethality during the Cold War years by the US than by the Soviet Union. Russia inherits from the Soviet Union a tradition of bomber forces entirely subject to destruction and submarines almost entirely vulnerable in port under conditions of normal peacetime readiness. Of course, Russian design bureaus and general staffs of the future are not necessarily fated to follow past Soviet practice. Investments can be withdrawn from ICBM modernization and devoted to bomber and submarine improvements, including improvements in the survivability of both types of forces.

However, the challenges are acute and immediate. Russian Navy representatives warn that the Navy must still be tasked for missions including nuclear deterrence and repelling nuclear or aerospace attacks, as well as for a variety of sea control missions well beyond the coastal waters of Russia itself.[45] On the other hand, it will be difficult to provide adequate resources in the future even to avoid slippage well below the standards of the early 1990s. According to Russian Rear Admiral A.A. Pauk, chief of the Main Naval Staff Center for Operational–Tactical Studies, Russia's status as a great sea power must be maintained and strengthened in the years ahead, but resource constraints may preclude this. Computations by Admiral Pauk suggest that at presently only about one-third of the ships in the Russian Navy are modern (have served less than half of their expected service life): in the next ten to 12 years, the Russian fleet will lose 67 to 70 per cent of its order of battle without any apparent guarantee of replacements.[46] In 1992 for the first time in 60 years not one new ship was laid down for the Russian Navy.[47]

If the political relationship between the US and Russia improves to the point at which neither targets forces against the homeland of the other, then the two parties can cooperate to modernize their slower second strike systems and to phase out systems capable of prompt launch and surprise attack. Nevertheless, as one study warns:

> Improving survivability and day-to-day alert rates is a costly and time-consuming objective. New systems and new ways of fielding existing systems must be developed and tested. Reduction in overall force levels should free some funds, but, in addition, time must be allowed in the transition to lower levels of forces for both sides to do this developing and testing if a secure deterrent balance at lower levels of force is the goal.[48]

My earlier assertion in favor of phasing out systems capable of prompt launch merits some qualification now. Single warhead ICBMs, including mobile ICBMs, might provide a prompt launch capability based on land which helped to reassure the two sides against an ASW or air and missile defense breakthrough. Single warhead ICBMs would not make a first strike against the other side's land-based missiles attractive, since the arithmetic would nullify any advantage for the attacker. Even 1,000 RV forces in two cases profited in flexibility and in survivability by diversifying weapons among land-based, sea-based and air-breathing delivery systems. Despite this qualification, it seems clear that the more stable components of any future US or Russian force will be those providing support for slow counterforce or countervalue strikes, presumably bombers and submarine-launched missiles. With regard to reassurance against surprise attack, the US and Russia might emphasize the future de-MIRVing of SSBN launchers and mutually agreed limitations on the lethality of submarine-launched weapons.

Most of the information here suggests that prudent modernization can be combined with arms control in favor of stable deterrence in the 1990s and beyond and at force levels much lower than those now deployed. Two caveats are in order, in addition to the uncertainties about Russian military modernization. The first possibility is that of technological destabilization of a stable minimum deterrence posture. This could come about if either the US or the Russians managed a breakthrough in technology for preclusive anti-submarine destruction of the other state's ballistic missile submarines. Technological destabilization could also come about by means of a one-side deployment of missile defenses which the other was without the means to match or overcome with existing offensive forces. The Bush-proposed GPALS (Global Protection Against Limited Strikes) system does not necessarily destabilize a US–Russian deterrent relationship based mainly on offensive retaliation and second strike survivability. However, the scope and character of GPALS must be managed so that it is in tune with Russian expectations of deterrence stability.[49] According to one analysis that most probably reflects Russian General Staff thinking, at lower levels of strategic nuclear arms, the possible effects of limited BMD deployments, third-party nuclear forces or potential losses in strategic forces during a conventional war become more important indicators of stability.[50]

Russian President Boris Yeltsin has indicated some willingness to discuss bilateral missile defense deployments, and joint delegations of experts have been meeting to explore the possibility. Any such agreement would also have non-proliferation implications (both conventional high tech and nuclear) not addressed here, but none the less significant. The data in this study suggest, but are very far from confirming, that even low levels of BMD are potentially destabilizing for minimum deterrent forces of 3,000 or 1,000 warheads.[51] Assessment of the implications of defenses for stable deterrence with reduced forces would have to consider changes in offensive target sets brought about by the existence of space or ground-based defenses; the relationship between missile defense components and command-control system viability; and the difference between penetration prospects with and without defenses for first and second strikers.[52]

The second caveat is that to get the US and Russia below 3,000 warheads, one must take into account the modernization plans of Britain, France and China.[53] This is not an issue of proliferation in the traditional sense, that is, horizontal proliferation from the nuclear haves to the have-nots: these states already deploy nuclear weapons of intercontinental range. The British and French systems together will provide, as a high estimate, some 640 survivable RVs by the mid-1990s if present modernization plans in both countries are played out.[54] Possible economies of scale and joint operations might be considered by London and Paris, with the aim of restraining both expenditures for military procurement and arms races. However, the future modernization plans of China are uncertain, and China has indicated no interest in coordinating modernization plans with those of other nuclear powers. Since limited BMD systems deployed by the US or by Russia (alone or jointly) would be intended for the mission of protection against accidental or deliberate small attacks, other nuclear armed states may conclude that BMD deployments are intended to restrain their deterrents while leaving those of Washington and Moscow in a position of international primacy.

The Gulf War of 1991 left no doubt in the minds of many analysts that conventional high-technology weapons could displace nuclear weapons for many assignments, and with obviously less collateral damage.[55] Precision guided munitions and improvements in sensing and in information processing now make possible the destruction of strategic targets to the depth of an opponent's defenses. Russian reflections on the outcome of Desert Storm draw exactly this conclusion about possible future competency of strategic conventional offensives.[56] It is also the case that the total withdrawal of Russian forces from Eastern Europe and the transformation of NATO into a more political than military organization could open the door to a pan-European security structure in which non-existent threats of aggression were buttressed by commitments to non-offensive defenses. In such an environment, extended nuclear deterrence of the kind provided by US and Soviet forces during the Cold War years would be unnecessary. US nuclear weapons could serve only as forces of last resort in cases of nuclear attack on the American homeland.

On the other hand, even in this favorable environment it is not obvious that nuclear weapons, so long as they remained in US and Russian arsenals, would be targeted only against cities or other 'soft' value targets. Since it takes very few weapons to cause historically unprecedented and socially catastrophic damage to urban areas, strategic planners might prefer to target most weapons à la carte against military targets of opportunity in regional contingency operations. Target planning of this type would call for dismantling the SIOP as it was known from 1960 to 1990 and replacing it with a 'dial an option' approach made possible by new information and control technology. Instead of a single integrated operational plan designed for one basic scenario, global war against the Soviet Union or Russia, the US could have flexible options based on recommendations of the various theater commanders (CINCs) and the Joint Chiefs of Staff for response to regional contingencies. Of course, it would be advisable to maintain Presidential control over nuclear weapons at all times, and the reduced fear of massive nuclear surprise might permit a shift in emphasis from prompt response to deliberate restraint in nuclear force application. Then, too, a more delayed and judgmental approach to nuclear use, deconflicted from Cold War planning for coverage of a virtually unlimited target set, could involve actors outside of the executive branch in the development of war plans.

NOTES

I am grateful to Michael Brown, International Institute for Strategic Studies; Joseph Coffey, Princeton University; Paul K. Davis, RAND Corporation; Richard L. Garwin, IBM Research Division and Committee on International Security and Arms Control, National Academy of Sciences; Daniel Goure, Competitive Strategies Office, US Department of Defense; William C. Martel, Harvard University; Michael Mazarr, Center for Strategic and International Studies; Jonathan Medalia, Congressional Research Service, Library of Congress; David E. Mosher, Congressional Budget Office; Gary Schaub, Jr., University of Illinois at Urbana-Champaign, and Terry Terriff, University of Calgary, for helpful suggestions and comments on earlier drafts of this study. They bear no responsibility for its arguments or opinions, which are those of the author only. Some of the calculations herein are also referred to in my article on the same topic which will appear in a forthcoming issue of the *Journal of Peace Research*.

1. Richard L. Garwin, 'Post-START: What do we want? What can we Achieve?', testimony published in US Congress, Senate Committee on Foreign Relations, *Hearings*, 102nd Congress, 2nd Session, pp. 130–47. See also Committee on International Security and Arms Control, National Academy of Sciences, *The Future of the US–Soviet Relationship* (Washington, DC: National Academy Press, 1991).
2. David Mosher and Michael O'Hanlon, Congressional Budget Office, *The START Treaty and Beyond* (Washington, DC: Congressional Budget Office, Oct. 1991). For other analyses of 6,000 and 3,000 RV cases, see Michael M. May, George F. Bing and John D. Steinbruner, *Strategic Arms Reductions* (Washington: Brookings Institution, 1988), pp. 42–59.
3. Ted Corbin, Arsen Hajian and Kosta Tsipis, *Nuclear Arsenals for the 21st Century*, Report #23, Program in Science and Technology for International Security, MIT (Cambridge, MA: Jan. 1991), p. 69.
4. Desmond Ball, *Targeting for Strategic Deterrence* (London: International Institute for Strategic Studies, Summer 1983), esp. pp. 23–5. Notional US and Soviet target lists are also discussed in William M. Arkin and Richard W. Fieldhouse, *Nuclear Battlefields: Global Links in the Arms Race* (Cambridge, MA: Ballinger Publications, 1985), p. 93. Sets of targets in the former Soviet Union are illustrated in Mosher and O'Hanlon, *The START Treaty and Beyond*, pp. 14–15. A current description of the US strategic nuclear targeting process is General Accounting Office, *Strategic Weapons: Nuclear Weapons Targeting Process*, GAO/NSIAD-91-319FS (Washington, DC: General Accounting Office, Sept. 1991).
5. Reasons for McNamara's shift in declaratory emphasis on counterforce and 'no cities' strategy (not identical, but related), to assured destruction are noted in Ball, *Targeting for Strategic Deterrence*, pp. 12–13. They included criticism of the first strike implications of the strategy within the US; the Soviet reaction to US declaratory damage limitation; unfavorable reactions from US allies; and, fourth, bureaucratic expansion of the US Air Force based on the damage limitation rationale for larger forces than McNamara actually sought.
6. Robert Jervis, *The Meaning of the Nuclear Revolution: Statecraft and the Prospect of Armageddon* (Ithaca, NY: Cornell University Press, 1989), Ch. 3.
7. Ball, 'US Strategic Forces: How Would They Be Used?', *International Security*, No. 3 (Winter 1982–83), pp. 31–60, and Ball, *Targeting for Strategic Deterrence*, passim.
8. For an account, see Scott D. Sagan, *Moving Targets: Nuclear Strategy and National Security* (Princeton, NJ: Princeton University Press, 1989), pp. 10–57.

9. The first estimates by McNamara were provided in 1965, the second in 1967. See Alain C. Enthoven and K. Wayne Smith, *How Much is Enough? Shaping the Defense Program, 1961–69* (New York: Harper and Row, 1971), pp. 207–10. Alternative criteria for assured destruction are presented in Michael Salman, Kevin J. Sullivan and Stephen Van Evera, 'Analysis or Propaganda? Measuring American Strategic Nuclear Capability, 1969–1988', Ch. 3 in Lynn Eden and Steven E. Miller (eds), *Nuclear Arguments: Understanding the Strategic Nuclear Arms Debate* (Ithaca, NY: Cornell University Press, 1989), esp. pp. 209–11. See also Gary John Schaub, Jr., *Strategic Nuclear Exchanges: An Assessment of the Literature*, unpublished paper, p. 21. I am grateful to Joseph Coffey for this last reference.

10. For estimates of assured destruction for attacks on the Soviet Union, see Barbara G. Levi, Frank N. Von Hippel and William Daugherty, 'Civilian Casualties from "Limited" Nuclear Attacks on the Soviet Union', *International Security*, Vol. 12 (Winter, 1987–88), pp. 168–89. Estimates for the assured destruction criterion for attacks on the US appear in William Daugherty, Barbara Levi and Frank Von Hippel, 'The Consequences of "Limited" Nuclear Attacks on the United States', *International Security*, Vol. 10 (Spring, 1986), pp. 3–45. For other estimates, see US Office of Technology Assessment, *The Effects of Nuclear War* (Montclair, NJ: Allanheld, Osmun and Co., 1980).

11. Although efforts were made by Pentagon analysts to quantify assured retaliation as part of the Carter administration debates over strategic modernization options. As part of the effort to develop operational definitions for assured retaliation, Carter defense planners examined whether US–Soviet strategic equivalence was meaningful, how equivalence in counterforce systems ought to be measured, and what kinds of hard target capability US forces really needed. The issue of second strike counterforce targeting was also considered at great length by internal Carter studies, and spirited debates took place within the government over the relative importance of slow compared to prompt retaliatory counterforce (maturing of cruise missile technology in the 1970s made this a very live issue). I am grateful to Paul Davis and to Leon Sloss for background on this issue, although they bear no responsibility for the interpretations presented here. See also Walter Slocombe, 'The Countervailing Strategy', reprinted in Steven E. Miller (ed.), *Strategy and Nuclear Deterrence* (Princeton, NJ: Princeton University Press, 1984), pp. 245–54.

12. McGeorge Bundy, 'To Cap the Volcano', *Foreign Affairs*, Vol. 48 (Oct. 1969), esp. pp. 9–10.

13. Kosta Tsipis, 'The Future of Nuclear Deterrence', Ch. 3 in Michael T. Klare and Daniel C. Thomas (eds), *World Security: Trends and Challenges at Century's End* (New York: St Martin's Press, 1991), pp. 45–67.

14. Frank N. von Hippel, Barbara G. Levi, Theodore A. Postol and William Daugherty, 'Civilian Casualties from Counterforce Attacks', *Scientific American*, No. 3 (Sept. 1988), pp. 36–42, citation p. 42. According to May, Bing and Steinbruner, the von Hippel, *et al.*, estimates are at the high end of the range of prompt fatalities from counterforce attacks: their estimates are provided in *Strategic Force Reductions*, pp. 60–9. The different estimates may be explained by some differences in scenario-targeting assumptions as well as differences in methodology. What is more important for our purposes is that both these studies confirm the great damage that can be accomplished against countervalue targets, especially urban targets, with numbers of warheads much smaller than those posited in exchange models requiring massive counterforce strikes.

15. This case is argued in Sagan, *Moving Targets*, pp. 58–97.

16. Background on the development of US targeting doctrine is provided in Desmond Ball, *The Evolution of United States Strategic Policy since 1945: Doctrine, Military Technical Innovation and Force Structure* (Canberra: Australian National University, Strategic and Defence Studies Centre, Jan. 1989), and Ball, 'The Development of the SIOP, 1960–1983', Ch. 3 in Ball and Jeffrey Richelson (eds), *Strategic Nuclear Targeting* (Ithaca, NY: Cornell University Press, 1986), pp. 57–83. On Soviet nuclear targeting and command and control, see Ball, *Soviet Strategic Planning and the Control of Nuclear War* (Canberra: Strategic and Defence Studies Centre, Reference Paper No. 109, Nov. 1983), and Stephen M. Meyer, 'Soviet Nuclear

Operations', Ch. 15 in Ashton B. Carter, John D. Steinbruner and Charles A. Zraket (eds), *Managing Nuclear Operations* (Washington, DC: Brookings Institution, 1987), pp. 470–534. How much of this transfers over to the post-Soviet military planning mind-set is unknown.

17. For background, see Leonard S. Spector with Jacqueline R. Smith, *Nuclear Ambitions: The Spread of Nuclear Weapons 1989–1990* (Boulder, CO: Westview Press, 1990), and Janne E. Nolan, *Trappings of Power: Ballistic Missiles in the Third World* (Washington, DC: Brookings Institution, 1991).

18. Richard Ned Lebow, *Nuclear Crisis Management: A Dangerous Illusion* (Ithaca, NY: Cornell University Press, 1987). James G. Blight argues that the experience of crisis management fragility may have improved the quality of official decision-making during the Cuban missile crisis of 1962. See Blight, *The Shattered Crystal Ball: Fear and Learning in the Cuban Missile Crisis* (Savage, MD: Rowman and Littlefield, 1990).

19. See James G. Blight and David A. Welch, *On the Brink: Americans and Soviets Reexamine the Cuban Missile Crisis* (New York: Hill and Wang, 1989) for insights into the perspectives of crisis participants. For background on Cuban crisis decision-making in Moscow and in Washington, see Raymond L. Garthoff, *Reflections on the Cuban Missile Crisis*, rev. edn (Washington, DC: Brookings Institution, 1989).

20. The best of these in my judgment is Freeman Dyson, *Weapons and Hope* (New York: Harper Colophon, 1984), esp. pp. 272–85.

21. The dynamic exchanges were simulated by using Sullivan's Instructional Operations Program (SIOP), developed by Kevin J. Sullivan, Michael Salman and Stephen Van Evera (Ithaca, NY: Cornell University Press, 1989). SIOP provides a very useful data base and modelling software for nuclear forces of the 1970s and 1980s. It can be adapted by the user to construct hypothetical forces in order to create 'what if' past scenarios or future conditions. Among other virtues, the model allows users to choose among four widely used formulas for calculating the single-shot kill probability of a reliable warhead against a hardened target. Each of these formulas assumes that single shot kill probability (SSKP) is a function of the relationship between the lethal radius of a weapon and its circular error probable (CEP). The formulas differ in their approach to calculation of lethal radius. The formula chosen in this analysis is the 'full GE' (for General Electric) formula, which uses four different equations depending on the hardness of the target. For the pertinent equations, see Eden and Miller, *Nuclear Arguments*, pp. 248–9, and Lynn Etheridge Davis and Warner R. Schilling, 'All You Ever Wanted to Know about MIRV and ICBM Calculations but Were Not Cleared to Ask', *Journal of Conflict Resolution*, 27 (June 1973), esp. pp. 213–14.

22. US military forces of the Cold War years, including nuclear forces, were described as having five levels of readiness or alert, from DefCon (Defense Condition) 5 under typical peacetime conditions to DefCon 1 (forces committed to combat). US Strategic Air Command was kept at peacetime status of DefCon 4. During the Cuban missile crisis, SAC was placed at DefCon 2, or imminent readiness for war; this was the highest alert level for US forces acknowledged in public sources. See Bruce G. Blair, 'Alerting in Crisis and Conventional War', Ch. 3 in Carter, Steinbruner and Zraket (eds), *Managing Nuclear Operations*, pp. 75–120 and Sagan, 'Nuclear Alerts and Crisis Management', *International Security*, 9 (Spring 1985), pp. 99–139.

23. Sagan, *Moving Targets*, pp. 166–73.

24. As Schaub notes, 'we would feel more secure about the robustness of the general conclusions of the literature if all of the forces had been tested in this more demanding scenario, rather than the more realistic ones where each nation is on a similar state of alert', Schaub, *Strategic Nuclear Exchanges*, p. 26.

25. There is almost no reliable information in the public record on Soviet strategic bomber alert procedures. Calculation of US bomber launch survivability is discussed in Congressional Budget Office, *Modernizing US Strategic Offensive Forces: The Administration's Program and Alternatives* (Washington, DC: Congressional Budget Office, 1983), Appendix E, pp. 99–110.

26. Ibid.
27. The Bush administration announced in 1992 that about 12 per cent of the US strategic bomber force would be dealerted. Continuation or acceleration of bomber dealerting would of course alter the above estimates even more.
28. Ibid., p.104. See also Mosher and O'Hanlon, *The START Treaty and Beyond*, pp.154–60, Appendix B, for a model which estimates US bomber survivability by relating the area of bomber dispersal to the area which could be barraged by an attacker with SLBM warheads. Barrage attacks on bombers are necessary in order to destroy those alert bombers flying away from base at the time of the attack.
29. The literature reaches no consensus on approach to the calculation of bomber survivability. Some analysts assume that all alerted bombers escape destruction (May, *et al.*, *Strategic Arms Reductions*). Others posit that approximately 15 per cent of alerted bombers can be destroyed while attempting to escape if enough warheads are used to barrage their bases (Michael Salman, Kevin J. Sullivan and Stephen Van Evera, 'Analysis or Propaganda? Measuring American Strategic Nuclear Capability, 1969–88', in Lynn Eden and Steven E. Miller (eds), *Nuclear Arguments: Understanding the Strategic Nuclear Arms and Arms Control Debates* (Ithaca, NY: Cornell University Press, 1989). Mosher and O'Hanlon develop a complex set of equations to estimate bomber survivability based on distance of attacking submarines from bomber bases, rates of bomber takeoff from bases, submarine missile launch rates, and other parameters (Mosher and O'Hanlon, *The START Treaty and Beyond*, pp.154–60). Other useful discussion of this problem appears in Schaub, *Strategic Nuclear Exchanges*, pp.33–4.
30. Mosher and O'Hanlon, *The START Treaty and Beyond*, p.155.
31. Ibid., p.154. The subject of Soviet SSBN vulnerability to US ASW is controversial. Mosher and O'Hanlon assume that Soviet SSBNs out of port are invulnerable because they are deployed in protection bastions in the Barents Sea or the Sea of Okhotsk (*The START Treaty and Beyond*, p.154). Salman, *et al.*, assume that US ASW would destroy about 20 per cent of Soviet SSBNs at sea (*Nuclear Arguments*, p.256). See also Schaub, *Start and Strategic Stability*, paper presented at annual meeting of the International Studies Association, Atlanta, GA, 31 March–2 April 1992, p.14.
32. Prior to the collapse of the Soviet Union a command for strategic forces, including land and sea-based and air-delivered long-range offensive forces, as well as strategic anti-missile and antispace defense forces, was discussed by some prominent Soviet military thinkers. Subsequent to Soviet demise, the Commonwealth of Independent States attempted for a time to establish a strategic forces command which included long-range offensive nuclear forces and nuclear and conventional forces thought necessary for strategic homeland defense (including, in the minds of some, the Black Sea fleet). The Commonwealth version collapsed when republic forces, including Russian forces, were nationalized by the spring of 1992. The Russian Ministry of Defense now includes a Strategic Forces Command which is essentially responsible for all nuclear forces, since intermediate and shorter range INF are banned by treaty and short-range nuclear forces are being withdrawn and dismantled parallel to the initiative by President Bush of September 1991 (to which Gorbachev immediately responded with reciprocal measures) to remove and dismantle many US land and sea-based tactical nuclear weapons. I am grateful to Daniel Goure, US Department of Defense, Competitive Strategies Office, for clarifying some pertinent points here, although he bears no responsibility for my deductions or arguments.
33. On problems of accidental or inadvertent nuclear war, see Sagan, *Moving Targets*, pp.135–75 and Thomas C. Schelling, *Arms and Influence* (New Haven, CT: Yale University Press, 1966), pp.97–8.
34. See the discussion of stratified crisis interaction in Joseph F. Bouchard, *Command in Crises* (New York: Columbia University Press, 1991), esp. pp.36–56. On the diverse understandings of orders, see also Graham T. Allison, *Essence of Decision: Explaining the Cuban Missile Crisis* (Boston: Little, Brown, 1971), *passim*.
35. Alexander L. George, 'The Tension between "Military Logic" and Requirements of

Diplomacy in Crisis Management,' Ch.3 in Alexander L. George (ed.), *Avoiding War: Problems of Crisis Management* (Boulder, CO: Westview Press, 1991), p.17.

36. Text of President Bush's State of the Union Message, *New York Times*, 29 Jan. 1992, p.A14. For further analysis of US force structure and arms control proposals announced by Bush, see Schaub, *START and Strategic Stability*, pp.6–7.

37. A seminal contribution is Glenn H. Snyder, *Deterrence and Defense: Toward a Theory of National Security* (Princeton: Princeton University Press, 1961). Deterrence before the nuclear age is discussed in George H. Quester, *Deterrence before Hiroshima: The Airpower Background of Modern Strategy* (New Brunswick, NJ: Transaction Books, 1986) who argues that the concept and terminology of deterrence, including mutual deterrence, can be found in the writings of airpower theorists between the world wars. Bernard Brodie's singular contributions to the study of US nuclear deterrence strategy are noted in Barry H. Steiner, *Bernard Brodie and the Foundations of Nuclear Strategy* (Lawrence, KS: University Press of Kansas, 1991): see esp. pp.12–14 on the development of Brodie's view of mutual deterrence.

38. See Lawrence Freedman, *The Evolution of Nuclear Strategy* (New York: St. Martin's Press, 1981) and Colin S. Gray, *Strategic Studies: A Critical Assessment* (Westport, CT: Greenwood Press, 1982).

39. For example, Thomas C. Schelling, *The Strategy of Conflict* (Cambridge: Harvard University Press, 1960), and Albert Wohlstetter, 'The Delicate Balance of Terror', *Foreign Affairs*, Vol. 37 (Jan. 1959), pp.212–34. For a succinct overview of the development of US strategic thought and its implications for policy, see Henry S. Rowen, 'The Evolution of Strategic Nuclear Doctrine', in Laurence Martin (ed.), *Strategic Thought in the Nuclear Age* (Baltimore: Johns Hopkins University Press, 1979), pp.65–79.

40. Major-Gen. S.K. Lopukhov, 'System of Strategic Leadership of the Russian Armed Forces', *Voennaya mysl'* (July 1992, Special Edition), pp.79–83, JPRS-UMT-92-012-L, pp.43–6.

41. Ibid., p.44.

42. Lt. Gen. L.I. Volkov, 'Strategic Missile Troops: Purpose, Missions', *Voennaya mysl'* (July 1992, Special Edition), pp.57–60, JPRS-UMT-92-012-L, p.31.

43. May, Bing and Steinbruner, *Strategic Force Reductions*, p.71. It is worth noting that reserve levels withheld in the simulations done for this study are smaller than those posited for the May, Bing and Steinbruner study, generally ten per cent of the force in the latter case.

44. Volkov, 'Strategic Missile Troops', p.31.

45. Rear-Admiral A.A. Pauk, 'Purpose, Missions and Makeup of the Navy Under Present Conditions and in the Future', *Voennaya mysl'* (July 1992, Special Edition), pp.71–5, JPRS-UMT-92-012-L, pp.39–41.

46. Ibid., p.41.

47. Ibid.

48. Ibid.

49. For background see US House of Representatives, Committee on Government Operations, Hearings before the Legislation and National Security Subcommittee, *Strategic Defense Initiative: What Are the Costs? What Are the Threats?*, 102nd Congress, First Session, 16 May and 1 October 1991. For historical perspective on SDI, see Donald R. Baucom, *The Origins of SDI, 1944–1983* (Lawrence, KS: University Press of Kansas, 1992).

50. Volkov, 'Strategic Missile Troops', p.31. The same presenter argued that BMD for protection of the US against limited strikes, actions by third countries and terrorists was as potentially destabilizing as a full-scale BMD system, 'inasmuch as a full infrastructure is created for a limited ABM defense (battle management, information equipment, antimissile weapons) which will allow building it up to any scale in the shortest time' (p. 32).

51. The implications of partial defenses for stability at lower force levels are discussed in CBO, *The START Treaty and Beyond*, pp.92–9.

52. May, Bing and Steinbruner, *Strategic Arms Reductions*, p.72.

53. On the relationship between nuclear multipolarity and minimum deterrence, see David W.

Tarr, *Nuclear Deterrence and International Security: Alternative Nuclear Regimes* (London: Longman, 1991), p.138. On minimum deterrence and proliferation, see ibid., p.143.

54. This assumes the following: France decides to maintain two SSBNs at sea at all times, and Britain keeps at least one and possibly two SSBNs at sea at all times. If the French replace the M-4 SLBM with the M-5 and if all M-5s are equipped with a maximum 12 warheads, then France would deploy 384 assuredly survivable warheads on ballistic missile submarines (2 × 16 × 12). The M-5 is not expected to begin deployment until 2005, and the French mobile IRBM program has been canceled. France would probably continue to deploy strategic or pre-strategic nuclear weapons in other basing modes, including fixed silo IRBMs on the Albion plateau, short-range ballistic missiles and air-delivered munitions. If Trident D-5 SLBMs replace all British Polaris A-3 and if the D-5s all carry the maximum eight warheads, then Britain with two boats would have a total of 256 assuredly survivable warheads (2 × 16 × 8). Actual totals deployed may be lower than these because the British government has stated its intention not to deploy the maximum number of warheads on the D-5, and France is judged by expert analysts as unlikely to deploy 12 warheads on each M-5. Approximately 300–400 assuredly survivable warheads would be a more conservative figure for estimating combined British and French survivable RVs in the first decade of the next century. I am grateful to Dr. Michael Brown, Senior Fellow, International Institute for Strategic Studies, London, for correcting earlier figures and for providing helpful additional information. He bears no responsibility for interpretations here.

55. The reduced utility of nuclear compared to conventional weapons for tactical missions was argued effectively by Richard L. Garwin, 'Reducing Dependence on Nuclear Weapons: A Second Nuclear Regime', in David C. Gompert, Michael Mandelbaum, Richard L. Garwin and John H. Barton (eds)., *Nuclear Weapons and World Politics* (New York: McGraw Hill, 1977), pp.83–147, esp. p.108. On the substitution of conventional for nuclear weapons in strategic missions, see Carl H. Builder, *Strategic Conflict Without Nuclear Weapons* (Santa Monica, CA: RAND Corporation, April 1983).

56. For interesting statements to this effect, see the draft Russian military doctrine appearing in the special edition of *Voennaya mysl'* (Military Thought), May 1992, esp. pp.3–9.

APPENDIX

FORCES IN THE ANALYSIS

Force characteristics, including operational parameters such as alert rates, are drawn from Michael Salman, Kevin J. Sullivan and Stephen Van Evera, 'Analysis or Propaganda? Measuring American Strategic Nuclear Capability, 1969–88', in Lynn Eden and Steven E. Miller (eds), *Nuclear Arguments: Understanding the Strategic Nuclear Arms and Arms Control Debates* (Ithaca, NY: Cornell University Press, 1989), pp.172–244, and Salman *et al.* 'Appendix: How Our Simulations Were Performed', in Eden and Miller (eds), *Nuclear Arguments*, pp.245–63, unless otherwise specifically noted. Force structures were derived primarily from these sources and from David Mosher and Michael O'Hanlon, *The START Treaty and Beyond* (Washington, DC: Congressional Budget Office, Oct. 1991), and Ted Corbin, Arsen Hajian and Kosta Tsipis, *Nuclear Arsenals for the 21st Century* (Cambridge, MA: Program in Science and Technology for International Security, Report 23, Jan. 1991).

START FORCES

I. US

ICBMs

A. 500 Small ICBMs (SICBMs) – 1 RV
B. 316 MM III – 1 RV
C. 50 MX – 10 RV
D. 35 MM IIIa – 3 RV

SLBMs

A. 18 Trident submarines with 24 Trident D-5 missiles (8 RV)

Bombers

A. 75 B-2 (Stealth)
B. 95 B-52H ALCM
C. 97 B-1B

II. Russia/CIS

ICBMs

A. 60 SS-24 (10 RV)

SLBMs

A. 10 Delta IV SSBN with 16 SSN23/boat (4 RV)
B. 6 Delta III SSBN with 16 SSN18/boat (3 RV)
C. 6 Typhoon SSBN with 20 SSN20/boat (6 RV)

Bombers

A. 70 Blackjack
B. 130 Bear ALCM

Mobile Land-Based Missiles (MICBM)

A. 36 SS-24M (10 RV)
B. 715 SS-25 (1 RV)

6,000 RV

I. US Forces

ICBMs

A. 200 SICBM (1 RV)
B. 50 MX (10 RV)
C. 86 MM III (I RV)

SLBMs

A. 8 Trident submarines with 24 Trident C4 missiles (8 RV)
B. 10 Trident submarines with 24 Trident D5 missiles (8 RV)

Bombers

A. 87 B-1B
B. 30 B-2 (Stealth)

II. Russian Forces

ICBMs

A. 115 SS-24 (10 RV)

SLBMs

A. 6 Typhoon submarines with 20 SSN20/boat (6 RV)
B. 10 Delta IV submarines with 16 SSN23/boat (4 RV)
C. 6 Delta III submarines with 16 SSN18/boat (3 RV)

Bombers

A. 50 Blackjack
B. 130 Bear-H

Mobile Land-Based Missiles (MICBM)

A. 600 SS-25 (1 RV)
B. 36 SS-24M (10 RV)

245

3,000 RV

I. US Forces

ICBMs
A. 208 MM III (3 RV)

SLBMs
A. 8 Trident submarines with 24 Trident C4/boat (3 RV)
B. 10 Trident submarines with 24 Trident D5/boat (3 RV)

Bombers
A. 90 B-1B

II. Russian Forces

ICBMs
A. 50 SS-24 (10 RV)

SLBMs
A. 6 Typhoon submarines with 20 SSN20/boat (3 RV)
B. 10 Delta IV submarines with 16 SSN23/boat (3 RV)

Bombers
A. 100 Bear-H

Mobile Land-Based Missiles (MICBM)
A. 500 SS-25 (1 RV)
B. 36 SS-24M (10 RV)

2,000 RV

I. US Forces

ICBMs
A. 300 MM III (1 RV)

SLBMs
A. 10 Trident submarines with 24 Trident C4/boat (1 RV)
B. 15 Trident submarines with 24 Trident D5/boat (1 RV)

Bombers
A. 90 B-1B

II. Russian Forces

ICBMs
A. none

SLBMs
A. 5 Typhoon submarines with 20 SSN20/boat (3 RV)
B. 5 Delta IV submarines with 16 SSN23/boat (3 RV)

Bombers
A. 100 Bear-H

MICBM
A. 500 SS-25 (1 RV)
B. 50 SS-24M (10 RV)

1,000 RV (CBO)

I. US Forces

ICBMs
A. 200 MM III (1 RV)

SLBMs
A. 8 Trident submarines with 24 Trident C4/boat (1 RV)
B. 10 Trident submarines with 24 Trident D5/boat (1 RV)

Bombers
A. 90 B-1B

II. Russian Forces

ICBMs

A. None

SLBMs
A. 10 Delta IV submarines with 16 SSN23 (1 RV)

Bombers
A. 85 Bear-H

MICBM
A. 500 SS-25

1,000 RV (TSIPIS)

I. US Forces

ICBMs
A. 300 SICBM (1 RV)

SLBMs
A. 30 Trident submarines with 24 Trident D5/boat (1 RV)

Bombers
A. 100 B-1B ALCM

II. Russian Forces

ICBMs
A. None

SLBMs
A. 30 Delta IV submarines with 16 SSN23/boat (1 RV)

Bombers
A. 100 Bear-H ALCM

MICBM
A. 300 SS-25 (1 RV)

7

Conclusions: Stability after the Cold War

This study considers how the international system of the post-Cold War period might differ from the Cold War system in its degree and kind of stability. By degree of stability is meant the probability of war or of outbreak of crisis with the potential to result in war. The kind of stability which is available in the European and international environment after 1990 depends on many factors both internal and external to territorial states. Although theorists have expended a great deal of energy arguing about whether 'system' factors or 'actor' attributes are more important for predicting system stability, in this study we adopt the common-sense and empirically validated approach that both matter.

Our conclusion is that neither of two widely cited and antithetical models for the future of European security is as probable as a third. The first of the two antithetical models is the vision of a demilitarized European security agenda. Liberal political pluralism and economic interdependence, in this model, would rule out any resort to major war in post-Cold War Europe. The same model assumes the diminution of nationalism, or at least the permanent disappearance of virulent nationalism linked to unrequited ambitions for territorial or other aggression. The second model, more or less opposite to the first, is based on the assumption that anarchy will follow in the aftermath of Cold War. The removal of US and Soviet forces from Central Europe and the inability or unwillingness of Russia and the United States to offer security guarantees outside of their respective borders returns fractious Europeans to an environment comparable with the political milieu of the 1930s.

The actual future of security in Europe is likely to resemble, if our assessment is correct, neither a debellicized security community nor security anarchy but security pluralism, supported by concert diplomacy. Security pluralism calls forth many and diverse approaches to preserving peace and to avoiding those kinds of crises that can lead to major power wars. Concert diplomacy is the means by which great powers act to confine civil wars within a single country or regional wars within a geographically confined region, in order to preserve the overall balance of power among the major state actors in

Europe. Concert diplomacy is neither scientific nor administratively neat, and it is also not based on equality of interest or commitment. Using a variety of institutions, the new Europe should rely upon the great powers of Europe and North America to act as a regional equivalent of the UN Security Council, marrying a virtual monopoly of major military force to the objective of pacific settlement and peace enforcement in Europe.[1] Evidence and argument provided in the preceding chapters also allows for a European response to challenges originating outside of Europe.

The disintegration of the Soviet Union and the reunification of Germany are the two most important geopolitical changes in European, and arguably world, politics marking the transition from the old era to the new. Like fourteenth- and fifteenth-century European seafarers hoping to discover new worlds, the political leaders and military planners of today are not buoyed by the certainty of old assumptions about world order. A new world has already been 'discovered' in Europe as a result of the Kohl–Gorbachev agreement of 1990 permitting German reunification. Another newly discovered world resulted in December 1991 when the Soviet Union was superseded by Russia and associated former Soviet republics in the Commonwealth of Independent States. Regardless of the fate of capitalism in Russia, the Gorbachev era and the abortive coup of August 1991 mean that Russians cannot go home again to the kind of Communist Party rule that existed under Lenin, Stalin, Khrushchev or Brezhnev. They could revert to other forms of authoritarianism, but right authoritarianism embedded in Russophilia is much more likely than left authoritarianism.

The downfall of communism and the breakup of the Soviet Union have left Europe more democratic but less stable. If a security community from the Atlantic to the Urals is to be created, it must be based on two pillars: democratic governments in place of formerly authoritarian ones; and, military potentials limited by multilateral arrangement to the capacity for repelling an attack but not for making surprise attacks on a large scale. The objective of keeping in place democratic governments where democratic roots are not necessarily strong taxes the strength of policy-making processes in East Central Europe and tests the commitment of newly liberated peoples to shared governance. The requirement for stable deterrence based on non-offensive defense inserts a requirement for adaptive military thinking into defense planning guidance among states formerly convinced that large, fast-moving offensives were the keys to victory.

Democratic institutions and non-offensive defenses will be hard enough to put into place in the new Europe. Events outside of Europe will also have to cooperate if post-Cold War stability is to obtain from Lisbon to Vladivostok.

250

First, the non-European parts of the former Soviet Union are now standing alone as states whose peoples' aspirations for economic achievement and security may outrun the capacity of their governments to provide for citizens' needs. Second, the 'Third World' as a potential arena of major wars, including multistate wars fought with high-technology weapons, will give the US and European powers no peace unless stability can be exported beyond the Eurasian heartland. Third, the most likely trend in US defense expenditures and overseas peacetime commitments is downward, as Bush- and Clinton-projected defense budget declines from fiscal year 1990 through 1997 make clear. In many instances the United States cannot serve as the guarantor of last resort, despite its singular status since 1990 as the only global conventional military superpower.

Stability based on essentially equivalent distributions of power among major powers is no longer as dependable a guarantor of peace as it once was. As Joseph S. Nye, Jr. has argued persuasively, the very nature of power in international politics is now undergoing revision.[2] Soft power is now as important as hard power: superior knowledge and technology are as necessary as are large industrial capacity and brute force. Tangible power remains important for states, but the relative importance of intangible power for future international relations cannot be ignored. Intangible power refers to the power that flows from a state's reputation for national cohesion, international cultural appeal and influence in international institutions.[3] For example, US influence in institutions such as the United Nations or the World Bank is significant, as is the appeal of US political institutions and political culture for peoples worldwide. Overall, power in the next century compared with the twentieth century will be less fungible, less tangible and less coercive.[4]

To say that power is less 'fungible' implies that it is less transferable from one kind of international regime to another. An international regime is a set of more or less predictable interactions among states, supported by norms, institutions and values they share, for a specific purpose. Regimes exist for the regulation of international fishing rights, for international telecommunications, for arms control and for other relations between states. Future power will be more regime-specific than power has been in previous eras because knowledge is more compartmentalized and specialized. This spells trouble for all persons who work in knowledge-related professions, but especially for military planners and political leaders.

Political leaders and military planners cannot get by, as most professional specialists can, by separating knowledge into isolated compartments and focusing only on each compartment one at a time. Political and military decision-making requires lumping of information into wholes as well as splitting it into parts, as historian John Lewis Gaddis once described the two basic approaches of academic historians.[5] The holistic view of the field of battle is what distinguishes the greater commander from the lesser, and today the holistic view of policy is all the more complicated by the information revolution that now supersedes the knowledge rules of the industrial age. The US information technology used in Operation Desert Storm is but a prelude to twenty-first-century successors that will change the nature of battle, of command and of political decision-making related to crisis and war.

There is a danger in applying the distinction between soft and hard power to the discussion of force and policy. Readers may infer wrongly that hard power is now insignificant or that it has been altogether superseded in importance by soft power. War is about many things, but mostly about the destruction of enemy forces in combat. This is a brutal subdiscipline of history, political science, economics, philosophy and other studies and requires of the student suspended disbelief. One must maintain one's analytical detachment to establish order amid the chaos of battle and crisis. On the other hand, the writer must never lose the sense of danger, exhaustion and suffering which makes battle distinct from other social phenomena.

Clausewitz, who established so many important points about the philosophy of war, noted that preparation for war is not the same thing as the actual conduct of war. One can make more scientific the process of military administration and logistics without rendering any more coherent or manageable the control over exchanges of fire and blood. Nuclear weapons brought about the ultimate divorce between the logic of preparing for war and the logic of fighting war. No state wants to engage in war unless it can do so at an acceptable cost to its political and social institutions. Nuclear weapons do not permit of fightable wars at acceptable cost. Therefore, a new strategy for 'using' nuclear weapons had to be advanced, or the weapons discarded from military arsenals.

Because nuclear weapons offered 'more bang for the buck' and saved money otherwise spent on additional conventional forces, they appealed to treasuries and defense departments alike. The new strategy for the use of nuclear weapons could not ignore their futility through overkill for battlefield use. Therefore, the new strategy of deterrence said that the value of nuclear weapons lay in their non-use. This non-military strategy had great political value if everyone could be made to believe it. Strangely enough, the people who mattered, political leaders of nuclear armed states of the Cold War era, did believe it and acted accordingly. Strictly speaking, as George Quester has reminded us, this strategy of deterrence through non-use was not altogether new.[6] It had its roots in the theories of strategic air bombardment which marked the period between the First and Second World Wars, and the logic of nuclear deterrence as it developed in the United States after 1945 owed much to the heritage passed along from airpower theorists.[7]

As much by inadvertence as by design, the logic of mutual deterrence got the US, the Soviet Union and the rest of Europe through the Cold War era, but it would be a mistake to suppose that this logic will apply with equal force to the late 1990s or to the next century. Although Russian nuclear weapons remain plentiful, Russian nuclear deterrence may be a vestige of its former self. Unless somebody undertakes the invasion of Russia against all odds or sanity, Russia's military problems will have more to do with its internal disintegration than with external invasion. Conflicts between Russians and bordering states with old scores to settle cannot be ruled out, and fellow members of the Commonwealth of Independent States are not all ready to follow the foreign policy lead of the Russian foreign ministry. Some problems with a potentially irredentist China, unstable Iran, assertive Japan or other neighbors are certainly within one standard deviation of political feasibility between now and the year 2000.

Regardless of its internal political oscillations between democratic and authoritarian tendencies, Russia cannot constitute a global military threat of the proportions of the former Soviet Union to US or allied NATO interests. This leaves much of US and NATO policy behind the times. NATO has a useful function to perform in aiding the transition from a Cold War stability in Europe to a post-Cold War stability based on something besides East–West polarity. NATO has both friends and enemies in the international political community, but among those who argue for diverse NATO futures, it is often difficult to tell the former from the latter. Well-meaning friends call for continuation of old NATO missions under new guises, as if NATO's problems could be resolved by improvements in 'interoperability' or by replacing a US SACEUR (Supreme Allied Commander) with a European one. NATO faces the more fundamental and problematical issue that the threat which called it into being has gone away, probably forever and certainly in the immediate future.

As hinted at in the preceding paragraph, this vanishing threat does not make NATO immediately obsolete. It has an important role to play in moving Europe from a security community based on a balance of terror toward a security community based on commonality of political purpose. A community of common purpose embracing former NATO members, former Warsaw Pact states, non-aligned and neutral European states, and formerly con-stituent republics of the Soviet Union requires rethinking of political grand strategy and military planning guidance. NATO is like the senior quarterback on a US professional football team whose last great years must include time for training his young successor. NATO must continue to hold at bay the forces of disintegration in Europe while transferring its expertise, experience and infrastructure into other hands. Whose might these be?

There are some who think that the reborn Western European Union (WEU) is such an entity to inherit the peacekeeping mantle of NATO. The WEU could function as the military–security arm of the European Community, itself injected with new life as a result of the Maastricht agreement to proceed to economic and political union in Western Europe. However, momentum for political and monetary unification has hit the rocks of currency disequilibrium, stagnation in some European economies, and obvious inequality in the economic potentials even within the current EEC membership. Should the ambit of EEC be extended to include newly independent states of East Central Europe, or even former republics of the defunct Soviet Union, the situation is more complicated still. Assuming for the sake of argument that the problem of political union can be circumvented, there is the appropriateness of military instruments to consider for the task of pacifying a future Europe.

If there is one lesson from the Cold War era outside of Europe which ought to be passed along to European planners of the next century, it is that conventional combat forces are not usually well suited to deal with civil war, revolution, insurrection, terrorism or other manifestations of irregular conflict. Irregular wars bogged down American fighters in Vietnam and Soviet forces in Afghanistan to no avail. Europe's leading colonial powers of the nineteenth century, including France, were summarily unable to maintain their grip on power outside of Europe despite, in the cases of Britain and France, adding nuclear weapons to their already large conventional military arsenals. British and French military power was not weak relative to the kinds of tests it might have had to face along with American allies in a conventional war in Europe. However, French, British and US power proved close to irrelevant in the circumstances of nationalist, ethnic, religious and tribal warfare which was thrust upon the developed states by the developing societies of the Cold War era.

The military defeats of the great powers outside of Europe in the Cold War years were partly the result of their sensible unwillingness to wage total war against developed societies (much to the dismay of military traditionalists in the US and elsewhere). Some theorists who failed to appreciate the deliberately limited political objectives of the US in Vietnam, for example, faulted US strategy for adopting a 'gradualism' introduced from outside military history by suspect social scientism.[8] But it was not social scientism

254

which caused the British to pull back east of Suez after 1956 (and more emphatically after 1968 when Labour made this policy more explicit) nor the French to withdraw from Indochina. It was that waging total war in Indochina would cause for the Americans or the French domestic political repercussions on the home front which were unacceptable prices for politicians to pay. In the case of Britain, its diplomatic success in writing off gracefully the crown jewels of Victoria's empire, as in India, aided its comparatively uncontroversial transition to post-imperial status. Negotiated transfers of power to British colonies avoided for the most part the fratricidal civil strife which engulfed French, Portuguese and other empires holding on to the remnants of past glory.

Britain's transition to post-imperialism was made easier by the security provided by bipolarity and US nuclear weapons. Peace in Europe was also more easily come by as a result of the locking of superpower nuclear arsenals into a situation of strategic military stasis. Against the prophecy that mutual deterrence would liberate conventional forces of NATO and the Warsaw Pact to fight one another below the nuclear threshold, it turned out that conventional war in Europe was perceived to be about as risky as nuclear attack. The assumption made by politicians was that conventional war might easily escalate into nuclear war; why else deploy nuclear weapons near the front lines of the East–West political divide? NATO and Soviet nuclear weapons deployments in Europe helped to make escalation neither certain nor impossible. Impossible escalation would have permitted safe conventional war fighting. Certain escalation would have guaranteed that no rocket rattling attendant on conventional war or crisis would be credible.

Escalation that was neither impossible nor certain in a strategic nuclear bipolar world helped to dampen regional conflicts into which the US or the Soviet Union might extend its reach. The end of bipolarity therefore reduces the reach of strategic duopoly, freeing centrifugal forces inside and outside of Europe to mount political and military challenges to the status quo. Nuclear proliferation had not developed by the 1980s to the extent that US pessimists of the 1960s had feared, but as the 1990s opened, the case of Saddam Hussein served to remind that non-proliferation remained a challenge for global and regional stability.[9] In addition, the spread of other weapons of mass destruction and ballistic missile technology to the Third World created the potential for destabilizing confrontations outside of Europe with potentially major implications for US and allied European security. The Iran–Iraq war of the 1980s was perhaps a first case study in the kinds of costly conventional wars which might take place outside of Europe in the 1990s or beyond that decade. A protracted struggle with an almost absurd commingling of First and 'Third'

World War strategy and technology, the Iran–Iraq war was followed by US and allied Desert Storm to liberate Kuwait.

The outcome of the Gulf War of 1991 has something in common with the problem of proliferation: both the outcomes of large-scale wars and the management of proliferation are related to the kinds of command and control systems which states and their military establishments possess. Iraq's defeat in Desert Storm was certainly due in part to the rapid collapse of its strategic military command and control system in the early days of battle. On the other hand, Iraq's command and control system functioned well enough to prevent Saddam's capture or liquidation, to forestall detection by the coalition of a great many mobile SCUD missiles, and to conduct postwar deception and cheating on UN-mandated sanctions with regard to weapons of mass destruction and launch vehicles.

Non-proliferation also raises command and control issues, until now relatively neglected in the understandable emphasis upon preventing weapons spread. The non-proliferation 'regime' of agreements, such as the Nuclear Non-proliferaton Treaty (NPT), and informal practices among supplier and possible nuclear acquirers, is a necessary condition for regional and global stability. Its accomplishments are already considerable. But it may not be sufficient for future stability. Non-proliferation may need to be supplemented by anti-proliferation measures: measures to reverse proliferation which has already occurred, and measures to stabilize the command and control systems of those states which have gone nuclear against the best judgments of the international community. Non-proliferation traditionalists argue against the idea of anti-proliferation measures, fearing that any compromise of non-proliferation objectives (keeping weapons out of bad hands) will result in the worst possible outcomes for stability (actual use of weapons by regional outlaws for reasons other than deterrence).

Recent history has presented a compelling case for anti-proliferation measures as supports for a non-proliferation regime: the breakup of the former Soviet Union. The result was four new states with *strategic* (of intercontinental range, by US definition) weapons: Russia; the Ukraine; Belarus; and Kazakhstan. Command and control arrangements for nuclear weapons deployed by member states of the Commonwealth of Independent States, the successor, at least for the time being, to the former Soviet Union, were still being worked out at the time of writing. US experts on nuclear weapons and Bush administration officials in 1990 and 1991 acted to reassure the US public that the problem of loose nukes in the former Soviet Union was under control. Agreements reached in 1991 called for all former Soviet republics to transfer their tactical nuclear weapons to Russian control by July

1992. Evidence suggested that most accountable weapons were transferred in compliance with this requirement, although not all weapons formerly thought to be in the arsenals were accounted for. Suspected illegal transfers of some weapons outside former Soviet borders or to dissident nationality groups could not be ruled out.

As for strategic nuclear weapons, the vast majority were held under Commonwealth command and, after Yeltsin's nationalization of the Russian armed forces in the spring of 1992, presumably under Russian command also (and in practice, Russian command period). The Ukraine announced in November 1992 (and repudiated in January 1994) its intent to retain control over some 150 SS-18 ICBMs deployed in that state by former Soviet forces. Holding onto those forces would make the Ukraine one of the world's major nuclear armed countries, disposing of about 1500 strategic nuclear warheads. This was more of a structural facade than a realistic indicator of power. The command and control of nuclear weapons, including the authorizing and enabling codes for actual nuclear release, remained in Moscow under the command of the Commonwealth and Russian defense ministers and general staffs. Presumably these defense ministers and general staffs would set in motion nuclear release only upon the authorized command of the President of Russia, Boris Yeltsin.

In a condition of civil strife and amid contention for control of a disintegrating Russian state, it might not be clear which commands were 'authorized' and which were not. Yeltsin's panache had carried him over the minefield of the attempted coup of 19–21 August 1991: some evidence exists that command and control arrangements were not altogether clear either to coup plotters or to their opponents.[10] Worse still would be the situation of small, non-survivable Third World nuclear forces poised for pre-emptive first strike at the first hint of enemy attack and subject to uncertain political control as a result of fractured civil–military relations. Command and control of high-technology delivery vehicles and mass destruction weapons has been thankfully dependable in the past. The Cold War Americans and Soviets never experienced a legitimacy crisis during a period of international tension possibly leading to war. And other nuclear armed states during the Cold War were not adventurist in seeking territorial gains at the expense of the superpowers or their allies, although some skirmishing in 1969 at the Sino-Soviet border rekindled Brezhnev's Sinophobia and could have escalated into a war between the two communist giants.

How stable would an Iraq, Iran or Libya armed with nuclear weapons be? The question seems ethnocentric: there is no logically deductive model by which Third World irresponsibility can be predicted unless one assumes a

257

correlation between authoritarianism and nuclear adventurism. However, this correlation did not hold up for the Soviet Union in the Cold War years, nor for China. Political legitimacy is one half of the equation of secure command and control; military obedience and disinterest in political rule by the armed forces is the second half. Cold War China and the Soviet Union met both halves of the requirement for secure and stable command and control over nuclear forces. It may be that future members of the nuclear club will be as responsible and stable in their crisis management behavior as current members. However, the experience of current members is less reassuring than it seems: close study of US and Soviet behavior during the 1961 Berlin and 1962 Cuban missile crises shows much stumbling and uncertainty in the efforts of both sides to walk away from the brink of war.

In a multipolar, decommunized and technologically well-armed world, it is reasonable to ask whether US–Russian nuclear deterrence need exist at all. Although too much reliance can be placed on deterrence as an all-purpose substitute for other means to stability, its contribution to Cold War peace and crisis management has been well documented. Some now propose that the US and Russia, for so long as political relations remain non-hostile but short of entente, disavow all but minimal nuclear arsenals and thereby reduce the threat of nuclear escalation or inadvertent nuclear war. Presidents Bush and Yeltsin in several initiatives in 1991 and 1992 reached agreement in principle that strategic nuclear forces of both sides could be reduced well below START levels, perhaps to an actual 3,500 to 3,000 warheads. Analysts in both the US and in Russia have called for reductions well below these levels, perhaps to 1,000 or fewer re-entry vehicles. It seems clear that momentum for further arms reductions will build as political relations between Washington and Moscow become more friendly.

It might seem obvious that lower levels of nuclear weapons are better than higher levels. And the nuclear non-proliferation regime embodied in the treaty of that name implies as much. The matter is not so simple: lower levels of US or Russian strategic arms are not necessarily more stable than higher levels. As reductions bring down the sizes of arsenals, reduced sizes also change the character of forces. A small force is even more dependent on the survivability of each individual component: a larger force can compensate for component failure with redundancy. Smaller US forces of the future can compensate for loss of redundancy by improving the survivability of second strike systems in which the US already has a considerable advantage, relative to the Russians. US bomber and submarine forces during the Cold War years were operated at more sustained tempos and would almost certainly have been more survivable against any surprise attack than their Soviet counterpart

258

forces. To some extent, these US relative advantages and Russian weaknesses may also characterize forces of the 1990s and thereafter.

It may not matter whether a stable balance of strategic nuclear weapons exists between the US and Russia so long as they are allies or non-competitive countries. Who worries now about the deterrent balance of British compared to French, or French compared to US, forces? In the absence of renewed hostility between the US and a post-Yeltsin Russia, one could argue that benign political relations between the two states makes nuclear deterrence irrelevant. On the other hand, Russia's leadership will certainly be aware that the US remains the only global conventional military superpower with pre-eminent non-nuclear forces capable of universal intervention. Only nuclear weapons confer major power status on a Russia too divided politically and weakened economically to restore its former Cold War predominance in European conventional land power. The draft Russian military doctrine of May 1992, perhaps indicative of Russian General Staff proclivities on this topic, warns both of strategic campaigns using conventional weapons and of the nuclear escalation which may result.[11]

Minimum nuclear deterrence as a pathway to stability requires not only the limitation of US and Russian strategic nuclear forces, but also the placing of constraints on British, French, Chinese or other acknowledged or unack-nowledged nuclear powers. The success of non-proliferation and anti-proliferation measures (reversing cases of proliferation, and assuring com-mand and control stability for those proliferators who cannot be stopped) is related to the probable success of minimum deterrence. In a world of think-tank analysis, the Cold War US and Soviet leaderships weighed carefully differences between their respective strategic forces such as relative throw weights and hard target accuracies. In the real world inhabited by political leaders, the destruction of several major cities would have constituted unac-ceptable and unprecedented national disaster. The result was that the threat to inflict unacceptable damage could be made good with even very small numbers of survivable weapons.

Minimum deterrence, like mutual assured destruction or assured retalia-tion, depends upon the second strike viability of nuclear forces. However, minimum deterrent forces could also send signals of non-bellicosity and trust between states with no immediate grievances against one another, but which were none the less sensitive to the security dilemma in which all armed states are inescapably located. The character of political relations between states which are dependent on self-help has driven their military equations toward war or peace since the dawn of the modern state system in 1648. Although political relations are in the driver's seat and not weapons characteristics, the

259

attributes of forces can help to avoid inadvertent war and to avoid excessive fear on the part of leaders of being subjected to a sudden and decisive surprise attack.

It is true enough that the role to be played by nuclear weapons in the post-Cold War world is for the moment very unclear. Can it be assumed that the weapons which helped to preserve the peace during about forty years of Cold War, although at great risk and at unimaginable potential cost, will also be more stabilizing than destabilizing in the world of the 1990s or beyond? Much depends on the numbers of states that acquire nuclear arsenals, on their governments' capacity to develop stable and secure command and control of nuclear forces, and on the threat perceptions of those aspiring or actual nuclear powers. If past is precedent, nuclear weapons will remain the weapons of choice for deterrence, and conventional weapons for actual war fighting. No one has offered a convincing argument that nuclear war can be limited to exchanges of a very few weapons with a strictly political effect, and even an intellectually convincing argument would find few national leaders among the takers.

NOTES

1. For one variant of this approach in Europe, see Charles A. Kupchan and Gregory F. Treverton, 'A New Concert for Europe', Ch. 8C in Graham Allison and Clifford A. Kupchan (eds), *Rethinking America's Security* (New York: W.W. Norton, 1992), pp. 249–66.
2. Joseph S. Nye, Jr., *Bound to Lead: The Changing Nature of American Power* (New York: Basic Books, 1990).
3. Ibid., p. 174.
4. Ibid., p. 188.
5. John Lewis Gaddis, *Strategies of Containment: A Critical Appraisal of Postwar American National Security Policy* (New York: Oxford University Press, 1982), p. vii.
6. George H. Quester, *Deterrence Before Hiroshima: The Airpower Background of Modern Strategy* (New Brunswick, NJ: Transaction Books, 1986 edition).
7. See Lawrence Freedman, *The Evolution of Nuclear Strategy* (New York: St. Martin's Press, 1981), esp. Chs. 1–3.
8. An argument to this effect is made by Harry T. Summers, *On Strategy: A Critical Analysis of the Vietnam War* (New York: Dell Publishing, 1982).
9. See Leonard S. Spector with Jacqueline R. Smith, *Nuclear Ambitions: The Spread of Nuclear Weapons 1989–1990* (Boulder, CO: Westview Press, 1990).
10. Richard F. Staar, *The New Russian Armed Forces: Preparing for War or Peace?* (Stanford, CA: Hoover Institution, 1992), pp. 3–7.
11. *Osnovy voennoy doktriny Rossii* (Proekt) (Fundamentals of Russian Military Doctrine) (Draft), *Voennaya mysl'*, May 1992 special edition, esp. pp. 3–13.

Bibliography

Allard, C. Kenneth. *Command, Control and the Common Defense*. New Haven: Yale University Press, 1990.

Allison, Graham T. *Essence of Decision: Explaining the Cuban Missile Crisis*. Boston: Little, Brown, 1971.

Art, Robert J., Vincent Davis and Samuel P. Huntington (eds). *Reorganizing America's Defenses: Leadership in War and Peace*. New York: Pergamon Brassey's, 1985.

Blight, James G. and David A. Welch. *On the Brink: Americans and Soviets Examine the Cuban Missile Crisis*. New York: Hill and Wang, 1989.

Bundy, McGeorge. *Danger and Survival: Choices about the Bomb in the First Fifty Years*. New York: Random House, 1988.

Enthoven, Alain C. and K. Wayne Smith. *How Much Is Enough? Shaping the Defense Program, 1961–1969*. New York: Harper and Row, 1971.

Friedman, Norman. *Desert Victory: The War for Kuwait*. Annapolis, MD: US Naval Institute Press, 1991.

Gaddis, John Lewis. *The Long Peace: Inquiries into the History of the Cold War*. New York: Oxford University Press, 1987.

Gaddis, John Lewis. *The United States and the Origins of the Cold War, 1941–1947*. New York: Columbia University Press, 1972.

Garthoff, Raymond L. *Deterrence and the Revolution in Soviet Military Doctrine*. Washington, DC: Brookings Institution, 1990.

Garthoff, Raymond L. *Reflections on the Cuban Missile Crisis*, rev. edn. Washington, DC: Brookings Institution, 1989.

George, Alexander L., David K. Hall and William E. Simons. *The Limits of Coercive Diplomacy: Laos, Cuba, Vietnam*. Boston: Little, Brown, 1971.

Gilpin, Robert. *War and Change in World Politics*. Cambridge: Cambridge University Press, 1981.

Herspring, Dale. *The Soviet High Command, 1967–1989: Personalities and Politics*. Princeton: Princeton University Press, 1990.

Holloway, David. *The Soviet Union and the Arms Race*. New Haven, CT: Yale University Press, 1983.

Huntington, Samuel P. *The Soldier and the State*. Cambridge, MA: Belknap Press/ Harvard University Press, 1957.

Ikle, Fred C. *Every War Must End*. New York: Columbia University Press, 1991.

Jervis, Robert and Jack Snyder (eds). *Dominoes and Bandwagons: Strategic Beliefs and Great Power Competition in the Eurasian Rimland*. New York: Oxford University Press, 1991.

Jervis, Robert. *The Meaning of the Nuclear Revolution: Statecraft and the Prospect of Armageddon*. Ithaca, NY: Cornell University Press, 1989.

Kennedy, Paul M. (ed.). *Grand Strategies in War and Peace*. New Haven, CT: Yale University Press, 1991.

Mandelbaum, Michael. *The Nuclear Revolution: International Politics before and after Hiroshima*. Cambridge: Cambridge University Press, 1981.

Miller, Steven E. (ed.), *Strategy and Nuclear Deterrence*. Princeton: Princeton University Press, 1984.

Nolan, Janne. *Guardians of the Arsenal: The Politics of Nuclear Strategy*. New York: Basic Books, 1989.

Pillar, Paul. *Negotiating Peace: War Termination as a Bargaining Process*. Princeton: Princeton University Press, 1983.

Prados, John. *Presidents' Secret Wars: CIA and Pentagon Covert Operations since World War II*. New York: William Morrow, 1986.

Sagan, Scott D. *Moving Targets: Nuclear Strategy and National Security*. Princeton: Princeton University Press, 1989.

Schelling, Thomas C. *Arms and Influence*. New Haven: Yale University Press, 1966.

Weigley, Russell F. *Towards an American Army: Military Thought from Washington to Marshall*. New York: Columbia University Press, 1962.

Index

270